A House Is
Not a Home

LExington 2-1099   New York City

POLLY ADLER

A House Is
Not a Home

Introduction by Rachel Rubin

University of Massachusetts Press
AMHERST & BOSTON

Originally published in 1953 by
Rinehart & Company, Inc., New York and Toronto
Copyright © 1953 by Polly Adler
Introduction and apparatus copyright © 2006 by
University of Massachusetts Press

Some of the names of persons and places, the dates of events and other descriptive details have been altered, and in some cases the persons are composites. But the basic events which make up the story of my life are as they happened. [Author's note from first edition] Grateful acknowledgment is made to the Frank Music Corporation for permission to quote a line from their song, "I'll Know," Copyright 1950, by Frank Loesser, from *Guys and Dolls*. [Author's acknowledgment from first edition]

LC 2006018584
ISBN 10: 1-55849-559-2
ISBN 13: 978-1-55849-559-3

Set in Adobe Caslon
Printed and bound by The Maple-Vail Book Manufacturing Group, Inc.

Library of Congress Cataloging-in-Publication Data

Adler, Polly, 1900–1962.
A house is not a home / Polly Adler; introduction by Rachel Rubin.
p. cm.
Originally published: New York, N.Y. : Rinehart, 1953.
ISBN-13: 978-1-55849-559-3 (pbk. : alk. paper)
ISBN-10: 1-55849-559-2 (pbk. : alk. paper)
1. Prostitution—New York (State)—New York. 2. Adler, Polly, 1900–
1962. 3. Prostitutes—New York (State)—New York—Biography. I. Title.
HQ146.N7A4 2006
306.7409747'1—dc22
2006018584

British Library Cataloguing in Publication data are available.

Frontispiece: Polly Adler's notorious calling card

To My Friends

Contents

Introduction

Polly Adler, "The Jewish Jezebel"

Rachel Rubin

What it comes down to is this: the grocer, the butcher, the baker, the merchant, the landlord, the druggist, the liquor dealer, the policeman, the doctor, the city father and the politician—these are the people who make money out of prostitution, these are the real reapers of the wages of sin.

—Polly Adler, *A House Is Not a Home*

In 1937, a popular radio host for WMCA's music show *Grandstand and Bandstand*, "Broadway's own" Smiling Jerry Baker, got into trouble with his station management although he was attracting plenty of listeners to the station. Baker had apparently been dedicating many of the songs he played to young women who, it turned out, were employees at Polly Adler's brothel, then legendary as the most "high-class" house of prostitution in New York.[1] This amusing, if minor, moment in American cultural history provides more than just a chuckle, for it epitomizes the ambivalent position Polly Adler occupied in 1930s New York. On one hand, she was an undeniable star of sorts, a personality just as familiar and celebrated as the radio announcer himself, and invoking her establishment was a way for him to claim cultural capital and hip cachet. On the other hand, though, there was the shame of "vice" associated with Polly Adler's name, requiring that the same public that ate up news of her also loudly condemn her activities.

Adler occupied this conspicuous and contradictory place in the American imagination for most of her life. During the 1920s and 1930s, she was well known to New Yorkers and other Americans by a slew of alliterative nicknames that simultaneously elevated and marginalized her. She was the Midtown Madam of Many Magdalenes. She was the Queen of Queer Street. She was the Jewish Jezebel. The tabloids assiduously tracked her, as did famous columnists such as Walter Winchell, who fed appetites for reports on her public appearances—whether in the police station or in an expensive nightclub. Celebrities such as baseball star Joe DiMaggio and comedian Milton Berle sought out her lavish "house" for entertainment—and let it be known that they did so. The "sophisticated" writers who made up the "Algonquin Round Table" (Dorothy Parker, Alexander Woollcott, Robert Benchley) spent time with her—and in some accounts actually worked at their writing in her "house." Meanwhile, Adler racked up more than 15 arrests, hid her face from hungry news photographers, moved her establishment from tony address to tony address to dodge the police, served a short jail sentence, and was ultimately forced out of business by a series of corruption investigations in which she figured centrally.

After closing her business for good in 1944, Adler moved from New York to California. According to her own account, she had always harbored an immigrant's hunger for education, and long maintained a fascination for writers. On the west coast, she enrolled at Los Angeles Valley College (eventually receiving her B.A.) and worked on her memoir. *A House Is Not a Home* was first published by Rinehart & Company in 1953, with a droll flyleaf reproduction of Adler's former business card. The book became an unexpected bestseller and ran through several wildly successful mass-market paperback editions. "Compared to writing a book," wrote Adler of the process, "running a house is a breeze." Although the book received its share of serious critical attention—in addition to its huge readership—*A House Is Not a Home* has been out of print since 1983. A remarkable account of New York's cultural history, a knowing and innovative immigrant tale, a significant meditation on sex and the marketplace, the book has nonetheless never been published in an academic edition.

By the time *A House Is Not a Home* was first published in 1953, the immigration narrative was a decidedly familiar form, its conventions firmly established decades earlier by such well-circulated autobiographies as Mary Antin's *The Promised Land* (1912), Andrew Carnegie's *Autobiography* (1920), and Edward Bok's *The Americanization of Edward Bok* (1921). Nonfiction was joined by fictional narratives in print (Abraham Cahan's short novel *Yekl: A Tale of the New York Ghetto* [1896], for instance, or Anzia Yezierska's 1925 novel *The Bread Givers*), and later on screens large and small. These narratives moved linearly from Old World to New World, with the process of "becoming American" organized as a series of acquisitions: language, possessions and money, a new family structure, knowledge of popular culture. With self-conscious deliberation, Adler mines this familiar territory, invoking the rules and requirements of the inspirational immigrant story; she also concretely refers to particular identifiable texts. Sketching a structure that her readers could be expected to recognize, she then tinkers with the familiar, injecting disruptive and irreverent elements (most often pertaining to morality) that challenge the strictures of the form.

The book's first chapter begins, conventionally enough, with the birth of the Russian-Jewish Pearl Adler in Yanow, Russia, in 1900. The story thus starts *ipso facto* with a historical moment when tsarist anti-Semitic policies were at a height. After the abortive Russian revolution of 1905—young Pearl would have been five years old—the

number and ferocity of pogroms, or violent attacks on Jewish neighborhoods or villages, increased sharply, with the complicity of the
government. Pearl's father, who was successful enough as a tailor to
be considered well off "by Yanow standards" (8), had traveled to the
United States, and in 1912 he decided that someone in the family
should move to America, with the idea that the rest would follow in
installments. Pearl, the oldest child at 12, was chosen. Her belongings in a potato sack, she boarded a ship to America, where (after
conquering sea-sickness) she was soon singing Russian folk songs
among a hopeful, polyglot group of new immigrants. Just like Mary
Antin, whose well-known narrative of immigration was published
the year Adler arrived in the United States, Adler recounts running
to the deck when the ship arrived to get a better look at the Statue
of Liberty; one of her shipmates lifts her to his shoulder and cries
out in Yiddish, "Look! . . . The American Lady! The Statue of
Liberty!" (13).

In this and several other ways, Adler takes pains to associate her
autobiography with the familiar tradition exemplified by Antin.
But while Antin's autobiography has many merits, it follows the
most predictable trajectory of immigrant narrative: from the darkness of tsarist Russia, Antin tells her story as a logically unfolding
narrative of education and uplift. *The Promised Land*, like so many
immigrant narratives, belongs to the class of works that constitute
what the historian Melvin Tumin has called the "cult of gratitude."
This autobiographical tradition privileges the "good citizen"; these
immigrants operate in the world of legitimate, educated, socially
secure Americans. As valuable as books like *The Promised Land* are,
the historical record is incomplete without works such as Adler's,
which reintroduce the darker world of the immigrant's demimonde.
In Adler's own words, "the picture will not be complete until all
precincts are heard from, and there are aspects of the scene on which
I am peculiarly well qualified to report—perhaps better qualified

than anyone now alive. . . . I could look into the underworld, the half-world and the high" (5).

Adler immediately sets up a tension between the standard immigrant narrative and her own commentary on that standard. The title of the first chapter is "'Goldine Madina' Means 'Golden Land.'" Here she quickly provides a structural model for understanding a story that is, on the face of it, quite familiar: old to new, represented by the translation of Yiddish to English. Furthermore, the phrase she has chosen to translate is by now a cliché of what the "Old Country" vision was of America, as the New World: what Antin biblically called the Promised Land, where the streets are paved with gold.

Directly below that chapter title, however, Adler places an epigraph taken from John Dos Passos's experimental 1915 novel *Manhattan Transfer*—a passage that is already using formal experimentation (here, deliberately non-standard English) to effect a world-weary tone that calls into question the immigrant myth:

> "I'd give a million dollars," said the old man resting on his oars, "to know what they come for."
>
> "Just for that, pop," said the young man who sat in the stern. "Ain't it the land of opportoonity?"

Thus Adler immediately signals that her own autobiography is to be written both within and against the immigrant tradition. For example, Pearl gets a factory job with other immigrant girls and develops a crush on the boss—a wealthier, more "American" example of success. But on their first "date," he rapes her, ultimately causing her to lose both the job and her home. Along the same lines, she describes how her own given name, Pearl, quickly becomes "Polly"—a move that Ted Morgan identifies as the all-American procedure of "shaking off an ethnic encumbrance."[2] But Adler also changes her name for less legitimate reasons, when she is arrested or seeking to avoid being arrested. She retains her interest in "working her way up," but consistently finds that being law-abiding and pious is not the way to achieve the American Dream: "I kept thinking that surely life must offer me other alternatives than a factory job and a [poor suitor like] Willie Bernstein" (23). She reads aphorisms from Benjamin Franklin (perhaps the most famous American autobiographer) to keep up her morale (and quotes him in her early chapters), but when she does attempt to "go straight," she is arrested anyway because of her reputation and soon finds herself "back in the whorehouse business" (55).

Ultimately, Adler's greenhorn girl does find the Golden Land—not through model immigrant behavior, but rather by earning enough black-market money to take advantage of class mobility and move to a better neighborhood. When she does this, she marshals the familiar language of gratitude to describe a more meaningful immigration, one based on class rather than geography: "There really was a 'Goldine Madina,' and it was right here on Riverside Drive" (32), she concludes, adding, "In many ways the difference between Second Avenue and Riverside Drive was greater than that between Yanow and Holyoke [Massachusetts]" (where Adler first lived as a young immigrant) (34). Thus, in *A House Is Not a Home* Adler joins rebellious Jewish writers such as the novelist Samuel Ornitz, who dubbed Polly's Riverside Drive "Allrightniks Row" for well-off immigrant Jews, and Daniel Fuchs, who chronicled the exploits of ambitious Jewish gangsters, in showing that crime may be the best path to assimilation and achieving the American Dream.[3] She proudly places herself in the Horatio Alger tradition of "making good" through her own pluck—but the pluck turns out to be the savoir-faire of the clever and bold criminal. Oddly enough, just at the moment in her life when Polly Adler reports coming to the conclusion that the American Dream for her will mean operating outside the law, she became a naturalized American citizen, on May 20, 1929.

Adler's "becoming American" came at a time when, as David E. Ruth points out in his study of the gangster in American culture, many Americans "came to believe that rampant crime was a defining element of their society."[4] As immigrants from Europe swelled the populations of American cities, commentators were obsessed with the Italian, Irish, and Jewish mobs who marked off city territory, generally according to ethnicity, and proceeded to amass huge fortunes from bootlegging and drug sales, prostitution, extortion, and loan-sharking. The Jewish mob in particular reached its peak of accomplishment during Prohibition, flourishing in ghettos on New York's Lower East Side and Chicago's West Side, and similar enclaves in Detroit, Boston, Baltimore, and other cities. Adler's generation of Jews contributed some of the United States' foremost bootleggers, racketeers, sexual procurers, and professional killers, culminating most famously in the Jewish-Italian criminal syndicate styled "Murder, Inc." by contemporary journalists. The ethnic criminal underworld has always fascinated Americans, and a huge amount of attention—academic, journalistic, artistic—has been paid to the gangsters who rose to great heights of power in large American cities in the early part of the "American Century." Mobsters made their splashiest appearance in hundreds of gangster movies of the 1930s, but when Adler was rubbing shoulders with the likes of Dutch Schultz, Legs Diamond, and George McManus, a broad variety of media institutions—newspapers, scholarly journals, government-sponsored reports, and the Motion Picture Academy—was acknowledging that they were a central force in American life.

The picture painted of the ethnic underworld, however, has been almost exclusively male. (Indeed, as I have argued elsewhere, one of the reasons that Jewish gangsters in particular have had such staying power in the American imagination, long outlasting their actual influence, is because they provide a readily available way to discuss Jewish masculinity.[5]) The example of Adler, who was described in court testimony as "a power in the underworld,"[6] offers one answer to the question "Where were the delinquent women?" Her memoir is a very unromantic, clear-eyed portrait of the Prohibition era's gangs of New York—from an unusual female perspective. Adler writes that her clientele "consisted mostly of gangsters and hoodlums, some of whom were to become the big shots of the day" (55). The Volstead (National Prohibition) Act of 1919 had provided an enormous business opportunity for gangsters, who controlled not only illegal alcohol sales, but also most of the clubs where people did their drinking. The mob Adler served was coming to resemble a "legitimate" corporation more and more, with an internal hierarchy of command, specialized jobs, and lawyers and accountants on retainer; popular gangster movies (starring the likes of Humphrey Bogart, Edward G. Robinson, and James Cagney) were making it plain that it wasn't so easy to tell the difference between mobsters and moguls. Adler captures this sense perfectly, portraying what she dubs "the more businessman type of hoodlum" (207).

The most notable of these "businessman hoodlums" was Arthur Flegenheimer, the king of Harlem crime better known as Dutch Schultz. Schultz and his gang used Adler's brothel to hide from police, which for Adler turned out to be a mixed blessing. Schultz tells Polly that she is "thumbs up with the mob" (209) and provides protection when she needs it (since appealing to the police for help was, of course, out of the question for her). But this didn't stop Schultz's gang from roughing her up on occasion—just for the brutal fun of it, according to Adler. She is frank enough about these frightening encounters to make their telling shocking, although, with her new authorial respectability probably in mind, she phrases them delicately—such as an occasion where she describes how gangsters "mishandle" a girl who was clearly raped (59), or when she recounts the gang's demand that if no girls are immediately available, they'll all "sleep with" Polly (83). Thus, not only does Adler's narrative fill a huge gap by writing female crime back into the story of the gangster era, but Adler also usefully interrupts a vision of the male gangsters that has too easily become romantic or at least glamorous—from accounts contemporary to Adler's career, such as Donald Henrick Clarke's slavish *In the Reign of Rothstein* (1929), to accounts contemporary to this edition of *House*, such as Nick Tosches's aggressively florid *King of the Jews*, also about Rothstein (2005). "Too frequently, they wrecked not only the house, but my nervous system" (80), Adler writes of the likes of Schultz, Legs Diamond, and Waxey Gordon. Instead of easily admiring the masculinity of the gangsters, she reflects philosophically on them as a subset of men, who have different ways of expressing patriarchal power. She wrote, "It was an odd thing—racketeers frowned on men of their calling who got serious with a prostitute, while men in legitimate businesses and intellectuals, especially the broad-A group, did not have this attitude and showed far more respect toward a prostitute than did any of the underworld inhabitants" (58). When a gangster named "Playful Joe" asked one of Polly's "girls," "Why do you work for this Jew bastard?" and the woman answered that it was because she liked Polly, he took off his belt and beat her viciously (82)—rendering his nickname horrifying rather than pleasingly colorful.

Adler recalls that at times she wanted to break away from the vice business—and the company of mobsters—and "go legit." At those times, Dutch Schultz dispensed to her the conventional wisdom (made famous by gangster movies including *The Godfather*) that breaking away from the rackets can't be done. Because gangsters remained at the center of her operation until she was forced out of business, Adler continued as a prominent fixture of New York's nightlife, simultaneously central and marginal, with her establishment a popular after-hours destination.

The culture of speakeasies, organized by criminal mobs and made possible by Prohibition, was key, as Lewis A. Erenberg has shown, in facilitating the United States' transition from the structured decorum of the Victorian period into the showy styles of socializing and consumption of what came to be known as "the Jazz Age."[7] Adler's New York, as the historian Ann Douglas has observed, was the center of "America's greatest takeoff" economically and culturally.[8] This takeoff began at the same time Adler, a twelve-year-old traveling alone from Russia, arrived in the United States; when Adler was twenty, the U.S. census indicated that the country was an urban nation for the first time—and New York was its center. Sketching New York in the 1920s, Douglas paints an "elated" time and an anti-puritan metropolis in which consumer culture was in the ascent. Prostitution, in which people are both consumers and consumed, and with its natural elements of both theater and commerce, becomes in *A House Is Not a Home* a perfect emblem for the America of the "Jazz Age," and Adler places her narrative right in the center of this picture. "My story is inseparable from the story of the Twenties" (5), she claims at the beginning of her autobiography. In one of her most concise and hilarious lines, Adler refers to America in the 1920s as "The Land of Plenty More Where That Came From" (201).

Adler's vision of New York offers a glimpse of a burgeoning culture of public amusement spaces, the birth of that central social activity that David Nasaw has dubbed "going out." As a teenager, Polly is saved from the unrelenting monotony of her factory job when she discovers the early twentieth-century ballrooms and dance halls. In the tradition of the "sweatshop poets," the first group of Yiddish poets in America whose own factory jobs provided the subject matter for much of their poetry, Adler writes that her job making corsets turned her into a "mole again, spending long days working and coming out of the factory into darkness" (17). She joins some factory friends one evening in a trip to the Nonpareil Dance Hall, and almost immediately becomes dance crazy. Polly begins going dancing every week, joining the dance rage of the 1910s that spread across New York, but especially among poor and working girls. Nasaw quotes the Christmas 1914 issue of *Variety* as claiming that "the very landscape of Broadway had been changed by the dance craze. North of Times Square, both sides of the street are lined with cabarets, Jardins, Gardens, Palaises and what not."[9]

In *House*, Adler recalls not only how crowded the dance floors had become with factory girls, but also the shock with which social reformers and settlement house workers regarded the new dating "scene":

> From their sanctified soapboxes, they expressed their horror at fashions in dancing which brought male and female bodies into such uncompromisingly intimate contact. They denounced the aphrodisiac quality of a new kind of music called "jazz"—music born (low be it spoken) in a New Orleans barrel house. They warned the parents of the nation to keep their daughters away from "the gilded hell of the *palais de danse*" in terms which strongly suggested that a sort of mass defloration was a nightly event in such places. (20)

A few years later, when Prohibition began, much nightlife was literally criminalized as illegal clubs where people could purchase alcohol proliferated. These speakeasies, according to the historian George Chauncey, "eroded the boundaries between respectability and criminality, public and private and between commercial space and home life, for the hosts welcomed patrons into their basement hideaways as if into their own homes, and encouraged them to mingle with the other guests and to spurn the conventions that normally governed their public behavior."[10] When Adler operates her own "house," she describes the environment there in this intimate way, picturing customers sitting around the table engaged in homey conversation: "My new customers did not always come to my house for sex. 'Polly's' was also a place to meet friends, play cards, arrange a dinner party, kill time" (96). Indeed, following one of Adler's arrests for running a disorderly house, she was quoted in a local newspaper as objecting vehemently: "This is my home! These are my guests!"

Adler describes the Prohibition-era club scene so astutely that *A House Is Not a Home* enters, in this regard, the territory of social history of leisure, anticipating the work of historians such as Erenberg and Nasaw. These clubs were generally owned by Irish, Italian, and Jewish gangsters but presided over by celebrities such as Broadway personality and Hollywood actress Texas Guinan, torch singer Helen Morgan, and comedian Jimmy Durante. Adler effectively conveys the new atmosphere in these clubs, centered on a master of ceremonies, whose personality dominated the scene and who interacted with customers. She is well aware of the profound impact that this new organization of leisure had on American society broadly drawn, pointing out that "Prohibition did much to knock the props out from under the existing social structure . . . inevitably, the intermingling of inhabitants of the top drawer, the demi-monde, and the underworld left its impress on the speech and manners of the day" (71).

As a business strategy, Adler—who detected and embraced the new importance of advertising—would stage appearances at these clubs, surrounded by her expensively dressed "girls." The result was that they would often be introduced by the master of ceremonies to the other patrons or mentioned the next day in the newspaper. Lewis Erenberg has pointed out that during the era, "publicity and celebrity—living a role the popular press desired—provided status in a competitive social order" (244). Adler knew this well, and turned it to her advantage—even, she claimed, generously advising other "madams" to do the same thing. She reaped the attention of gossip columnists such as Cholly Knickerbocker (who wrote in the society pages of the *New York American*) and Walter Winchell (who wrote in the entertainment pages of the *Evening Graphic*). She became a familiar figure in New York nightlife, a touchstone of both luxury and verve, mentioned in an array of intimate accounts of the period.

Adler also gives an account of the "slumming" fad and the "Negro vogue" in which white audiences indulged a fascination with Black America by making their way to clubs in Harlem to enjoy the spectacle of Blackness. These audience sometimes attended nightclubs patronized by African Americans, but generally visited white-owned clubs to sit in white-only audiences and watch Black performers who catered to their salacious expectations about oversexed and "primitive" Black people. Adler draws some parallel between the salacious expectations of her own customers and those of the "slummers," pointing out that after hours, spenders might head to her place—or they might head up to Harlem for a "slumming tour" to hear jazz musicians at a rent party or watch lewd performances at a neighborhood dive, where they would be supplied with "reefers and cocaine and morphine so that the 'upper clawsses' could have themselves a real low-down time" (73).

An important element of New York's bountiful vivaciousness was the spectacular appeal of sexual subcultures, as George Chauncey slyly summarizes in the title of his book *Gay New York*. Chauncey describes how the popularity of drag balls under Prohibition led to admiring attention even in conservative newspapers, which reported by the early 1930s, when Adler herself was most well known, that the number of society people and ordinary Harlemites attending these balls approached seven thousand.[11] Adler recounts the fascination of her upper-crust clientele with gay culture:

> The first to perform were three queer boys who were completely in drag,
> with wigs, false eyelashes, high-heeled pumps and beautiful evening
> gowns . . . the hit of the evening was their opposite number, Mabel, a
> big fat colored girl clad in white tie and tails, who flaunted a key ring
> on which was inscribed "With love" and the nickname of a well-known
> Park Avenue matron. (231)

Adler does not name most of her customers; instead, she merely
hints at and alludes to their social prominence. Chauncey confirms
that "pillars of respectability . . . along with Broadway celebrities"[12]
were often in attendance at drag events. Clearly, here gay culture
and drag in particular—and especially Black drag—provided ve-
hicles for "respectable" whites to express at least vicariously some
challenge to the decorum of the status quo. Adler dwells with some
drollness upon the inversions of social hierarchy facilitated by the
nightlife in general and the "vice" industry in particular, such as an
incident in her own "house" when, to impress a client, she arranges
for a drunken prostitute to pose as a European princess—which goes
over very well until the woman leaves the table briefly, then returns,
stark naked, to announce blithely that she peed on her dress, but the
butler is drying it out.

The popularity of speakeasies and clubs like the ones Adler
liked to patronize with her "girls" alarmed New York's self-
appointed moral guardians. According to the Committee of Fourteen, a citizens' association formed to investigate the spread of prostitution in New York, "speakeasies lend an atmosphere of apparent
respectability to prostitution."[13] Moreover, as Erenberg points out, they
were seen to encourage a rebelliousness that could well be extended
to other legislated public morality. The intimate world of speakeasies, coupled with the well-known role ethnic gangsters played in supplying alcohol to the saloons, advanced among certain New Yorkers
xenophobic fears that "native" Americans were coming into too much

illicit contact with immigrants. As a Jewish immigrant (a "Russian procuress" according to one tabloid account) who was associated with the clubs, Adler was perfectly situated to inherit a generation's worth of anxiety about sex and the city: the legacy of the late nineteenth- and early twentieth-century "white slavery" panic that had consumed public discussions of sex when young Polly arrived in the United States, casting every young woman as vulnerable to being forced or tricked into prostitution.

Adler's life story illustrates a new mobility on the part of young women, both to the United States and within it (as when Adler leaves her first American home in small-town Holyoke, Massachusetts, for the promises of New York City). This new mobility of women was the cause for some anxiety; in 1909, "white slavery" was established as a danger of international mobility when thirteen countries signed an agreement to fight it. The next year, the Mann Act addressed the connection between "white slavery" and movement within the United States by making it illegal to transport a woman across state lines for "immoral purposes." Urban reformers spun tales of sexually coerced "young women and girls, from thirteen years of age and upwards, of good moral character, [who] have, in a variety of ways, been led or driven, by deception, fraud, and force, into becoming victims of the white slave trade."[14] They also focused on the growing business of vice, turning their attention toward the modern city, with its mixed, mobile, and swelling populations.

   Jews figured as both victims and villains in these accounts, which frequently held that the suppliers of women for illicit sex had "French and Hebrew predominating" (according to an editorial in *Outlook* in 1909). At the same time, a number of commentators singled out Jewish girls as the "greatest supply" of innocent victims for white slave

traders, as George Kibbe Turner put it in a controversial essay called
"The Daughters of the Poor" in *McClure's* in 1909. Fiction and fea-
ture films in the early 1910s were full of crafty, skilled Jewish operators (often known as "cadets") and innocent Jewish immigrants (and
daughters of immigrants) who, despite "respectable" upbringing, fell
into their clutches. One of these, *Traffic in Souls* (1913), claimed to
have been based upon the *Rockefeller White Slavery Report*, a document that is also included as a kind of appendix to some editions of
Reginald Kauffman's white slavery novel *House of Bondage* (1910).

By 1914 the idea of white slavery came under widespread scrutiny:
Was it a myth? Had the public merely been gullible? By this time,
though, a firm connection had been established between Jewish
men and women and the business of prostitution—despite efforts of
"reputable" Jewish organizations to counter this association. Discussions of prostitution tended to pose a binary question: Was prostitution a result of the depravity or lax moral standards of the women
involved, or was prostitution rather due to young women being coerced or tricked into the practice? Only radicals were raising terms
of discussion that departed from the familiar vice paradigms. The
Communist writer Mike Gold, for instance, in his 1930 novel *Jews
without Money*, describes prostitution not as a freakish departure
from everyday morality, but rather as a normal (if poverty-driven)
part of Jewish tenement life. As the historian Ruth Rosen has convincingly demonstrated, employment opportunities were meager for
working women, and prostitution was frequently a viable means of
survival; furthermore, social workers and reformers bent on "saving"
young women from the profession were often blind or indifferent to
the perpetual economic predicament that confronted working-class
women.[15]

Adler's own philosophical outlook on prostitution, however self-
serving it might be, seeks to move the conversation away from the
question of "vice" and more toward practical terms of consideration.

Adler refers dismissively to self-appointed experts on prostitution and "white slavery" as "holders of a Sunday-supplement degree in sociology" (115). Having just recounted her first arrest for procuring, she writes, "to me it was a question of not morals but of economics—I knew the value of money, but how could I compute the value of a good name?" (44)[16]

Adler goes to some lengths to present prostitution as a job, and prostitutes and others in the industry as people performing labor. She describes the specialization of tasks in her "house"—from the maids and the cooks to the "girls" (her usual term) themselves, who also have differing areas of expertise. She discusses her hiring practices in terms of interviewing "applicants" who call to inquire about a "position." Noting that boredom with routine could be a problem for her employees, she writes that prostitutes naturally became fed up with the same routine—"as with the girls in any job" (111). Apparently, she was quite convincing in this regard when her book first appeared, for a few years after its publication Adler and *A House Is Not a Home* were listed in *American Life in Autobiography* (1956) in the section titled "Businessmen, Financiers, Industrialists."

Further, Adler draws connections between what women (and workers more generally) are expected to "sell" of themselves while working a "legitimate" job, and the job of prostitution, which, in her analysis, merely lays bare the dilemma faced by working women in general. She quotes a "girl" who wants to work for her as saying, "Every job I've ever had . . . the boss always tries to make me, and I'm getting sick and tired of getting chased around the desk. The way I look at it, if I have to sleep with some guy to hold a job, I might as well be a whore" (115). Adler ostentatiously notes that being chased around a desk is a "lark" in comparison to working as a prostitute, but she succeeds in making a poignant comparison nonetheless.

Adler also exposes the institution of marriage as an economic arrangement between the man, who provides money, and the wife, who provides domestic services including sex, commenting famously that the only difference between her girls and the average housewife was that her girls gave a man his money's worth (337). (And although Adler piously declaims that marriage is a prize she could never expect to win while she was operating a brothel, she isn't particularly convincing in this regard, and never did marry, even after leaving New York and the prostitution business.) Indeed, she sets the stage from the very first pages of her book for this comparison between marriage and prostitution, with marriage not always coming out more favorably. As opposed to her mother, who she says divided her time between the kitchen and childbed, Adler writes that she, by contrast, "did not want to be the perpetually acquiescent one" (10). The sex industry, for Adler, supplied a sense of agency that marriage could not—this despite the fact that she touts certain former employees of hers who go on to make "respectable" (and lucrative) marriages as great success stories. Adler's critique of marriage as an unsatisfactory, primarily economic arrangement has American antecedents at least as far back as the 1820s, when utopian communitarian efforts such as freethinker Frances Wright's Nashoba (in western Tennessee) were organized around the principle that marriage replicates the master-slave relationship and strove for "moral liberty" through free love. In the 1840s, the Boston literary figure Margaret Fuller urged women to reach their potential by freeing themselves from psychological subordination to men and characterized traditional marriage as a flawed institution. At the turn of the twentieth century, radical feminist activists such as Crystal Eastman, Charlotte Perkins Gilman, Jane Addams, and Emma Goldman argued that traditional marriage was one way in which women's emancipation was thwarted; Goldman, for instance, declared in an important 1910 lecture that marriage was "an economic arrangement, an insurance pact" that a woman paid for with "her name, her privacy, her self-respect, her very life."[17] There is a great deal of kinship to be found between Goldman's analysis and Adler's treatment of marriage and prostitution, although it is sometimes obscured by Adler's defensiveness; she tends to write harshly of the wives she imagines in this imbalanced economic arrangement, in an effort to prove that they are "no better" than the "girls" who work for her.

Adler is clear from the outset that one of the purposes in writing *A House Is Not a Home* is to provide some corrective to what she sees as the wrongheaded portrayal of prostitution. She complains that books portraying prostitution tend to be titillating and shaped according to male fantasy, or else shallowly moralizing and reliant on stereotypes. According to *House*, the "overwhelming proportion of writing on this subject—both fiction and what purports to be factual—is cheaply sensational, or distorted by prejudice or uninformed, often all three" (104–5). In particular, Adler vehemently disapproves of accounts that somehow set prostitution off from "mainstream" female experience. In language that reflects both her insistence on the agency of prostitutes and the racist primitivism of her time and place, she writes: "I resented the idea that the girls were a separate breed, like Ubangis or Hottentots. Many of my customers never seemed to realize that a prostitute is just as much a product of our so-called culture as is a college professor or a bootblack, and, as with them, her choice of occupation has been dictated by environmental and personality factors" (104). Unlike the reformers, who could see prostitution only as a "fall," Adler insists that women's reasons for becoming prostitutes, and the place prostitution held in relation to women's lives, were far more varied and complicated. Indeed, according to Adler, sometimes prostitution—or at least working in Polly Adler's house—*prevented* the ruin of women by increasing their financial options, such as the girl who was working to put herself though college and ultimately became a famous novelist (118–19), or the one who did have "legitimate" work as a Ziegfeld girl, but needed extra money because she was supporting a blind mother

("Honestly!" insists Adler about that last [152]). In fact, Adler saw a woman's move into prostitution as not necessarily unidirectional or permanent: it could, for instance, provide a fall-back option for show girls between jobs or performers who hadn't had their big break yet. According to Adler, prostitution could conceivably launch women back into "straight" life: "Most of my girls were of at least average intelligence and I don't think a one of them, in her right mind, ever had any intention of staying on in the business . . . the smart ones either saved their money against the day they would have to retire, or learned a trade, or worked out ways and means of snagging a rich husband" (108). Although she admits that most women don't easily move on from the business of prostitution, she lays the blame largely on society's moralizing attitude about prostitution. By becoming a prostitute, Adler writes, a woman becomes so socially isolated and deprived of legal rights that loneliness, not syphilis, is the "occupational disease of the prostitute" (125). In a more glancing way, Adler also gives a glimpse of the corrupt police racket of framing women as prostitutes which was able to thrive in no small part because of the paralyzing stigma attached to the charge of prostitution.[18]

Outspoken about the hypocrisy of those who shun prostitutes (and, for that matter, madams), Adler could not help but be aware of the difference between the way prostitutes were seen and the way their male customers were viewed. The facts support her in this regard. When Adler was arrested in 1935 along with three prostitutes after a raid on her East 55th Street apartment, a notebook allegedly containing the names of her regular customers was found in her apartment. The district attorney, William C. Dodge, reported that the book of names was found, but added, "There is no occasion to reveal the names in the book at this time. I do not think they are important. They are set forth as alleged patrons of the place and I am not going to blast the reputations of people just because their names are in the book of a notorious woman. . . . There is nothing illegal about being a customer of such a place" (*New York Times*, March 10, 1935). In staking her ground in *A House Is Not a Home*, Adler is constantly in dialogue—implicitly and sometimes explicitly—with newspaper stories and other portraits of her and her business that she saved in a scrapbook and carried with her into her "retirement," although they were as infuriating to her as they were gratifying.

The newspapers loved Adler, and she, in turn, seems to have had a passionate, if divided, attitude toward them. She covered her face when arrested, dodged reporters during her court appearances, and was whisked out of jail through a back door to avoid photographers after the only term she ever served. A Hearst tabloid, the *Daily Mirror*, was responsible for one of her arrests in 1935 by tipping off police about where she was hiding. As discussed above, she took fervent issue with sensational or superficially condemnatory versions of prostitution. Nonetheless, she gathered clippings assiduously from publications ranging from the reputable *New York Times* to the purple *Daily Tribune*. She quotes these pieces liberally throughout *A House Is Not a Home*, with a predictable mixture of pride, consternation, and outright denial. (To be fair, Adler had reason to worry about revelations in the newspaper: intimations that she was cooperating with corruption investigators would have gotten her into serious trouble with gangsters.) Adler's various press-given monikers are a treat of early twentieth-century purple journalism, from the ironic "La Adler" to the fanciful "Demi-Monde's Queen of the May" to the scolding "notorious harpy." Although by 1935 there was no need to identify Adler in newspaper stories beyond mentioning her name, accounts of her various appearances and arrests are most striking to us now for their characterization of three things: the

Missing Woman Witness In Court Inquiry Found

Polly Adler, Figure in Night Life, Questioned on Arrests

Polly Adler, a well-known figure in the city's night life, and wanted for months as a witness in the Seabury investigation of the lower courts to explain why she never was convicted although she had been arrested many times, was found and interrogated at length yesterday. Dressed fashionably, and well tanned, she explained to Harland B. Tibbets, chief counsel, that she had been in Florida.

Polly Adler's name came into the investigation in the testimony of John C. Weston, former representative of the District Attorney's office who admitted having been bribed to "go easy" once when she appeared before Magistrate H. Stanley Renaud and once before Magistrate Earl A. Smith. She was represented, he said, by lawyers who were in the habit of bribing him "to lay down" when their clients were concerned. Weston testified that a "Frank A. Geraghty" had spoken to Magistrate Smith in behalf of the woman and later corrected this name to one identical to that of a man he said he understood to be a public officer in the Bronx.

Coincident to the appearance of Polly Adler, it was learned yesterday that Referee Seabury plans, within the next two weeks, to report to the Appellate Division regarding alleged bribe-giving lawyers named by Weston. He also may report on the evidence adduced in private and public hearings dealing with three magistrates—Jean H. Norris, Jesse Silbermann and H. Stanley Renaud.

Polly Adler has appeared repeatedly in the lower courts as a defendant though so far as known has never passed a day in jail. Edward C. Perry, a process server for the investigation, served a forthwith subpoena on her in an apartment at Amsterdam Avenue and Seventy-seventh Street and upon her appearance at the County Court building she was questioned for more than an hour by Irving Ben Cooper and Philip Haberman, of the inquiry staff, as well as by Mr. Tibbets. The nature of her testimony was not divulged and she was told to return for further questioning.

New York Herald Tribune.
"Missing Woman Witness In Court Inquiry Found. Polly Adler, Figure in Night Life, Questioned on Arrests."
May 7, 1931.

JAIL FOR POLLY ADLER

Worried

POLLY ADLER

"Queen" faces maximum sentence of three years after guilty plea

Vice Queen Confesses Guilt

Polly Adler, the demimonde's Queen of the May, faces a maximum sentence of three years in the penitentiary as the result of her plea of guilty to the charge of possessing and exhibiting indecent films at her de-luxe mid-town bordello.

La Belle Adler was remanded for sentence on April 26 in Special Sessions after her lawyer, Samuel J. Siegel, failed to sell the three Justices of the court the idea of including a pending prostitution charge in the obscene picture plea.

Siegel informed the court that following a conference with District Attorney Dodge, he assumed the court would include the charge named, growing out of a recent raid, with the picture plea.

Justice Greiser, presiding, and his two associates, Justices Walling and Caldwell, cut that argument short. One plea at a time was their system, they informed Siegel, and on April 26, when she is sentenced on the first charge, Polly Adler must take her chances on the second.

Polly Adler, who for almost a quarter of a century was the most active disorderly house madame in New York, appeared terrified during the proceedings yesterday. She was dressed in a dark coat, around the neck of which was thrown a white muffler. She wore no jewelry. Her bail of $4,000 was continued until April 26.

The reels of motion pictures and the projection machines, which was clicking awn merrily for a select Adler clientele when police raided her apartment on March 5, was in the courtroom. Justice Caldwell announced the court would look at part of the reels before deciding on Polly's sentence.

The March 5 raid on Polly's apartment resulted in a number of sensational departures from the routine way of handling prostitution cases. For one thing, Magistrate Jonah J. Goldstein, before whom Polly first appeared in Women's Court, insisted on learning the names of the two men who were present in the apartment at the time of the raid.

Their identities were never fully revealed, but it was known among the inmates of Polly's establishment, they were called "Uncle Louie" and "Sterling Silver," both middle-aged and married.

Following the discovery that two of the girls who were maintained at Polly's apartment were suffering from social disease, Magistrate Goldstein ordered the men as well be given thorough physical examinations.

All three of Polly Adler's yeights were found guilty, Eva Moore, Eva Acosta and Dorothy Walker. They were given suspended sentences and two remanded to a city hospital for treatment.

Daily Mirror [New York]. "Jail for Polly Adler." April 16, 1935.

POLLY ADLER SEIZED;
POLICE CRITICIZED

Valentine Irked at Deference Shown the Woman and Orders Inquiry.

New York Times. "Polly Adler Seized; Police Criticized." July 11, 1936.

Polly Adler was arrested early yesterday as a procurer. The arrest was the sixteenth in her career. Deference said to have been shown her by the police so angered Commissioner Lewis J. Valentine that he ordered an inquiry.

"I have ordered Chief Inspector John J. Seery to make a thorough investigation," said the commissioner. "I can see no reason why such a woman, an alleged disorderly housekeeper, should receive that special consideration.

"Don't they know there has been a change in this department? I vigorously resent fraternizing by men of this department with people of her alleged character. The probe will cover all phases."

At 4 A. M. yesterday Plainclothes Patrolmen James MacCarthy, Raymond Stilley, and Joseph DeVito of the commissioner's staff, rapped on the door of the Adler apartment on the sixth floor of 65 Central Park West, and, when a maid answered, forced their way in. They found the Adler woman, a 25-year-old blonde named Billie Tinsley, and two men sitting at a table drinking.

The men told the arresting officers that Miss Adler had procured the girl.

About noon they were then taken downtown for arraignment before Magistrate George B. DeLuca in Women's Court. He fixed bail at $1,000 for the Adler woman and $500 for the other. Neither was represented by an attorney and both entered pleas of not guilty.

"I can't possibly furnish that much," said Miss Adler. "I'm broke now and I owe a lot. Besides, I'm innocent of this charge." Her protest, however, made no impression on the magistrate. A hearing was set for Monday.

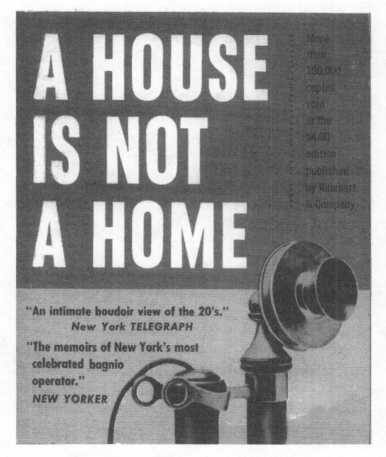

POLLY ADLER

A HOUSE IS NOT A HOME

More than 100,000 copies sold in the $4.00 edition published by Rinehart & Company

"An intimate boudoir view of the 20's."
New York TELEGRAPH

"The memoirs of New York's most celebrated bagnio operator."
NEW YORKER

Cover for mass-market paperback edition of *A House Is Not a Home* (New York: Popular Library, 1954).

Publicity poster for the movie *A House Is Not a Home*. From *Exhibitors' Show-manship Manual* (Embassy Pictures, 1964).

Polly Adler, ca. 1955. Associated Press caption for this photograph reads: "Polly Adler, authoress and one time New York Madame, died June 9, in a Hollywood, Ca., hospital, of cancer. She was 62. She chronicled her career in the book 'A House is Not a Home.'" (Courtesy, AP Images).

"high-class" nature of her business, her Jewishness, and her underworld stature. The last made perfect sense, since most of Polly's press coverage came during two investigations into government corruption in which she was a key witness as the state tried to prove how it came about that she had been arrested as many as sixteen times but never convicted.

The lavishness of Adler's establishment was evidently a source of both titillation and frustration, supporting her own characterization of the era as one when more class mingling occurred than was comfortable for some observers. At times Adler refers somewhat derisively to her catered-to customers, calling them the "breakfast-eating, Brooks Brothers type" (59), the "broad-A group" (58), and so forth. Newspaper accounts made a point of mentioning such details as "All were expensively dressed" (*New York Times*, March 20, 1935, on the arrest of Adler with three other women) or "as usual, her place was well stocked with choice liquors and food" (*New York Times*, January 16, 1943). Although "Polly's" was known as the most posh establishment in town, not everyone was sanguine about these characterizations. For instance, in 1937, during a discussion of a medical campaign among prostitutes in Harlem, a patrolman was quoted saying proudly, "We are doing our bit in Harlem." The magistrate promptly asked, "Why should such an economic line be drawn? The wealthy are as likely to become infected with disease as the people of Harlem. Nearly all of Polly Adler's 'expensive girls' were found to have been diseased" (*New York Times*, July 19, 1937). Despite objections like these, however, there seems to have been an unlimited interest in the conspicuous consumption that was the hallmark of Adler's operation.

Although a *Daily Mirror* columnist did refer to Adler as a "Jewish Jezebel" (May 8, 1931), Adler's Jewish identity was generally repressed in the papers or else encoded in more indirect ways. A tabloid account of a government corruption investigation in which Adler was called to testify, which she quotes in her book, points out that she broke into "indignant outbursts of Yiddish before grudgingly admitting the truth" (186). Other depictions used words like "pushy" and dwelled upon her height (under five feet) and plump figure or "mature" appearance as signs of her immigrant status; for instance, in 1935, when Adler was thirty-five years old, a *Daily Mirror* front page caption tags her as "fat, fiftyish, gaudy in her dress, a bit arrogant." (Jewish girls were considered to "mature early" and become too voluptuous to meet contemporary beauty standards, leading legendary Broadway producer Florenz Ziegfeld to exclude them from his famous choruses.) Such indirection is not surprising, for not long after the white slavery scandal and the outcry of response by Jewish organizations, outright references to Adler's Jewishness were dicey. Later, however, Jewishness would be written back into depictions of Adler. A prime example is true-crime writer Vincent T. Bugliosi's *Lullaby and Good Night*, a corruption/murder story in which Adler appears as a minor character. Bugliosi dwells upon Adler's manner of speaking, which he represents as stage-Jew vernacular; a brassy woman, she repeatedly says, "Listen to me, dollink." In 1964, the casting of Shelley Winters to play Polly Adler in a movie version of *A House Is Not a Home* served to emphasize Adler's Jewishness considering that, as J. Hoberman writes, "No actress since Gertrude Berg has been more associated with the Jewish mother than Shelley Winters."[19]

Pointing up the odd hypocrisy of tabloid journalism is at the heart of Adler's own quite sophisticated authorial strategy. She uses these accounts not only to quibble over details about what "really happened" but also to comment with amazing self-consciousness on the cult of celebrity in which she lived and operated. In fact, it is self-consciousness that most strongly characterizes Adler's book. *A House Is Not a Home* ends with the process of Adler writing her autobiography, so that in a sense the book is its own product. (In fact, in a formally intriguing move, the first and last sentence of the book are the same.) Adler coyly describes all the books she *could* have written—books others urged her to write:

> I was told that the book would be meaningless without a detailed account of my family background and childhood—and that nobody would be interested in my pre-madam years; that I should include a "good big picture" of the Twenties—and that the Twenties had been done *ad nauseam*; that the gangster material was old hat—and the Dutch Schultz chapter the best in the book; that I should avoid anything smacking of *True Confessions*—and that the confessional slant was sure fire; that the treatment should be semi-fictional and the tone light and frothy—and that my approach should be clinical, stressing the sociological implication of my story, and annotated by a psychiatrist, social worker, or legal eagle. (370)

By cataloging the books she could have written, Adler calls our attention here to the innate dishonesty of autobiography, and indeed, this is not a totally honest book. She leaves any relationship with her family out of it, for instance, while newspaper accounts have her accompanied by her brother, Sol Adler, to court to pay back taxes (a typical arrest for gangsters!) in 1935 and receiving money by wire from another brother, Benjamin, when arrested. She rather blithely spins a completely unbelievable yarn about how pornographic movies ended up in her brothel (as if an explanation beyond the obvious were needed) and how she came to be showing the movies, which led to her being charged with possession of a lewd film. (She was holding them for a friend, apparently, and what she had been intending to show was innocent footage she'd shot of her last vacation. Whether the connection this draws between American travel narratives and pornography is intentional is difficult to say.)

Thus, rather than a straightforward rectification of the record, Adler has written a book that is extraordinarily externally referential, factually slippery, and chock-full of sly hints about its own intention and toolkit. Indeed, the best stylistic description of the book is found in Polly's description of the mixture of styles—an Egyptian-styled bar, a Chinese room, period French furniture—in which she decorated her first whorehouse. "Now, of course," she writes, "such a mixture of styles seems laughable, but in those early Twenties to us in America the whole world seemed like a big toy shop, and in our travels abroad we helped ourselves at random to all the glittering odd things that took our fancy" (63). *House* is certainly a coherent tale, but it also is a wonderful collage of writerly concerns and styles. Most striking in this regard is Adler's remarkable use of epigraphs, which range from "high" to "low," from artistic to scientific, from whimsical to journalistic—and invoke pretty much all the different kinds of writing she catalogs in her list of books the memoir "could have" been.

Adler's own writing similarly ranges over a "mixture of styles." Like many "serious" writers about organized crime, she has assimilated the "hard-boiled" language of popular culture. For instance, she has a crooked cop snarl words that can only be imagined coming from Edward G. Robinson in one of his dozens of movie gangster roles: "The thing is, you're newspaper copy, sister. When Adler's is raided, that's headlines, see? And my boss goes for headlines, and he goes to bat for the boys that grab 'em off for him. So when I'm lookin' at you, Polly, I'm lookin' at a promotion" (146). Her ready-made quotability (and in fact, Adlerisms do appear in many collections of "great quotations") is like deliberate showing of the authorial brushstroke: "And if it might seem that I have got Polly Adler confused with Pollyanna, I can only say that I am one of those people who just can't help getting a kick out of life—even when it's a kick in the teeth" (31). At the same time, "high" literary aspirations mark the book; indeed, Adler refers to "high culture" as a second "Goldine Madina" and notes her "stockpile of knowledge about music and literature and art and history" much as she does her growing bank account when she first sets up business. In a startling, formally experimental move, she titles a chapter with a phrase from Dutch Schultz's delirious deathbed monologue, which, with its compelling montage of evocative phrases, came to fascinate later writers including William S. Burroughs (*Last Words of Dutch Schultz*, 1970) and E. L. Doctorow (*Billy Bathgate*, 1989). In short, *A House Is Not a Home* reminds us that not only is it "reporting" on gangsters, nightclubs, policemen, celebrities, and politicians of the 1920s and 1930s, but it is also commenting on the cultural work done by these figures and the way they have been imagined (in books, movies, newspapers, political rhetoric, and the like). It is at once a snapshot—and a wink.

Contemporary reviewers of *A House Is Not a Home*, apparently sobered by its foregrounded strategies, for the most part took it quite seriously, resisting the "nudges and winks" or disapproval one could imagine greeting an immigrant madam's self-penned life story. At least one reviewer states that he has it on good authority that the book was not ghost-written.[20] The *Saturday Review* columnist Lee Rogow called the book "extraordinary" and compared it, fascinatingly, to the Sacco-Vanzetti letters. He credited it with presenting "unblinkable facts about our civilization." The *Newsweek* reviewer found *House* to be an "eerie, impressive, offbeat volume" that avoids the pitfalls of most books on the subject. One of the *New York Times*'s resident Pulitzer Prize winners, Meyer Berger, saw fit to review the book; he treated it more negatively, although his characterization of it as a "harsh, straightforward account of the tribulations of running a bordello" is not necessarily disparaging. The book, meanwhile, was a nonfiction best-seller when it came out in 1953, rivaling the Bible, Norman Vincent Peale's *The Power of Positive Thinking*, and the Kinsey report on female sexuality.

Serious reviews notwithstanding, although *A House Is Not a Home* was first presented to the reading world as a "quality" hardback, it quickly reappeared as a mass-market paperback with a lurid cover. In this form, the book was received in some quarters as scandalous—which, given the subject matter, is hardly surprising. In the first place, its publication in 1953 coincided with the accelerated deepening of the Cold War, which directed intense scrutiny toward language and literature that could be considered "subversive," and with legislation that increasingly targeted the distribution of "obscene" materials. Furthermore, the national obsession with containing communism internationally was accompanied by a strong move to protect the "American way of life" by preserving the status quo domestically. This meant, among other things, containing women in the home, as Elaine May has well established in her book *Homeward Bound: American Families in the Cold War Era*. In a political climate that demanded ideological conformity and gender orthodoxy, books like Adler's (and, for that matter, the Kinsey report) could operate as challenges to the "normal," as outlets for talking about sex, and—simply because they were seen as departures from the "polite"—as very early rumblings of what would come to be called the "sexual revolution" little more than a decade later.

After the highly visible initial release of *A House Is Not a Home*, its major public moment occurred when a film version was released in 1964, directed by Joseph Levine and starring Shelley Winters as Polly Adler. (This was Winters's second straight role as a madam, after 1963's *The Balcony*.) Unfortunately for the book, there was immediate and almost unanimous agreement that the movie was poor, and it sank directly into lasting obscurity. This, no doubt, contributed to the loss of interest in Adler's fascinating book (although it did briefly resurface in a paperback edition in 1982). Publicity material for the movie indicated that the it would, indeed, pander in a way the book did not; the portrayal of "Polly's girls" included the casting of starlet Raquel Welch, the dissemination of promotional posters of scantily clad beauties (with very little visible effort to represent period detail in their clothing and hairstyles), and slogans urging viewers to "visit Polly's girls." Nonetheless, the movie is not without its hardboiled, campy pleasures, as in a scene where two prostitutes sit side-by-side in front of a mirror, discussing the difficulty of getting a john to spring for dinner. Says one, "There are two types of men, those who want to eat before, and those who want to eat after." The second woman rejoins wisely, "Oh, I see you haven't met the third kind yet."

Promptly, the *New York Times* reviewer bemoaned the movie as "so abysmal, it could set movies back 20 years." Calling it a piece of "maudlin fakery" and a "meretricious picture," the same reviewer tipped his rather moralizing hand in a later piece in which he listed the movie as one of many that prove that there is "no guard against the projection of sex emphasis" and making "a life of vice . . . look luxurious." Other newspapers of the time were similarly concerned with the moral implications of the film. The *Valley News* in Van Nuys, California, for instance, trumpeted, "Dark Era Recalled" and characterized the movie as a portrait of "the sin-ridden 1930s." The movie's theme song, "A House Is Not a Home," written by the successful composer Burt Bacharach and sung by the popular soul singer Brook Benton, stalled at the bottom of the Billboard charts. The movie has still never been released on VHS or DVD. And a musical based on *House*, reportedly in the works around the same time as the movie version, never made it to Broadway.

So here is Polly Adler, in all her unruly glory, telling her own story, without the dubious benefit of the Hollywood dream machine. She is nobody's Jewish mother, nobody's princess, nobody's noble social worker, nobody's grateful schoolgirl. And we need her story—for its sharp angle on the evolution of the United States' most important city. We also need her story so that Jewish women's history doesn't become mired in piety—and American gangster history doesn't become enveloped in masculine nostalgia. One would be hard pressed to think of many Jewish women famous for being "bad" to keep Adler company. This reveals a shocking elision in conventional American history, but perhaps it's one Adler herself wouldn't mind. As she said herself about writing this book, "too many cooks spoil the brothel" (373).

NOTES

Thanks to Daniel Rodriguez and Jon Went for their research assistance.
—Rachel Rubin

1. In Geoffrey O'Brien, *Sonata for Jukebox: An Autobiography of My Ears* (Counterpoint Press, 2004), 89.

2. Ted Morgan, *On Becoming American* (Paragon House, 1988), 77.

3. See Samuel Ornitz, *Haunch Paunch and Jowl: An Anonymous Autobiography* (Rinehart, 1923), and Daniel Fuchs, *Summer in Williamsburg* (1934), in *Three Novels* (Basic Books, 1961).

4. David E. Ruth, *Inventing the Public Enemy: The Gangster in American Culture, 1919–1934* (University of Chicago Press, 1999).

5. Rachel Rubin, *Jewish Gangsters of Modern Literature* (University of Illinois Press, 2000).

6. Quoted in *New York Herald Tribune*, July 23, 1931, 6.

7. See Lewis A. Erenberg, *Steppin' Out: New York Nightlife and the Transformation of American Culture, 1890–1930* (University of Chicago Press, 1981).

8. Ann Douglas, *Terrible Honesty: Mongrel Manhattan in the 1920s* (Farrar, Straus and Giroux, 1995), 3.

9. David Nasaw, *Going Out: The Rise and Fall of Public Amusements* (Harvard University Press, 1993), 105.

10. George Chauncey, *Gay New York: Gender, Urban Culture, and the Making of the Gay Male World, 1890–1940* (Basic Books, 1994), 308.

11. Ibid., 259.

12. Ibid., 310.

13. Qtd. in ibid., 307.

14. Stanley W. Finch, *The White Slave Traffic: Address before the World's Purity Congress*, 1912.

15. See Ruth Rosen, *The Lost Sisterhood: Prostitution in America, 1900–1918* (Johns Hopkins University Press, 1983).

16. Fascinatingly, Adler here echoes the words of a Jewish ex-prostitute in Philadelphia at the turn of the century, Maimie Pinzer, whose letters were collected in 1977. Pinzer wrote, "Respectability too often means a cheap

room with cheap surroundings" (*The Maimie Papers*, ed. Ruth Rosen and Sue Davidson. [Feminist Press: 1977], xxviii)

17. Emma Goldman, "Marriage and Love," 1910. First published in *Anarchism and Other Essays* (Mother Earth Publishing Association, 1917), 234.

18. For a "true crime" novelization of this racket, which was ultimately brought to light under the corruption investigations headed by Judge Samuel Seabury in 1931, see Vincent T. Bugliosi's *Lullaby and Good Night* (New American Library, 1987). Bugliosi's book also features Polly Adler as a character.

19. J. Hoberman, "Shelley Winters," in *Entertaining America: Jews, Movies, and Broadcasting*, ed. J. Hoberman and Jeffrey Shandler (Jewish Museum, New York, in association with Princeton University Press, 2003), 176.

20. In a typewritten letter to Sam N. Behrman (September 23, 1960), a long-time University of Nebraska Press editor named Virginia Faulkner claims to have ghost-written the book in the course of a cross-country trip. However, there is no documentary evidence of this in her papers (or contemporary references to it beyond this letter and Behrman's reply to it): no correspondence with Adler or with the publisher of *House*, no drafts of the book, no record of Faulkner having met Adler, etc.

Proper Names Mentioned

HARRY RICHMAN (28)—Broadway singing sensation in the 1920s; introduced some standards into the American popular song canon.

ARNOLD ROTHSTEIN (32)—Jewish gambler thought to have "fixed" the 1919 World Series.

MABEL NORMAND (36)—Comic actress from silent movies.

ROSA PONSELLE (51)—Operatic diva.

HOLBROOK BLINN (60)—Successful actor, director, and producer from the stage and silent movies.

IZZY EINSTEIN and MOE SMITH (70)—Prohibition agents working from 1920 to 1925. Closed many speakeasies using a variety of (sometimes elaborate) disguises.

AL CAPONE (71)—Probably America's best-known gangster; leader in organized crime in Chicago during Prohibition.

JOE MASSERIA (71)—Sicilian-born gangster in New York's bootlegging industry. Executed by members of his own gang in 1931.

OWNEY MADDEN (71)—Gangster and operator of the Cotton Club, a whites-only nightclub in Harlem in the 1920s. His nickname was "the Killer."

MAURY PAUL (71)—Famous columnist who wrote under the name "Cholly Knickerbocker." Coined the term "Cafe society" for New York's fashionable world of leisure.

WALTER WINCHELL (71)—Emerged in the 1920s as a gossip columnist whose syndicated daily column and weekly radio broadcast reached an audience of millions. Winchell is credited with changing the nature of celebrity by introducing personal revelations into his columns.

EMILY POST (71)—Authority on manners who published ten editions of her book, *Etiquette,* as well as writing a syndicated newspaper column and hosting a radio show.

JACK "LEGS" DIAMOND (71)—Gangster who was the front man for Arnold Rothstein and the chief rival of Dutch Schultz. He survived 17 bullets over the course of his career.

DUTCH SCHULTZ (71)—Leader of Harlem bootlegging, gambling, and enforcing. Cooperated with Italian mob (led by Lucky Luciano) to form crime syndicate known as Murder, Inc.

TEXAS GUINAN (72)—Born Mary Louise Cecilia Guinan. Broadway personality and Hollywood actress. Famous in clubs for greeting guests with "Hello, Sucker!" Long-time target of Prohibition agents.

HELEN MORGAN (72)—Wildly popular singer in speakeasies in the 1920s.

LOU CLAYTON, EDDIE JACKSON, JIMMY DURANTE (77)—A comedy trio that launched comic Jimmy Durante as a vaudeville and radio star.

GEORGE MCMANUS (81)—Gambler indicted, and then acquitted, in the murder of Arnold Rothstein.

HARRY SINCLAIR (87)—Industrialist who transformed the oil industry and began to build a $350 million company, the Sinclair Consolidated Oil Corporation, which would control all aspects of petroleum production, from exploring to retail sales. By World War I his was the largest independent oil company in the country.

WAXEY GORDON (91)—A major New York bootlegger who went on to lead a heroin ring after World War II, when in his sixties.

EARL CARROLL, JOYCE HAWLEY (95)—Carroll was Ziegfeld's chief competition in the "beauty chorus" business, and Hawley his most famous star. Hawley would take champagne baths onstage, which led to Carroll's arrest under Prohibition and jailing for perjury because he said under oath that it was water Hawley bathed in.

DEMPSEY-TUNNEY FIGHT (95)—The match between boxers Jack Dempsey and Gene Tunney in 1927 was arguably the most famous bout at that time, drawing what was then a huge gate of $2,658,660. Dempsey pummeled Tunney in the first six rounds but eventually lost the match.

DEMPSEY-SHARKEY FIGHT (100)—Another famous boxing match of 1927, in which Jack Dempsey beat Jack Sharkey.

FRANK COSTELLO (102)—Mastermind bootlegger and gambler, said to have exercised more political influence than any other syndicate boss.

KIPLING (104)—Rudyard Kipling was an Indian-born English writer, much of whose work appeared during the late nineteenth-century heyday of British imperialism. The poem Adler refers to is "The Ladies."

ZOLA, DOSTOIEVSKI, MAUGHAM (104)—Writers Emile Zola (French), Fyodor Dostoievski (Russian), and Somerset Maugham (English) all published important works about prostitutes: Zola's *Nana* (1862), Dostoievski's *Crime and Punishment* (1866), and Maugham's "Rain" (1921).

TOMMY LYMON (111)—Cabaret performer of the 1920s. Said to have coined the phrase "torch song."

SING SING (136)—New York's most notorious prison.

IVAR KRUEGER (144)—Swedish financier who engaged in construction operations in the United States before returning to Sweden, where he formed a trust to control all match production, first in Sweden, then in the world.

SAMUEL INSULL (144)—A powerful Chicago-based utilities magnate.

JOHN J. RASKOB (144)—Financier who played important roles in building the General Motors Corporation and DuPont and published a 1929 article in *Ladies' Home Journal* titled "Everybody Ought to Be Rich." Raskob is also remembered for spearheading the construction of the Empire State Building.

MAE WEST (145)—Risque vaudeville and burlesque performer born Mary Jane West. West was arrested in 1927 on morals charges after appearing on Broadway in a play she wrote titled *Sex*, but she always regarded openness about sex to be a human rights issue.

RUTH SNYDER (145)—A Queens housewife who conspired with her lover to murder her husband. After the trial, Snyder was executed, becoming the second woman to die in the electric chair at Sing Sing Prison.

JUDGE SAMUEL SEABURY (145)—New York City judge who presided over the biggest investigation into political corruption in American municipal history.

IRWIN O'BRIEN (151)—Police contact of Adler's whose real name was Irwin O'Leary. O'Leary was fired in 1931 for his association with Adler.

VALENTINE'S DAY MASSACRE (161)—The most notorious gangland "hit" in American history took place in Chicago in 1929, when Al Capone's gang lined up seven of rival Bugs Moran's gang and mowed them down with machine guns.

"THE GREAT ENGINEER" (163)—Nickname for President Herbert Hoover.

FIORELLO H. LA GUARDIA (166)—Elected mayor of New York in 1933, signaling an end to the power of the Democratic political machine known as Tammany Hall.

VIVIAN GORDON (173)—A prostitute (who, despite Adler's denials in *House*, evidently worked for her) murdered in 1931 by a strangler just before she was set to testify in the vice corruption investigations.

STEPHEN S. WISE (181)—U.S. rabbi and Zionist leader who engaged in social justice work. Wise was a friend to Franklin Delano Roosevelt.

REVEREND JOHN HAYNES HOLMES (181)—Preacher at Community Church in New York, known for his social justice work. Holmes was a founder of the National Association for the Advancement of Colored People, the League for Industrial Democracy, the India League of America, the Fellowship of Reconciliation, and the American Civil Liberties Union (of which he was a director for 40 years and chairman of the board for 10).

IRVING BEN COOPER (185)—Special council, New York City Department of Investigation. Cooper went on to become a federal judge in 1962.

ZIEGFELD FOLLIES (201)—Legendary "beauty revues" staged by producer Florenz Ziegfeld, who declared his dedication to "glorifying the American girl."

ADOLPH MENJOU (205)—Silent film star.

VINCENT COLL (205)—Irish gangster and rival of Dutch Schultz. Known as reckless and violent; finally killed by Schultz's men. His nickname was "Mad Dog."

CHAMBER OF REST AT FRANK CAMPBELL'S (206)—Funeral parlor on Madison Avenue.

BILL DWYER (270)—Known as "Big Bill Dwyer." An early Prohibition bootlegger who formed a partnership with Frank Costello.

DOROTHY KILGALLEN (274)—Trial journalist in the Hearst Publications who would go on to be a radio and television personality and an open critic of various government institutions (including, most famously, those involved with investigating the assassination of President John F. Kennedy).

THOMAS E. DEWEY (289)—New York City prosecutor who helped to convict gangster "Lucky" Luciano (of Murder, Inc.) in 1936. He went on to be the governor of New York State and the Republican presidential nominee in two elections (both of which he lost).

jkbvgcx

ROBERT BENCHLEY (292)—Writer and humorist for *Vanity Fair* and the *New Yorker*, he was considered the organizing force behind the Algonquin Round Table, a group of New York City writers, actors, critics, and other sophisticates. Adler claimed Benchley as a great friend and one of the people she admired most.

DOROTHY PARKER (292)—Writer and poet known for her sharp tongue and caustic wit. She was a part of the Algonquin Round Table.

LUCKY LUCIANO (294)— Legendary New York mobster who is considered to have masterminded the National Crime Syndicate.

BUGSY SIEGEL (295)—Benjamin "Bugsy" Siegel (born Siegelbaum) was a gangster popularly considered to have conceived the idea of Las Vegas. Sent to California to develop connections there in the gambling rackets, Siegel managed to gain entrance to Hollywood's inner circle.

VIRGINIA HILL (295)—Reputed mafia courier and long-time mistress of Bugsy Siegel. Siegel was shot to death in her mansion.

EVERLEIGH SISTERS (310)—Born Ada and Minna Lester, they operated the most successful brothel in Chicago starting around 1900.

STANLEY KETCHEL (313)—Born Stanislaus Kiecel, he was the world middleweight champion in boxing in 1908.

GENTLEMAN JIM CORBETT (313)—First heavyweight champion of the world in boxing.

JOHN BARRYMORE (314)—Famous Shakespearean actor regarded by many as the greatest actor of his generation.

GROVER WHALEN (328)—New York chief of police, known as a ruthless enforcer of Prohibition.

WALLY BEERY (330)—Wallace Beery, a Hollywood actor in mostly comic roles. Known for alcoholism and violent behavior.

H. ALLEN SMITH (332)—Humorist writer popular in the 1940s and 1950s.

WOLCOTT GIBBS (351)—Parodist and drama critic for the *New Yorker* magazine.

FANNIE BRICE (354)—Stage name of Fania Borach, a comic star of the New York stage. Her signature song was "My Man."

GENE FOWLER (354)—Journalist, playwright, and screenwriter.

Appendix B

Timeline for Situating *A House Is Not a Home*

1900: Polly Adler is born in Yanow, Russia.

1903: Kishinev pogrom leaves about 120 dead and about 500 injured.

1905: Odessa pogrom leaves 299 victims.

1908: New York Police Commissioner Theodore Bingham writes report claiming that at least half of New York's criminals are "Hebrews."

1909: Emma Goldman publishes *The Traffic in Women*.

1910: "White slavery" scare peaks. Special grand jury appointed in New York to investigate the white slave traffic.

1910: Mann Act passed.

1910: Reginald Wright Kauffman publishes *House of Bondage*.

1911: Dillingham Commission (U.S. Immigration Commission) Reports document immigration to the United States and subsequent welfare of the immigrants.

1912: Adler comes to the United States (age 12).

1912: Mary Antin publishes her memoir, *Promised Land*.

1919: The 18th Amendment and the Volstead Act make sale of alcohol illegal.

1920: Adler first starts arranging "dates."

1921: Adler opens legitimate business, a lingerie shop. It folds after one year.

1921: Quota Act of 1921 limits entrants from each nation to 3 percent of that nationality's presence in the United States as recorded in the 1910 census.

1924: Immigration Restriction Act reduces the annual immigration ceiling to 160,000. It further reduces quota for Jews and immigrants considered less desirable to 2 percent of the group's representation in the 1890 census.

1924: Statue of Liberty becomes a national monument.

1927: National Origins Act (which took full effect in 1929) reiterates quota approach to immigration restriction.

1928: Jewish gambler Arnold Rothstein killed. The murder is never solved.

1929: Adler becomes a naturalized U.S. citizen.

1930: Mike Gold publishes *Jews without Money*.

1931: Dutch Schultz and gang hide out in Polly's apartment.

1933: Prohibition is repealed.

1935: Adler sentenced to 30 days in jail; serves 24 days.

1935: Adler seized as fugitive in Chicago.

1935: Dutch Schultz killed.

1936: Forced out of the brothel business by Dewey and Seabury corruption investigations, Adler starts operating on an outcall basis.

1938: Federal government files income tax lien against Adler.

1943: Adler arrested for the last time (charges were eventually dropped).

1953: Publication of *A House Is Not a Home*.

1957: Adler enrolls in college.

1961: Adler is quoted in *Webster's Third New International Dictionary* under the entry for "shake" as a verb: "There's no shaking off the press."

1962: Adler dies of cancer at age 62.

1964: Movie version of *A House Is Not a Home*, directed by Joseph Levine and starring Shelley Winters, released by Embassy.

2003: museumofsex opens in New York; premiere exhibit includes Polly Adler.

A House is not a Home

Who Is

Polly Adler?

Her career has made her name synonymous
with sin.

THE DAILY NEWS

During the twenty-five years I ran a house, it often seemed to
me that my time was about equally divided between answering questions and avoiding answering them. Customers and
cops, reporters and prosecuting attorneys, kept me constantly
on the receiving end of a fusillade of queries which ranged
from the routine to the dynamite-packed, from the naïve to
the knowing, from the obscene to the ridiculous. But one
question I never was called on to answer—and which, frankly,
I never dreamed there would be any need for anybody to ask
—is the one which heads this page. Because of my numerous
personal appearances in the headlines (to say nothing of
the even more numerous informal allusions to me in stories
which achieved mass circulation without benefit of newsprint), I just took it for granted that "Polly Adler" was a
household word.

So we live and learn. When the publication of this book
came up for consideration, one of the first points to be discussed was the question of what my name means to the general public. "I would venture," wrote the editorial chief,
"that ninety per cent of people below the age of thirty-five
never heard of Polly Adler."

Never heard of Polly Adler. Those words—why deny it?—

gave me quite a jolt. After all, the clippings in my stack of scrapbooks do not date back to the days of the horseless carriage. It was in 1945—*not* 1845—that I closed the doors of "New York's most famous bordello." Yet barely seven years later it seems that "the most highly publicized procuress in the country" who—it says here—"enjoyed a power in politics, with the press and among the best night clubs that probably never has been matched" already has become the Forgotten Madam.

Now for years I have yearned for the day when, on being introduced to some fellow citizen, the utterance of my name would not inevitably touch off such facial reactions as the quirked eyebrow, the dropped jaw, the tightened lip, or—more vexing still, particularly since I am no longer in business—the leer. Indeed I have firmly believed and frequently stated there was nothing I would welcome so much as a little obscurity. But while its advantages in private life are inestimable, the switch from notoriety to anonymity takes a bit of getting used to. And to find the waters of oblivion closing over your head on the eve of bringing out a book of memoirs is, if nothing else, darned inconvenient.

Actually, I have been (and still am) written about quite a lot—in hard-cover books as well as newspapers and magazines—and not merely because of the public's perennial curiosity about my former profession, but because, like Jimmy Walker and Texas Guinan and Peggy Joyce and Scott Fitzgerald, I played a conspicuous role in the comedy-melodrama of an already legendary decade, the Golden Twenties. My name first became news during the years of that cockeyed national sleigh ride which ended in the crash of '29. Although my career as a madam was by no means ended with prosperity (neither depressions nor wars have an adverse effect on the whorehouse business), still in many respects I was a creation of the times, of an era whose credo was: "Anything which is economically right is morally right"—and my story is inseparable from the story of the Twenties.

While much has been written about this period in America, the picture will not be complete until all precincts are heard from, and there are aspects of the scene on which I am peculiarly well qualified to report—perhaps better qualified than anyone now alive. From the parlor of my house I had a backstage, three-way view. I could look into the underworld, the half-world and the high. What I saw may shock or disgust some readers, but it was there to be seen, and it belongs on the record.

Chapter 1

"Goldine Madina" Means "Golden Land"

> All along the rail there were faces; in the portholes there were faces. Leeward a stale smell came in from the tubby steamer that rode at anchor with the yellow quarantine flag drooping at the foremast.
>
> "I'd give a million dollars," said the old man resting on his oars, "to know what they come for."
>
> "Just for that, pop," said the young man who sat in the stern. "Ain't it the land of opportoonity?"
>
> *John Dos Passos* MANHATTAN TRANSFER

I

I was born in Yanow, a White Russian village near the Polish border, on the second Sunday before Passover, April 16, 1900. Isidore, my father, was a tailor, a talkative, temperamental man with big ideas and a correspondingly large sense of his own importance. In his eyes, as in the eyes of the village, a wife's place was either in the kitchen or in childbed, and Sarah, my subdued self-effacing little mother, alternated uncomplainingly between them. I was the eldest of their nine children. After me were to be born one girl and seven boys.

By Yanow standards we were well off. Our house was large and airy, standing in a big yard. There were vegetable and flower gardens and a barn for the sled horses and the cow. The house also served as headquarters for father's "fine custom tailoring"; during the day the living room doubled as a fitting room and at night the adjacent cutting room became a dormitory for Pavel, father's apprentice, and Katrina, the Polish peasant girl who was our maid-of-all-work.

When I was a year old, my father set off on the first of the many odysseys which have punctuated his life. He must be, I have often thought, a lineal descendant of the Wandering Jew. This first voyage took him to America—called by the villagers "Goldine Madina," the Golden Land. Though he was gone only a few months, it was long enough for him to become an authority on all things American. In the course of the next eight years, he made three more trips—to Warsaw, to Berlin and to New York again—and became an authority on everything.

His journeys never seemed to take him anywhere in the neighborhood of the pot of gold, but they did provide him with material for travelogs which he had no scruples about spinning out to soap-opera length. (As not more than a dozen people in Yanow had ever been even to Pinsk, he always was sure of an audience. Maybe that's why he came home.) For the most part, his tales were listened to with open-mouthed attention and duly swallowed whole. However, on one occasion the villagers' incredulity touched off a top-blowing which had repercussions permanently disturbing to the peace of our household. Reporting on the wonders of "Goldine Madina," father described a new invention called the telephone. But when, instead of ohing and ahing, the audience reacted with winks and knowing looks, his collar began to sizzle. By heaven, he swore, he'd show 'em—he'd build a telephone! Alexander Graham Bell had nothing on my pop. The next day he installed an iron pipe leading from the living room to his bedroom on the second floor and—after a couple of test hails—summoned the skeptical citizenry to see (or hear) what Adler had wrought.

Although the "telephone" never really caught on in Yanow, in our house at least it had come to stay. From then on father spent much of his time in bed, bawling orders down the pipe like a ship's captain. As he had a sonorous and flexible voice, which the speaking tube amplified to foghorn volume, even a placid request for a glass of tea took on apocalyptic overtones. When he was excited or angry the sound effects could be palely approximated if an unusually amorous bull moose were compelled to sit out opening day of the mating season.

Mother was the only one who ever "answered" the telephone. Neither Pavel nor Katrina wanted any part of Pop's invention. If Katrina were anywhere near the pipe outlet when he started to broadcast, she would throw her apron over her head and plunge blindly toward the nearest exit, caroming against chairs and tables and, more often than not, leaving the floor strewn with my little brothers who had to learn early either to dive for safety or be bowled over like so many ninepins. Pavel would stand cowering until the commotion subsided, then trot out to the hall and call upstairs requesting a playback. He could not, he claimed, understand a single syllable that came out of the speaking device. Father, who did not take kindly to criticism of his invention, declared that Pavel was (among other things) a poltroon with wax in his ears, and went right on running the household by phone. It was, after all, his nickel.

I have inherited many of my father's traits—his restlessness and quick temper, his adventurous and inquisitive spirit, his stubborn refusal to be satisfied with second best. It seems to me that at a quite early age I began identifying myself with my father—if by identifying is meant preferring a role in life which would not confine my horizon to the boundaries of Yanow or limit my activities to cooking, sewing, scrubbing and childbearing. I did not want to be the perpetually acquiescent one, forever overshadowed and pushed into the background. I wanted to get out and see the world and mingle with people and have my say about what went on.

As long, almost, as I can remember I have been driven by a fierce desire to get an education. By the time I was twelve all my hopes and plans for the future hinged on my winning a scholarship to the Gymnazia at Pinsk. I knew I was starting with a couple of strikes against me since only one scholarship was available to the Jewish children in Yanow and custom decreed it should go to a boy. But I screwed up my courage and sought help from the most learned man in our village, the Rabbi. Every day after school he tutored me in Russian, Hebrew history and mathematics, and at the end of a year's intensive cramming my head was so bulged out with knowledge it's a good thing I didn't own a hat. I wouldn't have been able to get it on.

What a temptation to say that hard work and persistence paid off, and that as the villagers cheered and the family wept for joy I was handed the scholarship (who's going all the way to Yanow just to make a liar of me?) by Rasputin in person. But the truth is I never did know how I made out, for when prize day came around I had already traveled many miles along a road which did not lead to Pinsk.

My father, who was always toying with the idea of transplanting the family to America, finally had hit upon the plan of sending us over in installments, and when he heard that a cousin of ours was about to set sail for the Golden Land, I, as the eldest, was elected to accompany her. A husband's word, of course, was law, and my mother's tears, her protests that I was only a baby, cut no ice with father. At first I was upset at the thought of leaving home, but once I grew used to the idea, I was excited and eager to be on my way. After all, it wouldn't be long before we were all together again—at least so father said—and I tried to comfort my mother by reminding her of this while she packed my belongings in a potato sack (the Yanow substitute for a Vuitton trunk).

Father took me to the next town, which was on the railway, and after embracing me solemnly, turned me over to the travel broker and departed—probably fearing that if he hung around to see me off he might succumb to his chronic wanderlust. Once I was put aboard the train, I promptly fell asleep—not that I was blasé about traveling, but it had been a long day—and when I awoke, I found my cousin sitting beside me. She was a pale, sad-eyed woman, with an air of mournful abstraction—a character (though I didn't think of it that way then) right out of Chekov. However, unlike most Chekov characters, she appeared to have taken a vow of silence, so after a while I gave up my attempts to be sociable and devoted the rest of the journey to looking out the window.

Since there were young men in our group who had not done their military service and would have been turned back by the border guards, we left the train at Danzig and sneaked into Germany through dark muddy tunnels. The tunnels were scary, but we were in no danger, as the travel broker had paid the necessary bribes when he arranged our passage.

Emerging in Germany, we boarded another train and went on to Bremen, our port of embarkation. The arrival there was all bustle and confusion—so many papers to show and questions to be answered. I was more exhilarated than frightened, but my cousin became increasingly confused and at last broke down completely. "I am afraid," she wailed. "I cannot go to a strange land. We must ask the official for permission to go back. You ask him, Pearl; you're little. He won't be angry with you."

When I saw it was useless to argue with her, I made my first adult decision. Let my cousin go back; *I'd* go on! I went over to the emigration officer, turned on the tears, and talked him into giving me a re-entry permit—one only. Then I marched back to my cousin, thrust it into her hand, and told her of my determination to go on to America. Though she put up a token resistance, the one thing on her mind was getting the hell out of there and back to Russia, so it wasn't long before she kissed me good-bye and went her dim and distracted way.

I sailed that night on the ship *Naftar*. Being the youngest passenger, I rated penthouse accommodations—the top bunk —which served both as bedroom and dining quarters. The food served in steerage was not as good as we gave our animals back in Yanow, and I thought how lucky it was that my mother had tucked four loaves of black bread, four salamis, garlic and apples into my potato sack.

My fellow passengers—all going to seek their fortunes in the Golden Land—were a mixture of nationalities: Russian, Polish, Danish, Swedish and Italian. Since the voyage was very rough, nearly everyone was seasick, but not me. It was my first taste of freedom, and my spirits were high. I would stay up most of the night snacking on salami and singing Russian folk songs—to the annoyance of my ailing shipmates who quite often rewarded my vocalizing with a cussing-out. But when the epidemic of seasickness subsided they made a pet of me, and for the rest of the voyage I had it—as the saying goes—good.

The climax of the trip came one morning when everyone rushed to the rail and began screaming and waving. I was certain that we were sinking and stayed where I was, too frightened to move. Then one of the men grabbed me and set me up on his shoulder.

"Look!" he shouted in Yiddish. "The American Lady! The Statue of Liberty!"

And in a moment I was shouting as wildly as the rest of them. We had come to the Golden Land.

II

From the time we docked, I was swept on by a wave of excitement which carried me through such arrival ceremonies as being deloused and having my papers okayed. The formalities completed, an immigration officer put me on the train for Holyoke, Massachusetts, explaining in Yiddish that I must sit still. He could have saved his breath. Of course I would sit still. I was too scared to move a muscle.

The train was much bigger and noisier than any I had seen in Russia, and when an American lady (nothing like the statue) took the seat beside me, I could not help staring at her strange clothing. After a while it dawned on me that maybe *I* was the one who was dressed peculiarly, and I tried to push my potato sack out of sight. The lady smiled and spoke to me, but I could only shake my head dumbly. All during the trip I listened to the voices around me, trying to sort out what they were saying.

Excitement sustained me till I was in the depot at Holyoke. Standing by the ticket window, I watched as the other passengers were greeted and hugged and kissed. Then the train puffed away and I, left alone with my potato sack, discovered that I was tired and hungry and homesick. Although I kept reminding myself that it was not just a dream, I was really in America and all my friends in Yanow would give their eyeteeth to be in my shoes, my attempt at a pep talk was not very successful. All I wanted to do was cry. The station master came over and looked at the identification tag pinned to my coat. Speaking to me in German, which I could understand a little, he said not to be frightened, I was sure to be met, and he gave me a piece of candy. Feeling a little better, I settled down to wait, but my morale was completely shattered when it grew dark and the big electric signs flashed on. I had never before seen anything like them, and I was petrified.

At long last, the Grodeskys—the people with whom I was to stay—came bustling up to claim me. After making sure I was all in one piece, Mr. Grodesky slung my potato sack over his shoulder and motioned to Mrs. Grodesky for us to follow him. I remember looking back and smiling at the station master, who waved good-bye.

The Grodeskys had come to America five years before and, though not acquainted with my family, were friends of friends. Father had arranged to send them a sum monthly in advance for my keep and schooling, but as I arrived in mid-December, it was too late to enroll me for the current term. So Mrs. Grodesky suggested that for the time being I help her with the housework, explaining that Nadja, the eldest of their numerous children, was preparing for college and was not much use around the house.

My relationship with the Grodeskys was a curious one. I was fed and clothed and taken care of. No one struck me or

spoke to me harshly. No one was unkind. Instead their attitude toward me was one of complete indifference. All my
life I had been an affectionate child, demonstrative and out-
going. Now, surrounded by the unresponsive Grodeskys, I
had to learn to live within myself.

My first friends in America were the MacDonald sisters
who lived next door. They invited me to join their games,
told me the English words for things, and never made fun
of me. After I started school, I found another friend in my
teacher, Mrs. O'Sullivan, who was kind and patient and took
extra time to help me catch on to American ways. But perhaps the most valuable thing she taught me was to take a
joke. Thanks to Mrs. O'Sullivan, when the other kids laughed
at the slips I made, I could laugh with them. Being a woman
of heart, she understood that for people who have had little
opportunity to acquire the social graces, laughter sometimes
can be the saving one.

I worked hard in school, but when at the term's end I came
home brandishing a report card glittering with A's, Mr.
Grodesky signed it without comment. Pats on the head were
not included with room and board. However, as consolation
there was a letter from father saying the family soon would
be sailing for America.

That was in June, 1914. A few weeks later the First World
War was in full swing, and this effectually scuttled my
family's travel plans. Moreover, it meant money no longer
could be sent out of Russia, and Mr. Grodesky ruled that I
could not go back to school. Since I was only five months
away from a diploma, I pleaded with him to allow me to
finish, and in the end he relented enough to allow me to
attend summer school. But there was a condition: though I
was only fourteen, I must ask my father to send me a nota-
rized certificate that I was sixteen. Since I could not pay for

my keep, I must go to work—and in the Golden Land you have to be sixteen to get a job.

The day after the necessary papers arrived, I went to work in a paper factory. The wages were three dollars a week, and I worked there two years. There is not much to remember about those years. I joined a library and spent my free time reading and writing to my family. I heard that my only sister Slawa had died of malnutrition, and that the Germans had taken our horse, Gabba, and our cow and killed our chickens. But happenings in far-off Russia were unreal to me, and gradually the passing of time took from me the thought of being with my family.

How I was to go about it I had no idea, but I knew that I must make a life for myself. I hated the confinement, the humdrum routine, the narrowness of life in the Grodesky house. America was a whole big country, not just one town called Holyoke. Why shouldn't I see some of it? Was I to spend all my days like a mole, hidden away from the sun, buried behind the dark walls of a factory?

Father had written that I had a cousin living in Brooklyn, New York, and one night at dinner, as I looked around at the stolidly chewing Grodeskys, I decided to toss a bombshell.

"I'm going to New York," I blurted, and waited tensely for their reaction.

"Pass the mustard, Nadja," said Mr. Grodesky.

III

When I arrived in Brooklyn, I was startled by the signs of poverty in the neighborhood where my cousins lived. The Grodeskys had not been rich, but compared to the Rosens their house was the Taj Mahal. Nonetheless, I was glad I had come, for after I'd explained who I was, my cousin Lena really made me feel that I was being welcomed from the heart. Pulling me over the threshold, she gave me a big bear hug, the children kissed me and patted me and fussed over me, and Lena kept exclaiming she couldn't wait until Yossell, her husband, came home and found the wonderful surprise. The Rosens were poor; they lived in what amounted to a tenement, but they lived like human beings with warm blood in their veins, not like cold fish.

Almost immediately, I found a job in a corset factory. I made five dollars a week, out of which I paid three dollars for room and board and a dollar twenty for carfare and lunches. That left eighty cents for clothes and shoes and all the things a growing girl needs. I learned to shop for remnants from the bearded pushcart men on Dumont Avenue, and sewed blouses and skirts and underwear for myself by hand. I had to get up at six to be at the factory on time, and I came home just in time for supper.

Though I was happier with the Rosens, I was a mole again, spending the long days working, coming out of the factory into darkness. And I felt strongly that it would always be like this for me unless I got more education. So I enrolled in night school. This meant that after working all day I'd walk a mile to school and a mile back again, not, believe me, because I was any fresh-air fiend or out to take the walking record away from Eleo Sears, but because if I squandered a dime on carfare I couldn't afford lunch the next day. Sometimes I'd be so beat that I'd flop down and go to sleep fully dressed. I slept on a hard leather couch with no mattress, and it was my dream that someday I would own a real bed and be able to climb into it right after supper and stay there the whole night.

Usually, on Sundays I all but slept the clock around. I'd get up for dinner, wash my hair, and then go back to sleep again in spite of the fact that the Rosens' little boys practiced the fiddle all afternoon. Since I loved music, I wanted to get into the act too. I borrowed the violin and persuaded a neighbor to teach me for twenty-five cents a lesson. A dollar and a half later the lessons stopped. I couldn't afford them.

As my cousin's plumbing business began to prosper, I gave up my Sundays' rest to help him with his books. The Rosens praised me for my mathematical ability and were so generous in their compliments that Anna, their eldest daughter, became resentful and took to pouting. It was then that I learned my first lesson in diplomacy. I gave Anna little jobs to do in connection with her father's business papers—enough to make her feel important and keep her busy while I was going over the books. With the jacking up of her ego, the pouting ceased as if by magic.

In April, 1917, when the United States entered the war, the corset factory closed down, and I found a new job in a Blake Avenue factory which manufactured soldiers' shirts. At first I was doing all hand work, but as soon as I had learned to operate a machine, the foreman put me on piece work, saying I could work overtime if I wanted to make more money. I worked overtime.

Along with my hunger for an education, I had developed a new craving—I wanted finery. There was a Japanese mink (dyed cat) cape in a store window on Pitkin Avenue, and every day I walked an extra two blocks just to see it. I used to go over and over my budget, trying to figure out a way of getting that cape. But of course it was a pipe dream—I was doing well to own more than one pair of drawers.

Now, at seventeen, I had matured physically. I had reached my full height of four feet eleven, and my chest had taken on a new look. In those days life would have held little for the columnist Earl Wilson since bosoms were out of style and the boyish figure all the rage. In order to make myself as flat in front as possible, I used to bind myself with strips of white cloth—so tightly that sometimes when I was bending over my machine I'd nearly pass out. It was only after the girls at the factory found out about my "mummy wrappings," and as a result of much kidding, that I finally unpent myself.

Sidonia did most of the kidding. She was a heavy-set redhead, full of bounce and wisecracks, and rumor had it that she was a bit of a rounder. One day after work she announced that she had a date lined up with a couple of sports, and how about me coming along? When I hesitated, she laid her hand on my arm.

"Listen, kiddo," she said, "I know you're a good girl, and no guy's gonna get fresh with you or give you drinks while I'm around. You tell your folks not to worry—Big Sidonia's lookin' after you."

So that night after supper I joined Sidonia and her friends and we went to the Nonpareil Dance Hall. Technically, I guess, this was my début as a "painted woman," for I had daringly dusted my nose with cornstarch and rouged my lips with coloring obtained by soaking red tissue paper in a bowl of water. It was also my début on the dance floor, and after five minutes I was convinced that was where I wanted to spend the rest of my life. Before the evening was over, I had mastered the waltz and one-step, the two-step and the cake-walk, and had been informed by my partner that I was a "real cute little trick" and had "the makin's of a nifty stepper."

The next time Sidonia asked me on a date there was no need to twist my arm. But when the band struck up "Oh, You Beautiful Doll" and Sidonia and her beau whirled out onto the dance floor, my guy—the clod—just stood there chomping on his Spearmint. It wasn't, he said, that he couldn't dance, he just "dint wanta." Finally, in desperation, I asked Sidonia if we could trade dates.

"Sure," she said cheerfully. "One man's as good as another."

Although I was too inexperienced to challenge this statement, I quickly learned it didn't hold true—on the dance floor anyway—and from then on seldom double-dated with Sidonia unless she could guarantee an escort with educated feet. Dancing was the only aspect of dating which interested me—all the flirting and "jollying" seemed a waste of precious time.

At that time—the fall of '17—dance halls all over America were crowded as never before, and reformers and blue noses viewed the scene with alarm. From their sanctified soapboxes, they expressed their horror at fashions in dancing which brought male and female bodies into such uncompromisingly intimate contact. They denounced the aphrodisiac quality of a new kind of music called "jazz"—music born (low be it spoken) in a New Orleans barrel house. They warned the parents of the nation to keep their daughters away from "the gilded hell of the *palais de danse*" in terms which strongly suggested that a sort of mass defloration was a nightly event in such places. Well, if so, I never got in on any such doings. Far from being a "gilded hell," the Nonpareil was more like a gymnasium, and, as in a gymnasium, the goings on though strenuous were disciplined.

Since no escorts were necessary, I began going there Sunday afternoons with a girl from the factory, and before long we made friends with the "regulars"—the kids who, like us, were dance mad. By dint of spending every spare moment practicing, I got to be very good (in fact, almost as good as I thought I was) and entered all the dance contests, competing for candy, kewpie dolls, cups and sometimes even cash. It was considered very hot stuff to jump into a split in the middle or end of a number, and my favorite partner was known as Jack Split because of his skill in this department. I danced with other boys, of course, but it was understood that the contest dances belonged to Jack. Like other teams, we had a small but devoted "fan club," an unofficial claque, who did their best to applaud us into the prize money when we appeared at the Halsey Theatre on amateur nights. Mostly we finished second, but on a few banner occasions copped first.

Although my acquaintance with Jack Split was a hundred per cent unsentimental—I couldn't even have told you the color of his eyes—my cousin Lena, observing my growing interest in my appearance along with my passion for dancing, came to the conclusion it was high time she found me a husband. I was not yet eighteen, still in Russia many girls no older had two or three children. Lena, who believed in leaving nothing to chance, already had picked out my suitor, a neighbor boy named Willie Bernstein.

The whole family co-operated in setting the stage for Willie's wooing. Anna was to spend the evening with a girl friend, and the small fry were packed off to a carnival under orders not to return till nine o'clock. Lena and Yossell would be in the parlor to greet Willie, then suddenly remember urgent business in the kitchen.

After all the scheming and build-up, Willie in person turned out to be quite a letdown—scrawny and pale, with a bad case of acne, and wearing an ill-fitting uniform. (This last was a blow to Lena—he'd been inducted only three days before.) Of course looks aren't the whole story, but poor Willie was by no means the Personality Kid, and it did not add to his charms that he considered dancing sinful. But he played piano and he tried to be pleasant, and we settled down to going steady, which meant that Wednesday, Saturday and Sunday were "Willie's nights."

We knew that Willie would soon be going overseas, and on the night he told us he had received his orders, Lena gave me a poke and look which said plainly, "Close the deal at once." Willie seemed to be in a hurry too, for the minute Lena and Yossell closed the kitchen door, he grabbed me in his arms and kissed me hard on the lips. Well, I knew this was supposed to be my shining moment, but my only thought was that Willie's complexion didn't look any better close up. I drew back and he must have thought I was offended at his freshness, for he hastened to make clear that his attentions were honorable.

So, just as my cousin had planned, Willie had taken the bait. Now all I had to do was to say one little word, and the trap would snap shut. But if I said "Yes," it wasn't only Willie who would be caught—I too would be trapped. There was nothing to do but tell him I didn't love him and wouldn't marry him. When he finally got it through his head my turn-down was on the level, Willie said good night stiffly and stalked out.

Lena was furious, and prophesied gloomily that I was sure to end an old maid. She couldn't understand why I had gone right down to the wire and then balked at the finish line. But how could I explain my feelings to her? My reason for rejecting Willie wasn't only that I didn't love him. Even more than that, perhaps, it was because I so hated the one thing we had in common—our poverty.

I got a raise at the factory and was promoted to a more difficult machine. For a few days I was proud of myself and felt like quite a career girl. Then it dawned on me that I was still sleeping on the leather couch, still grindingly poor, still minus an education, still without a place in the sun. I was restless and discontented. I kept thinking that surely life must offer me other alternatives than a factory job and a Willie Bernstein.

One day a new foreman came to work. His name was Frank, and whenever he walked past my machine I got weak in the knees. If he so much as looked at me, even though his glances were impersonal and cold, my heart thumped like a tom-tom. He affected the other girls the same way. They all raved about Frank—how handsome he was, how sexy, what a spiffy dresser. When I saw him swagger down the aisle between the machines, every girl giving him the eye, when I saw the lordly way he acknowledged their homage and disdained it—well, let's face it, I was a dead pigeon.

Up to that time I had never even thought of making a play for anyone, but this was different, this was love, and I bragged to Sidonia that Frank was as good as in the bag. Sidonia looked me over appraisingly. "Well, if you can't be good, be careful," she said. "You sure got mischief in your eyes."

That day I really gave out every time Frank was in the vicinity, and finally he sauntered over by me and bent down as if he were inspecting my work.

"Come to my office right after lunch," he said.

I almost strangled. From then until noon hour I was on

tenterhooks. He had been so businesslike I didn't know whether he was going to fire me or ask for a date. But when I went into his office there was no longer anything cold or impersonal about the way he looked at me. What he wanted to see me about, he said, was would I care to go out to Coney Island with him that night?

Would I? My voice has always been low and husky, but it dropped a full two registers on that "Yes."

Frank asked me if I'd mind coming along while he picked up some clothes he'd left in a cottage out there. It was the end of the season and the place was being closed for the winter. We arranged to meet.

As I went back to my machine, walking on air, I gave Sidonia the high sign, and she passed the word around to the other girls. All afternoon my conquest was the only topic of conversation, and when one girl—trying, I guess, to figure out what I had—said, "Well, you know, Pearl does look kinda like Theda Bara," my cup was full. I felt like the *femme fatale* of all time.

It was a long walk from the station to the cottage where Frank was to pick up his things. The boardwalk was deserted, and there were shutters on the concessions. An icy wind flattened against us as we walked along, and by the time we reached the cottage, I was shivering with cold and glad to get inside where it was warm.

We kidded about mutual acquaintances at the factory while Frank packed. When he closed the grip, I stood up, ready to leave.

"What's your hurry?" he said. "The evening is young."

He put a record on the talking machine—a comedy song, Scotch brogue (I think now it must have been Harry Lauder). Then he sat down on the couch and patted the place beside him, beckoning for me to come and sit there. I complied, and after a moment he leaned over and began pulling the pins out of my hat. All of a sudden I got scared. I jumped up from the couch and said it was time to go. Instead of answering, he went over to the door and locked it.

When I resisted him, he knocked me cold.

The next morning I told Lena I was too sick to go to work. Since my jaw was badly bruised and my eyes swollen nearly shut from crying, I kept my face hidden from her in the pillow. Later I made up a story about falling down, and she seemed to believe it.

I stayed away from work the next three days. It seemed to me I could never face the girls at the factory again, and even worse was the thought of seeing Frank. On the evening of the third day, Sidonia came to inquire about me, and I poured out the whole story. She called it rape, and though I winced on hearing this ugly word, still it did reduce what had happened to a size where I could handle it. I had heard the girls talking about it, I had seen the word in the headlines, and the knowledge that I was not the only one who had been through such an experience helped to restore my sense of proportion. I accepted that such things happened and still the world did not come to an end.

After I had been back at work a month, I discovered I was pregnant. Though my feelings about Frank were the same I would have for a dangerous reptile, only more so, the child inside me was his, and I asked him to marry me. His answer was to kick me out of his office.

So what was there left to do? Sidonia and I talked it over, and she took me to a doctor for an abortion. But his fee was a hundred and fifty dollars and all I had was the thirty-five dollars I had been accumulating toward the Japanese mink cape. Again Frank refused to help out, and at last Sidonia found a Dr. Glick who would do the operation for what I had saved. But when he heard my story, he would only accept twenty-five and told me to take the rest and buy some shoes and stockings.

I tried to put all this nightmare behind me. But though I went through the motions of living, I was changed—I had lost heart, I no longer had hope. Even the excitement and exultation of Armistice Day failed to lift me out of my despairing mood, and when Frank began to pursue me again, it seemed the last straw. Unless I came to see him, he said, he would tell my family what had happened, and I knew he was just the type of man who would enjoy doing it. I went into a huddle with Sidonia, and she advised me to move away. We made a date to meet in Manhattan on Sunday and hunt me a place to live.

Friday I bought some material from one of the pushcart men and basted up a smart dress—black satin with a lace tunic. I didn't have enough time to stitch it, but I wore it anyhow. I met Sidonia in the lobby of a hotel at Twenty-eighth and Broadway, and while she was admiring my finery, a tall, good-looking chap kept circling around us. Sidonia liked his looks, so she smiled at him and he came over.

He introduced himself. His name was Harry, and he was a dress salesman. Harry proved to have a very funny line, and Sidonia roared at his jokes. Presently he invited us to join him at a night club—as I remember, the Bal Tabarin. Sidonia said she had a previous engagement but that I could go with him.

"Alone?" I said—meaning, was he really all right?

"Sure," said Sidonia. "Harry'll be good for what ails you."

This was my first time in a night club, and I was amazed

to find that everybody seemed to know my escort. Hat-check girls, waiters, the mâitre d', some nicely dressed people at one of the tables—they all spoke to Harry and smiled at me. It made me feel as if he were a duke and I his duchess. The music was good, the atmosphere friendly and gay, and Harry kept saying one funny thing after another. At first, I laughed just to be polite, but later, when I got into the spirit of things, with genuine enjoyment. Up to that time I had never had anything stronger than soda pop, but when Harry asked me if I would have a highball, not wanting him to know how small-timish I was, I said "Yes." Since I drank the whisky in big thirsty gulps, like soda pop, it wasn't too long before from being just a duchess I felt as if I'd been promoted to queen.

When Harry asked me if I danced, I didn't hesitate to boast about how many cups I'd won. But as we fox-trotted out onto the floor, my knees felt as if they had an extra joint in them and I tripped over Harry's feet. He looked at me questioningly. I gave him a brave smile, and we danced on. A wave of dizziness hit me, and I clung to him with both hands. The ceiling spun round and round, the walls wavered back and forth, the floor began to behave like a seesaw. Though I managed to stay upright, somehow or other my high heel caught in the hem of my dress. The hastily whipped up seams had already been subjected to more of a strain than they could stand. As Harry struggled to disentangle me, the whole dress came apart and hung around me in fluttering bits and pieces.

However, Harry was—and is—no man to be daunted by an emergency. Quicker than you can say "Minsky," he had whisked me off the floor, wrapped me in my coat and steered me out of there. Once we made the sidewalk, he leaned me against a building and wiped his brow.

"Now then, my little Irene Castle," he said, "where do you live?"

I tried to pull myself together. When I looked at Harry, he seemed to have a twin brother, and his voice came from very far away. He had to repeat his question.

"Brooklyn," I told him.

"Everything happens to me," Harry said grimly.

He called a cab, and I settled down in it among my pieces of finery. He asked my street address, but I couldn't tell him. I had passed out.

But Harry, as I have said, was resourceful. I later learned he took me to a hotel where he was acquainted with the management, got me a room, and turned me over to the night maid. I have a vague recollection of being thrown into a tub of cold water, then blackout again. When next I opened my eyes, it was bright sunlight. Still in a fog, I got up and wobbled over to the dresser. Lying there were all my belongings —powder, rouge, union card, and capital of fifteen cents. There was an envelope containing a note from Harry. He explained that he couldn't see me home because he didn't know where I lived, and he enclosed money for my hotel bill.

It was many years before I saw Harry again. Then I ran into him one night at Reuben's, and we both got a lot of laughs out of recalling our first encounter. By then quite a few people knew the name of the notorious madam, Polly Adler, but people all over the world knew the name of that great Broadway star, Harry Richman.

When I got back to Brooklyn, Lena did not mince words. I had stayed out all night, my dress was in rags, she was not interested in hearing my story. All she wanted was for me to get out—and to get out as of that minute. I did not argue with her. I wrapped my clothing in a newspaper and went.

In the subway station, my bundle came undone and all my belongings spilled out on the floor. As I scooped up the blouses and stockings, I could not help thinking that at least when I left Yanow I'd had a good stout potato sack in which to carry my possessions. I began to laugh—I couldn't help it. So far, I had certainly racked up a row of goose eggs in the Golden Land. I had failed in my quest for the education I might have gotten in Pinsk, I had lost my virginity, my reputation and my job. All I had gotten was older.

So far, the joke was on me.

IV

I found a room on Second Avenue and Ninth Street which I rented for ten dollars a month, payable in advance. Did I say room? It was a windowless hallway leading to the basement flat occupied by the janitor and his family. But I bolstered my morale by remembering what the teacher in night school had told us about Benjamin Franklin—how as a mere boy he had arrived alone in Philadelphia without a penny in his jeans and almost no contacts. And here was I starting out thirty-nine dollars more solvent than Ben, plus the rent paid for a month.

Next day, bearing firmly in mind that "God helps them that help themselves," I set out to look for a job. By the end of the week both the soles of my shoes and my faith in the adage had worn a little thin. But, although I had not found a job, I had made a friend. This was Abe Shornik, a man about my father's age, who worked as a cutter in a dress factory. Abe took his evening meal at the same restaurant I did, and one night when it was crowded we shared a table. After that we often ate together. Abe had come over from Russia in the early nineteen hundreds, he had lived in a village very much like Yanow, and it worried him that I was alone in New York. All unknowingly, I had selected a very tough neighborhood in which to reside, and the restaurant was a hangout for streetwalkers and hoodlums. While briefing me on the perils of the big city, Abe pointed out the hustlers, and I eyed them covertly, embarrassed even to be caught looking at them. I wondered how any woman could sink so low.

When another two weeks had passed, and still no job, I stopped going to the restaurant. My capital had dwindled to fifteen dollars, ten of which had to be reserved for the soon-due rent, so I economized by restricting myself to one-course meals (choice of stale rolls, spoiled fruit or peanuts), which I ate either *chez moi* in my boudoir or *al fresco* near the place of purchase if I was too hungry to hold out till I got home. I was still on the "early to bed, early to rise" kick recommended by Franklin. Yet so far it certainly hadn't panned out. Although maybe I was getting a little wiser, I was fast losing ground financially and as for staying healthy, well, in B. F.'s own words, "It is hard for an empty sack to stand upright."

Fortunately, before the empty sack collapsed altogether, I ran into Abe one day on Second Avenue. He asked why he hadn't seen me at the restaurant. When I explained I couldn't afford it, he not only bought my dinner but stuck a five-dollar bill under my plate. Either his kindness changed my luck, or having eating money in my poke gave me more assurance—the next day I landed a part-time job at the Trio Corset Company.

I hung on there for a little more than a year—from December, 1918, until January, 1920. Now, looking back at those months, the only impressions which remain are of unrelieved drabness, of hurry and worry and clawing uncertainty. In view of the fact that my life was so soon to take the turn which it did, perhaps I should make something more of this—perhaps I should lay it on about what a bitter, hope-quenching, miserable sort of existence it was for a girl of nineteen. But after thinking it over I've decided to skip it. (For one thing, probably the reader would too.) Sure, it was a tough life, it was a hell of a life, but—as I hasten to point out before everybody else does—no tougher for me than for plenty of other poor working girls who *didn't* become madams. In any case, whatever meaning or value my story might have depends first and foremost on my presenting a true picture, and memory does not always hand back the whole truth. So even though my recollections of this period are all of the stench and sourness and dirty-grayness of poverty, of the panicky day-after-day struggling to keep my head above water, it doesn't mean that the sun never shone for me. I know myself well enough to be positive that I couldn't have lived through a whole year, or even a whole week, without finding something enjoyable about being alive, something that made it more than just surviving. And if it might seem that I have got Polly Adler confused with Pollyanna, I can only say that I am one of those people who just can't help getting a kick out of life—even when it's a kick in the teeth.

For me 1919 was a year spent on a treadmill, but if I had looked around me—or, more accurately, looked at a paper— I would have found plenty of indications that the world was not standing still. Aviation was in the headlines—this was the year of the first Atlantic flights—and the Dove of Peace was hovering over Europe, preparing to lay the egg of all time at the Versailles Conference. But it was in the reports of domestic developments that (had I been operating a crystal ball) I might have seen signs and portents of my own future. On January 29, 1919, it was announced by Congress that the Eighteenth Amendment, making illegal the manufacture, sale or transportation of intoxicating liquor, would be in full force on January 16, 1920. This also was the year of the Black Sox scandal, which brought into national notoriety the name of a man whom I was one day to know well. Although all the facts in the case have never been disclosed, it has long been believed that the gambler Arnold Rothstein was the big wheel in engineering the World Series fix.

Like the old year, 1920 began for me with the same day-to-day uncertainty as to where I stood. When business is slow part-time workers are the first to be laid off, and I begged Abe's help in finding a steady job at the dress factory. But there were no openings and no prospects of there being any. Finally, as a last resort, Abe took me to see the daughter of a friend who had come to America when he did. She had married a well-to-do dress manufacturer, a Mr. M., and Abe thought that maybe for old time's sake she might ask her husband to employ me.

The M.'s lived in an apartment on Riverside Drive, which, in 1920, was as plushy an address as Park Avenue is today, and my visit there was an eye opener. Probably the M.'s apartment was no more luxurious than that of any upper-middle-class New York family, but to me it was a revelation of how people—the people in the sun—could live, a miracle of richness and comfort. Now at last my nebulous longings came into sharp focus and crystallized, now I saw the goal I must set myself. There really was a "Goldine Madina," and it was right here on Riverside Drive.

It seemed only fitting that the Golden Land should be inhabited by a Golden Girl. Since Mr. M. was related to the head of a big theatrical supply house, he was acquainted with a number of theater people, and it was at the M.'s I met Joan Smith. In the years since that night I have seen many beautiful girls, but no one who could measure up to Joan. She was tall and blonde, with sapphire-blue eyes and a radiant smile: when she smiled, you felt as if not just the room but every corner of your heart had been lighted up. The word "charm" has taken an awful kicking around, but there really was something magical about Joan. To me she was both the enchanted princess in the tower and the fairy godmother who made your wishes come true. I don't know how to say it—any more than I know how she did it—but she made you feel *good* about yourself. When you were with Joan, it was a wonderful world.

At that first meeting what impressed me almost as much as her beauty was the fact that she was on the stage. She had come on to New York from Chicago, where she had been singing in the same night spot as the Yacht Club Boys, and was soon to be featured in a Broadway musical. But with all this glamorous background, Joan did not put on airs. Her friendliness was so spontaneous and her gaiety so contagious that it was impossible not to respond to it. When she gave me her address and said to drop in the following Sunday, I was in seventh heaven. After that, I could take in my stride the news that Mr. M. knew of no job for me (and even hinted gloomily that if business didn't improve the whole garment business was doomed).

On Sunday, when I went to Joan's apartment, I met a number of her friends—Broadway characters and people in show business. Since I had never been to a musical comedy or a play, my contributions to the conversation must have been naïve to a degree, but I misunderstood their laughter, and was convinced I was a card. I was invited to come again, and it wasn't long before Joan knew all there was to know about me. Then one day, about a month after we had first met, she suggested that I move in with her until I could find a steady job. I thought she was kidding, but she explained she had just leased a nine-room apartment on Riverside Drive, as she was expecting a visit from her mother and dad. Until they arrived, she said, she'd just be rattling around in that big place, and I would be doing her a favor to come and stay. That was how Joan operated. She wouldn't be content merely to give you the shirt off her back; she would hand it to you on a gold platter and make you feel you were saving *her* life by taking it.

If the next few weeks didn't seem like a dream, it was because I suddenly found myself transported into a world which, until then, I wouldn't even have been able to imagine. In many respects the distance between Second Avenue and Riverside Drive was greater than that between Yanow and Holyoke, and for days I went around popeyed and dangle-jawed in a trance of wonder and delight. Joan's show, a Shubert musical, had not yet gone into rehearsal, and the new apartment quickly became a gathering place for her many friends. They liked me, I think, because being so naïve I made a good straight man. Also, I was an eager and uncritical audience. Nearly everyone who came there could perform in some way, and as an actor without an audience is like ham without eggs, I was constantly being called on to watch (and, of course, applaud). But it was no hardship to be an onlooker, I loved it, and most of all when Joan played the guitar and sang. My favorite number was "Moonshine Valley," and I pestered her for it constantly.

Oh, I was in clover all right, but unfortunately—for Joan, tragically—there were poppies growing in that particular clover patch.

I made this discovery one day when I happened to admire
a beautiful Chinese robe—black satin embroidered with a
scarlet dragon—that Joan was wearing. I had never seen anything like it, and she told me it was her favorite costume
when she went on a hop party. I must have looked puzzled
for she held up her sleeve for me to smell. The cloth gave off
a curious acrid aroma.

"What kind of perfume is that?" I asked.

"Not perfume, honey, hop," she said. And when I still
didn't get it, "Opium—don't you know?"

At first I thought she must be joking—how could anyone
speak so lightly of taking drugs?—but she proceeded to explain in detail about the stick, yenhok, lamp and pills. Yet
even then I refused to believe it. She knew how gullible I was
and how the others always were stringing me along, so I tried
to tell myself this was just another gag.

However, I couldn't keep on kidding myself much longer.
Now that she had confided in me, Joan was much more open
about her habit. She began to have hop parties almost
nightly, and would be peeved at me for not joining in. Up to
this time I had put off job-hunting, but now when I spoke of
it Joan begged me not to desert her. What could I say? She
had been so wonderful to me and still was, except when she
was lying on her hip. It was a nerve-wracking, even dangerous
situation, but I thought surely when her mother got there
the parties would have to stop.

But when the family finally did arrive, I was in for another shock. "Dad" turned out to be a young man hardly
older than Joan. I could not help commenting on this and
Joan explained, between shrieks of laughter, that he was her
mother's gigolo. Since I had no idea what a gigolo might be,
I kept watching, expecting to see I don't know what sort of
wild and outlandish stunts, but to my disappointment he did

nothing unusual. When I learned the meaning of the word, it was quite a letdown.

The hop parties did not stop with the arrival of Joan's family. They simply moved over to the apartment of Mary Jane W. on Eighty-sixth Street. There was no reason I had to go, but I tagged along with Joan. I would not smoke opium, but I was dazzled by the parties and by the state in which Mary Jane lived.

Mary Jane was then the mistress of a well-known Wall Street man, and her establishment put Joan's in the shade. She had a car and a chauffeur, gorgeous clothes, a platoon of servants and a duplex apartment which was, in more ways than one, like something out of the Arabian nights. In the middle of the drawing room was an enormous white fur rug on which Mary Jane usually was reclining, and stretched out on divans around her would be an array of celebrities—stage and screen stars (the late Mabel Normand was one), directors and writers and composers—all hitting the pipe.

People at these parties seemed to regard me as a sort of mascot, and I received the nickname "Hop Toy" because I was so small and because I was always hopping up and down in my eagerness not to miss anything. One of the most famous stars maintained I had eyes like Nazimova's and offered to get me a screen test. But I said (calling my shots better than I had any idea) that probably the only pictures I'd ever pose for would be taken for the Rogues' Gallery.

Mary Jane liked me, and I followed her around like a puppy dog. She was not nearly so beautiful as Joan, but there was a certain air about her which Joan lacked—a finish, an authority. Her allowance was two thousand dollars a month, and she told me there was a hundred thousand dollars in trust which would become hers whenever she decided to marry (and I *don't* mean marry her lover). Naturally enough, the thought occurred to me that I couldn't make two thousand dollars in a factory if I worked overtime for five years. And as for a hundred thousand—well, I just didn't believe there was that much money in the world.

Although Mary Jane was a far more aloof person than Joan, she demonstrated her friendliness by showing me a more becoming way to fix my hair and how to apply lipstick, and by teaching me table manners and wising me up on various points of etiquette. When not taking drugs, she was kind and discerning and fastidious—a woman who bore no resemblance whatsoever to the crazy slut that was herself hopped up.

She often warned me against using drugs. "Look at Joan," she would say. "Joan has great talent, and it's going up in smoke at these parties. It's a crime a girl like that should be an addict. Don't let it happen to you." Yet whenever there was a party Mary Jane was always the first to start smoking. And it was not as if she was unaware of the consequences. One time, she told me, she was sleeping with two well-known Broadway characters whose first names were the same, and she got so charged she committed the *gaffe* of calling one Georgie by the pet name of the other Georgie at the most inexcusable moment. Another time she awakened from a drugged sleep to find her Japanese houseboy climbing into bed with her. She ran from him and telephoned a friend for help, knowing that she had neither the strength nor the will to keep off any man who chose to take advantage of her self-induced helplessness.

If I had not heard these stories and if I had not seen what dope did to Joan and Mary Jane, I might have sought this escape during the frantic, hectic years to come. But I was always mortally afraid of drugs, and later was to become well known for my aversion to addicts and my bitter hatred of drug vendors.

I last saw Mary Jane in Chicago in 1937. She had married, and she and her husband had lived high and hard while the hundred-thousand-dollar settlement had held out. But the money was soon gone, and Mary Jane went into Bellevue for the cure. Free of the drug habit, she had rejoined her husband and they had a baby. Later they moved to Chicago where Mary Jane got a job selling lingerie and, when I saw her, seemed quite happy.

I asked about the cure. "Was it as bad as I've heard?"

"Worse," said Mary Jane. "Worse than anything you can imagine. They had to keep me in a strait jacket. I would have committed murder for just one shot of morphine."

"And now that you're cured, does the craving ever come back?"

Mary Jane smiled. "In the winter," she said. "When it snows."

At Mary Jane's parties, there was a young man named Ernie Levin who became interested in me. He was an out-of-towner, from Cincinnati, good-looking, well-bred, a college graduate. He didn't smoke opium either, which was a bond, and finally we began to duck the parties and go for long drives. He said he was in love with me, and certainly I was attracted to him, but this time I was wiser than I had been with Frank. Instead of tossing my hat over the mill, I looked him over and said to myself, "Here is a nice Jewish boy, educated and all, the kind of man my parents would approve of me marrying." So I began to drop hints that I would like nothing more than to settle down and raise a family.

I had known him about two months when he called and asked if he might come over, as he had something very important to tell me. I was sure this was it and spent the interval before he appeared rehearsing various becoming ways of accepting a proposal of marriage. However, it turned out that Ernie wanted me to be the first to know that he was engaged to a perfectly lovely girl in Cincinnati. They were to be married soon, and he was the happiest guy in the world.

So that was another lesson learned the hard way. I realized how foolish, how unrealistic, I had been. I wasn't pretty, I wasn't well educated—how could I ever expect to buck "the girl back home"? I may fall in love again, I told myself bitterly, but so help me the next man I get starry-eyed over is going to have to lay his cards on the table before I'll pick up my hand.

I continued to live with Joan and her family through the spring of 1920. This was at her mother's request. Joan had begun using stronger drugs, cocaine and heroin, and had become very hard to handle—sullen and nasty, sometimes violent. Soon she was missing rehearsals and when we pleaded with her to think of her career, she turned on us with wild accusations. After repeated warnings by the director, Joan was replaced in the show, but even this had no effect on her. There was nothing I could do. Just talking never got anyone off the junk, and I had neither the authority nor the knowledge to take stronger measures. Moreover, when Joan began to display Lesbian tendencies toward me, I knew I had to get out of there.

I talked over my troubles with a fellow named Tony, a bootlegger and later a well-known gangster. At that time he was having an affair with a rather prominent woman; she was married and they had to be careful. He said if I would take an apartment and allow him to meet his friend there, he would pay the rent. I jumped at his offer.

Now that I can look back over the whole story, it seems obvious that this was my first big step down the so-called primrose path. But then it never even occurred to me to think of Tony's plan and my part in it as being moral or immoral. It did not touch me personally. It simply paid my rent. I didn't think, Now I'll be a madam and run a house of assignation. I thought, Here's Tony willing to pay my rent just so he can use my apartment a few times a week. I am aware that in the judgment of the stratum of society which decides these things I should have drawn myself up and said, "No thank you, keep your dirty money! I'd rather sew shirts for five dollars a week." But I am not apologizing for my decision, nor do I think, even if I had been aware of the moral issues involved, I would have made a different one. My feeling is that by the time there are such choices to be made, your life already has made the decision for you.

With the money Tony gave me I rented a two-room furnished apartment on Riverside Drive and moved in at once. I had progressed from a potato sack to a battered old theatrical trunk, presented me by Joan's mother, and my wardrobe had been augmented by odds and ends of finery given me by Joan and Mary Jane, including a bird of paradise, which was my pride and joy. I still have it.

It was a thrill to have a place of my own, but my thoughts were tempered with sadness. For the date was the twenty-fourth of June, and that night Joan's show opened its New York run without her.

Chapter 2

The Stage Is Set

There is a real sense in which the
American respect for law has of itself begotten
lawlessness. For the effort to control every
field of human conduct by statute—an obvious
deposit of the puritan heritage—with the result that the sale of liquor and tobacco can
be prohibited, meant that a group of men would
arise to supply these wants to which the law
refused satisfaction. The more widespread the
want, the greater would be the profit in
supplying it, and the more earnest would be
the zeal of those responsible for applying the
law to see that it was enforced. Out of this
there developed quite naturally a sense of satisfaction in outwitting the lawmakers. And once
there is that kind of tension in the social environment, which this generation has witnessed
in the conflict between those who regarded prohibition as almost an article of religious faith
and those to whom it was a wanton interference
with personal freedom, the stage is set for
the breeding of violence by the attempt to
compel obedience to the law.

Harold J. Laski   THE AMERICAN DEMOCRACY

I

I had not been in the new apartment very long before Tony's
romance went on the rocks, and he asked if I could find a

new girl for him. His request didn't shock me—far from it. Since I had begun to travel with the crowd at Joan's and Mary Jane's, I had met plenty of girls who made no bones about their being available for a fee, and when Tony said he would give me fifty and the girl a hundred I really believed there was a Santa Claus. Right away I got in touch with a pretty blonde called Lucy, and she was delighted to keep the date.

Tony was making a packet in those days bootlegging, and he began spending at least two nights a week at my apartment, sometimes with Lucy, sometimes with other girls whom I had arranged for him to meet. He used to arrive about six in the evening, loaded with chickens from the rôtisserie and bottles of Dago red, and it was all very cozy and *gemütlich*.

With a hundred or more a week coming in, I was able to do as I pleased. I got myself some nice clothes and on my free nights went to dance halls and speakeasies. Soon I was meeting a lot of money men and when I saw the way they flung their dough around I thought to myself: Why shouldn't some of it be flung my way? So I gave my address to the ones whom I thought would be discreet, and it wasn't long before three girls were coming in several nights a week to entertain acquaintances I had made along the Gay White Way.

It was in this informal, almost casual, fashion that I began my career as a madam. Of course I didn't think of it then as a career or of myself as a madam. I suppose, in the way people do, I managed to sell myself a bill of goods—I didn't invent sex, nobody had to come to my apartment who didn't want to, I was really doing them a favor—that sort of thing. But I had a bad conscience when I thought of my parents, and I used to have terrible nightmares in which my father

would chase me down the streets yelling, *"Kirva! Bliad!"*
("Whore! Bum!")

Although I had broken off with my Brooklyn cousins, I
never had stopped writing to Yanow, or sending home whatever money I could spare. I had kept my Second Avenue
mailing address while I was staying at Joan's, and I did not
change the arrangement after I moved to my own apartment, fearing my father might be suspicious if I suddenly began writing from a swank neighborhood. I accounted for the
money orders, which I now sent monthly, by saying I had a
job managing a corset factory.

But no matter how I viewed my conduct, to the world
I was the proprietress of a whorehouse, and this was soon
brought home to me in no uncertain terms. Billie—one of
my girls—and I were sitting in the living room one evening
when there was a knock on the door, and I opened it on two
policemen. They asked if I was Pearl Adler, and I admitted
it readily. Never having been arrested before, I didn't grasp
the seriousness of the situation, and the boys in blue were
not, as yet, my personal bogeymen. One of them kept hold of
me while the other looked around the apartment (fortunately only Billie and I were there); then I was hustled
down the stairs to the patrol wagon.

I had not yet learned to cover my face with my arms, and
all the people of the neighborhood were gathered outside,
pointing at me and gaping. I think it was in that moment I
finally realized in what category I had placed myself. Just so
had *I* gaped in the restaurant that time when Abe pointed
out the prostitutes.

At the station after I had been booked I was allowed to
call Tony. He arranged for a bondsman to bail me out and
hired a lawyer to defend me. Although the case was dis-

missed for lack of evidence, I could no longer gloss over the facts. I had been arrested for running a disorderly house, and in the police files I was listed as a procuress. And now I had to make a choice between keeping what name and reputation I had left or taking my chances on making money fast. To me it was a question not of morals but of economics—I knew the value of money, but how could I compute the value of a good name? As I saw it, it came down to this: Did I want to leave my apartment on Riverside Drive and go back to a hole on Second Avenue? What other alternative was there? Factory work was the only kind I knew.

I made up my mind quickly. So far as I was concerned the Golden Land was still Riverside Drive, and I was determined to stay there. However, like everyone I've ever heard of who has gone into this business—be she madam or prostitute—I regarded it as just a temporary expedient, a means to an end. I'd quit when I had enough capital to finance a legitimate enterprise.

Having made this decision, I began to do things in a more businesslike way. To build up a bigger clientele I patronized more night clubs and let it be known to headwaiters and captains that my apartment was now a house, cautioning them to send only those who could afford to pay twenty or more. Since my objective was to make my stake as quickly as possible, I took care of my phone twenty-four hours a day, and never said no to anyone who was out to spend, regardless of the hour. It meant that I had to be on the job all the time, and I began to find out how much work and thought go into the preparation of an evening's pleasure. My only recreation was watching my bank roll grow, and, as Tony was still spending about three hundred a week, the money was really rolling in.

Pressure of business had kept me from seeing much of old

acquaintances, but Joan's mother, Helen, had kept in touch with me and called every now and then to sing the blues about her troubles with Joan and "Dad." One morning about five months after my trial, I was awakened by a call from her. She was crying so hard she was almost incoherent and insisted that I come round at once. I arrived to find Joan charged to the gills, Helen hysterical and "Dad" nowhere to be seen. He had forged a check, drawn out Helen's savings, and left them high and dry with the rent overdue and the bills piling up.

Joan, of course, was not working. All she cared about in the world was drugs. Now she took the opportunity to shack up with the peddler who was supplying her, while Helen came to live in my house. She was a very striking blonde who looked ten years younger than her age, and she became a great favorite with the men who frequented my place.

Subsequently Joan's peddler threw her out into the street; not even he could put up with her temperament, especially when she ran out of money. She moved into a cheap furnished room, and Helen gave her the money to live, including enough to pay for her daily ration of drugs. I wondered what kind of a mother it was who would work in a whorehouse to keep her daughter supplied with narcotics, and one night Helen told me of the happenings which had brought them both to such a pass.

"It's all my fault that Joan is what she is," Helen told me. "She was three years old when her father died. I was sorry to lose him and thought I had loved him, but not long after his death I fell in love with another man and married him. I was crazy about Hal, but terribly unsure of him and so unreasonably jealous that if he so much as looked at a woman who passed him on the street I wanted to rush over and stab her.

"He was devoted to Joan and treated her as if she were his own child. Every night he would tuck her in and stay with her until she went to sleep. At first I was grateful for his kindness, but when Joan had reached the age of twelve, and he still continued this practice, I began to be suspicious. It seemed to me that he stayed with her too long each night. I tried to fight down the horrible thought which occurred to me, but one night I sneaked up the stairs and saw them. My husband was in bed with my child.

"I should have left Hal right then and there, but instead I took it out on my own flesh and blood. I asked Joan to leave our house the next day. She looked at least sixteen and had a beautiful voice, so she went to Chicago where she found a job as a table-singer. One time after that she came back to visit her grandmother—my mother—but I was still so madly in love with Hal and so jealous of Joan that I refused to see her.

"I did not lay eyes on Joan again until she was eighteen. Meanwhile my husband had left me, and I had remarried again—another wrong man. The marriage did not last long, and when I finally realized the awful wrong I had done Joan, and was hoping that in some small way I could make it up to her, it was her turn to shut the door on me.

"Before she got in with a fast crowd and started to take drugs she had several good parts in shows—but you know what's happened to her career. What you don't know is that it was not until she became an addict that she let me come and visit her. By that time she herself had become so degraded that what I had done to her no longer seemed so bad."

All this time Helen had been talking with the tears running down her face. Now she reached out and grabbed my hand. "Let me bring her here, Pearl. I know you hate drug addicts, but please, please make an exception in her case. She was good to you. Let her come and stay until I've saved enough to take us back to Ohio."

There was a risk in having a drug addict around, and, in addition to that, I knew what a devil she could be when she was coked up, but I agreed to take Joan in. And that was how a mother and daughter came to be working side by side in my house. It was also how I became aware that in some people sexual gratification is obtained in dark and terrible ways. For when the relationship between Joan and Helen was discovered, there were men who would pay double and triple for the kick of having a mother and daughter in bed with them.

I was relieved when Helen decided to go back to Ohio. She talked it over with me, and I convinced her that her only hope lay in finding other work, as it was insane for a woman of her age to go on prostituting herself. For a while Joan stayed on with me, but I kept after her to take the cure and —tired, I think, of my constant harping on the subject—she left the house a few weeks after Helen did.

The next time I saw Joan, the only thing I recognized about her was her beautiful smile. She had become a dere-lict. My heart broke to see her in such a condition. I took her home with me—she had been locked out of her room for days—and bathed her and fed her and put her to bed. Again, I begged her to take the cure, offering to pay the hospital bills, and she promised to begin the following week. I gave her money for her hotel bill and food and clothes. This was a mistake. Several weeks passed before she returned. When she did come back, she promised faithfully she would go to Dr. Gould's sanitarium on the West Side. I gave her a hun-dred dollars, saying I would visit her as soon as she was al-lowed to see anyone.

However, when she left I followed her. And, sure enough, an elderly woman was waiting for her under a lamppost on the corner. Joan made a beeline for the woman and quickly handed over the money, receiving in return a packet containing a fresh supply of drugs. I swooped down on them, jerked Joan away, and screamed every vile word I could think of at the old woman, who, needless to say, did not wait to hear most of them. Then I told Joan I was through believing in her and not to attempt to see me again.

"If you ever want to be cured," I said, "let me know, and I'll take you to the sanitarium myself and stay with you till it's over."

She would not look at me, and as soon as I let go her arm, walked away from me down the dark street. I never saw her again.

Several years later I met a friend of hers, a song-writer, and he told me that she was down in Chinatown, living with a Chinese. In August, 1925, I saw in the papers that she had been arrested for illegal possession of narcotics, and a few months after that she was dead. I was glad to know she was out of her misery.

When I hear the song "Moonshine Valley" I think of Joan as she was when I first saw her—so shining and debonair. She weighed only fifty pounds when she died.

II

Life in a house is pretty insulated from all but the most earthshaking outside happenings, and at this stage of my career I cannot say that I made any particular effort to broaden my outlook. It did not even stir me when I heard that women now had the right to vote. I was too busy running a house to spare a thought to running the country. Also, the type of customer I had then was, for the most part, parochial in his point of view, so I heard what was cooking on Broadway and that's about all. If I had an intellectual idol in those days, it was the famous criminal lawyer, Bill Fallon. Among others, he defended Nicky Arnstein, husband of the great comedienne, Fannie Brice, and in his behalf employed the "constitutional grounds" strategy—the refusal to testify on grounds that it might incriminate or degrade—which later became almost S.O.P. in the various vice and racket investigations. In fact, I've used it myself.

Nowadays when we think of the Twenties, it is always as a period of prosperity, but for the first two years of the decade the going was rugged. There were cartoons in the papers about the High Cost of Living (little did we know!), and it was then, I believe, that a forerunner of Elsa Maxwell invented the Hard Times party. There was even an explosion in Wall Street—some disgruntled character tried to blow up the Morgans. But after eight years the Republicans were back in the saddle again and, in the words of President Harding, we could expect a "return to normalcy." Nonetheless, 1921 was a year of recession in which nineteen thousand small businesses folded.

But mine was not one of them, and by the spring of the following year I had saved six thousand dollars. Now it seemed to me I had enough in the kitty to justify embarking on a new business venture—and this time the business was to be legitimate. I had a friend whom I called Neddie, a widow who had no connection with the world I had been living in, and we pooled our resources to open a lingerie shop. Dun & Bradstreet gave us a rating of ten thousand, and although in terms of cash our investment may have been a bit less than that, in terms of work the sky was the limit. We leased first-

floor space at 2487 Broadway and knocked ourselves out preparing for the grand opening. I designed the silks, and Neddie handled most of the book work.

One sizzling July day, shortly before we were scheduled to
open, we spent hours in the wholesale district shopping for
merchandise. Tired and hot we returned to the apartment,
showered, and collapsed on the bed, wearing practically nothing. The outer door had been left ajar so the breeze from
the river could blow through the apartment, but something
else blew in besides the breeze—namely, two cops who came
marching straight into the bedroom.

Neddie screamed and dragged the spread over her while I
grabbed a towel. "What's the big idea?" I demanded, glaring
at them.

"Whadaya think?" said one copper. "Climb into your glad
rags, girls. You're coming to the station for a little visit."

So now I began to realize what it meant to be a marked
woman. It was taken for granted that I was running a house.
While we were being booked I could not look at Neddie, I
was so ashamed that her association with me had brought her
this humiliation.

Even though the charges were trumped up, I had no way
of knowing when I appeared for trial that I would not be
found guilty. In desperation, I appealed to Inspector Boland
for help. I produced the bills of sale for the merchandise that
we purchased the day of the arrest and explained that I
planned to open a store within a few weeks. Sympathetically,
he listened, and for all I know he may have interceded in my
behalf. On the day of the trial the case was dismissed.

This incident momentarily took the edge off my enthusi-
asm for honest enterprise, but I cheered up when I saw our
sign lettered in gilt on the window: POLLY'S LINGERIE
SHOP. (After this time, nearly everyone called me Polly in-

stead of Pearl, which is my real name.) It was our dream
that this shop should be the first of a country-wide chain, like
the Lerner shops, and we worked from nine in the morning
till midnight, buying and selling during the day, designing
and manufacturing at night. I used to nearly burst with
pride when I overheard people at Pomerantz's restaurant
remarking on our beautiful window display. We hoped to
draw our clientele from the entertainment world, and among
our best customers were Rosa Ponselle and her sister.

For the first year we held our own. We didn't do any
branching out, but we were breaking even. However, we had
no cash in reserve, and the minute business slacked off we
felt it. Along with the rent, there was a pay roll to be met
every Saturday (we had a salesgirl and a porter), and Neddie and I each had a drawing account of forty a week. This
mounted up to too heavy an overhead and, on top of everything else, our clientele seemed to consist largely of shoplifters. Neither Neddie nor I knew that boosting was a common practice among afternoon shoppers. Nor did we know
their technique of "lifting" articles with the aid of a handbag or a coat sleeve. Consequently, Polly's Lingerie Shop was
a heaven for the girls and our stock melted away under their
light fingers.

There was one woman whom I did have my eye on, but
she was so smooth I finally decided I must be mistaken.
Many years later at Hot Springs I spotted the same woman
in the company of a character named Maggie, whom I knew
to be a crook. More to check up on the accuracy of my memory than anything, I asked her if around about 1923 she
hadn't been a blonde, and if she hadn't owned a very large
diamond solitaire.

"Why, yes," she said. "But that was nearly twenty years
ago. How did you know?"

"Well, you see," I said, "I was running a shop then, and I remember you as one of the customers. Or maybe customer isn't the right word. But you came to the shop all right, and after each of your visits we were always short several boxes of hosiery."

She was very apologetic. "Why, dearie," she said, "I didn't dream you were 'regular,' or I never would have done it."

I told her at the time in question I was trying desperately to make a go of a legitimate business, but—since a few boxes of stockings could hardly have tilted the scales one way or the other—I let bygones be bygones and we had a drink together.

Even though in the end Polly's Lingerie Shop failed, I shall always consider it was time and money well lost, if only because it protected my relationship with my family. For while the shop was still a going concern my father turned up in New York, and the fact that I was in a legitimate business enabled me to face him.

The landlady at Second Avenue had given him my forwarding address, and he was waiting outside the apartment one evening when Neddie and I came home from work. Whatever suspicions he may have had about the source of my comparative affluence were quickly dispelled when he learned I had a shop on Broadway (with a real telephone). He was staying with my cousins in Brooklyn, and it seemed that Lena had given him an earful about me. She had told of my refusal to marry Willie Bernstein and about the time I stayed out all night and came home with my dress torn to pieces. But father had told Lena that if I came to a bad end the blame was his. He should not have sent me away from home when I was a mere child. Consequently, once he had seen the shop, he could hardly wait to get back to Brooklyn and boast about how well I was doing. He really was proud of me, but of course my "success" let him off the hook too. His judgment was vindicated. There was no need for self-reproach.

I must admit that many times in my thoughts I had blamed my father, thinking that things wouldn't have happened as they did if I'd had a home and parents to turn to. But what is done is done and no amount of second-guessing can change it. And though in moments of bitterness I'd vowed if I ever got the chance I'd humiliate him with the knowledge of what had befallen me, his daughter, whom he'd shoved out into the world at the age of thirteen, now that I had the opportunity I saw how cruel and useless it would be. It doesn't really make a hurt less to hurt somebody else, especially if you love him. So instead of making father feel bad, I did my best to make him feel even better. I told him that I was engaged to a nice Jewish boy, a Rabbi's son (In cases like this why not make it good? It costs no more.), and I explained my "fiancé's" absence from New York by saying that he was on the road selling dresses.

Pop said the news of my engagement would make Mother very happy, and I think he was peaceful in his mind about me when he sailed. (I later wrote the engagement was broken.) Fortunately his visit was a brief one. I guess he just came over for the ride—that old wanderlust rearing its head again. For I wasn't to be in a legitimate business much longer. A month after father's departure for Yanow the sign Neddie and I were so proud of was replaced by one reading: For Rent. (It is probably typical of my topsy-turvy existence that in the first year of "Coolidge prosperity" I went broke.)

In the fall of 1923 my assets consisted of my furniture, my chow dog, Nicko, and eight hundred dollars. Being well aware that eight yards cannot be stretched out to last forever, I was trying to figure a way to turn a quick buck when I happened to meet two friends of mine (at least I thought they were friends), Tim Michaels and Mike Fogarty. I knew that by profession they were cardsharps, but I made no effort to steer clear of them, never dreaming they would pick me for a mark.

It seemed they had a poker game on and a good sucker to take over, and they suggested that I lend a helping hand. The idea was for me to sit in, and Mike or Tim would signal what cards the sucker was holding. We had a brief dress rehearsal. Then they produced the sucker. He looked the sap type all right, even had a patch on one eye—maybe to show me that he'd be able to overlook a full house if he drew one.

I had been given a thousand to play with, and, as the sucker kept waving more dough in my face, my eyes got bigger and bigger, and in my mind I was already spending my third of the take. With the help of my confederates, I was really cleaning up and everything went along smoothly till the big pot came along. Then Mr. Sap kept on raising me until suddenly I had nothing left to call with. Tim beckoned me to one side, and, after a brief consultation, I agreed to furnish the money needed. I told them to hold everything, my bank was just around the corner on Ninety-eighth and Broadway.

The teller knew me, and I instructed him to fork out seven of my eight hundred, boasting that I'd be back in a flash and make a big deposit. He tried to stop me from withdrawing the money, sensing that something was not kosher, but I wouldn't listen. I jutted around the corner and back to the game, shoved my dough into the center of the table, and called the hand. . . . Ah, well, live and learn! All your life you have it dinned into you that you never get some-

thing for nothing, but you won't believe it till you have found
out the hard way.

Come to think of it, that's about what I said to Mike
Fogarty the next time I saw him. Five years had passed when
I spotted him one day on Forty-seventh Street. I called him
a name (to be specific, a cheap louse) and asked him if he
was still living on the seven hundred he clipped me.

He grinned. "Aw, now Polly," he said, "you're not going
to beef about that after all these years!"

I said, "Of course not. You have to have larceny in your
heart before you can be taken. I want to thank you for making me wiser when I had so little to lose. If it hadn't been
for you boys, maybe I would have been taken when I had a
lot more. I consider it a very cheap lesson."

III

With only a hundred left, I made up my mind to go back in
the whorehouse business and this time not to quit until I was
really heeled. I called some of the men I'd had before, and
they brought their friends with them. Also I made some new
contacts on my own, and my enterprise was off to a prosper-
ous start. My clientele consisted mostly of gangsters and
hoodlums, some of whom were to become the big shots of
the day. Most of them died with their boots on. One of the
gang was a character called Sammie the Schnook, but why
they called him Schnook I don't know. He was smarter than
they were—he's still alive.

The crap games were running wide open in Yorkville, and
the boys would all wind up in my apartment to finish the
night. Money meant nothing to those fellows; they sometimes

spent five hundred or more in an evening. Whoever won the crap game payed the bill.

It had not occurred to me to sell drinks until one of the bunch remarked that I was a sap to let them buy their booze from a bootlegger and cart it up to my apartment. Why didn't I get smart and sell them drinks at a buck a throw? I took his advice, and, in his own words, cut myself in for a nice piece of change.

They were a wild bunch all right. They used to check their rods with me as they came in, and I usually hid them in the stove, figuring it wasn't likely anyone would get a yen to bake a cake. They liked a joke—when it was on someone else. I had no maids then, except for a house-cleaner, and I served the drinks myself—whisky for the guys, tea in highball glasses for the girls. Since I was kept on the jump, running back and forth with trays, it was inevitable that sooner or later I'd get the glasses mixed and a guest would draw the wrong type of drink.

There was one gambler named The Lug who had a habit of keeping his hat on, pulled down low over his eyes. He was inclined to be a troublemaker, and I always kept an eye on him. On this particular night, he helped himself from the tray, took a long swallow, and then made a terrible choking noise. I knew what had happened even before he swivelled around and hurled the glass against the wall, splattering tea far and wide. Of course he knew he had got the drink meant for his girl of the evening, and at the rate he was paying, each drink cost more than several pounds of tea. There was a tense silence, but after a moment The Lug relaxed.

"Okay, Polly," he said. "So you got to make a living. . . . Well, fix me another drink."

But that wasn't the end. The Lug couldn't stand being played for a sucker. He had to get even. And the next night, with the help of the other boys, he doctored a tray of drinks. Two of my girls and several of his pals drew mickey finns. The guys spent the night being sick in the alley, and the girls felt too ill to work for three days.

I had a big important project those days. I was saving up to buy a mink coat. I talked about it so much that when a guy was trying to make a point at craps, he'd holler, "Come on, little Joe! This is for Polly's mink coat." They told me it brought them luck.

"How many minks have you saved now, Polly?" they'd ask. "How's trapping tonight?"

Since it was my first mink, I instructed the furrier to let himself go, even if it meant decimating the mink populations of the world. I didn't care how big and bulky the coat was, I wanted to be swathed in mink, dripping it, trailing it.

The night I came home with the coat (acres and acres of mink, all mine), the gang examined it carefully. "Yeah, nice coat," one would say. "Warm, I bet." Another would scrutinize it soberly. "Mink, huh?" he'd say. "Looks like skunk to me. Smell it if you don't believe me."

I kept laughing, pretending to be sore and going along with the gag, but nervous for fear the coat would get burned by a cigar butt or spilled on. I was relieved when I could put it away in the closet, but I kept a watchful eye on the closet, afraid, I guess, that my precious coat would suddenly grow a set of little mink paws and run away.

When I came back from an errand in the kitchen, one of the boys said to me, "Put your coat on, Polly. We'd like to see it again." I didn't need a second invitation. I was ready to wear it around the house all day. But when I opened the closet, no coat. They all swore up and down they hadn't seen it, and pretended alarm so convincingly that I became panic-stricken. Saying they would help me search for it, they looked under the rug, behind a vase, in the flower-pots, the icebox, the oven (finding the rods but not the coat), lifted up saucers in the pantry, opened doors, unscrewed light bulbs, and clowned around generally. But I was so upset I couldn't realize it was a big act. Then one of them yelled, "You little dope, why did you put it out on the fire escape?" And that's where it was. What a laugh they had! I laughed loudest and longest of all—with relief.

Sometimes the stunts they pulled were not so harmless, but there was nothing I could do about it. I had chosen running a house as my profession and whatever the customers did, I had to take it and keep smiling.

Dave, one of the gambling crowd, began to pay a lot of attention to Celia. She was a beautiful girl who had not been with me long and whom I liked a lot. I noticed her talking with Dave in the hall one night, and the next evening he took her out on a date. After that he began to hang around my place when the gang wasn't there. Then he took her with him on a trip to New Orleans.

When they came back, Dave asked me to see to it that she did not sleep with any of the gang, and also to keep from them that he was in love with her. (It was an odd thing—racketeers frowned on men of their calling who got serious with a prostitute, while men in legitimate businesses and intellectuals, especially the broad-A group, did not have this attitude and showed far more respect toward a prostitute than did any of the underworld inhabitants.) Dave said whatever money Celia and I lost by this arrangement he would gladly make up to us.

I told the boys Celia was no longer with me, and sent her out of the house when I knew they were coming. Then one night they dropped in late unexpectedly. I shoved Celia into

a closet, but the gang sensed something fishy in the air.
The Lug marched over and pulled open the closet door.
When they saw Celia crouching there, they dragged her out
and mishandled her, and I got pushed around for lying to
them. They made such a racket that I was asked to move.

Dave was wild when he heard what had happened. "The
hell with those bastards," he said. "I'm going to marry her
and take her out of the damn business."

He did, too. Dave and Celia lived together happily for
many years until he was shot. I used to see them sometimes
at Hot Springs, Arkansas, and I'd be careful to pass by without speaking, not wanting to mar their happiness by reminding them of the past. But a lot of the so-called respectable
women who were married to racketeers tried to humiliate
Celia whenever they could. After Dave was killed, Celia married again, a nice chap in a legitimate business. I used to
see her sometimes in the shopping district, and, if there
was no one around, we would smile. I got a thrill out of
knowing that she had found happiness, and not once but
twice.

IV

Since, as a result of the brawl over Celia, I had to move, I
took an apartment in the West Seventies, some twenty blocks
farther downtown. I was hoping to draw a better class of
customer. I knew a businessman clientele would be a lot
quieter and far easier to handle than the hoodlums. There
would be no rods to stash away, no being pushed around. But
though I did attract the quiet solid-citizen type of businessman ("the breakfast-eating, Brooks Brothers type"), they seldom had the kind of money I was interested in—or, if they

had, they didn't spend it. The gamblers helped popularize my name, but they played a little too rough. The business-men had better manners but not big enough bankrolls to get me to the top. What I really was shooting for was the patron-age of the upper brackets of society, of theater people and artists and writers (the successful ones). As I have said, I am never satisfied with second best, and since I was a madam I was determined (to paraphrase Holbrook Blinn's famous line) to be "the best goddam madam in all America."

But I had not yet reached the point where I could pick and choose my clientele, and in the meantime there was work to be done. I was running on a twenty-four-hour sched-ule—up all night, disturbed all day. I just couldn't say no to a man who was out to spend, for I realized I'd better get all I could while the getting was good. I never knew when there would be a raid, and every such disturbance set me back several thousand. Nevertheless, it was these early raids which made me wise and cautious and were in great part responsi-ble for my achieving what the *New York Times* later re-ferred to as "the astuteness and prosperity which enabled Polly Adler to run a house for fifteen years before an arrest could be made to stick."

Of course, just fast talking was not enough to stave off the cops when they came snooping around, but back in 1924 it didn't take too much to get rid of them. I'd cup a C-note in my palm and go around shaking hands, and the cops would take themselves off, all smiles, to pinch some other madam who hadn't developed the gentle art of handshaking to such a fine pitch. Also, I had an "in" with many of the big gam-blers. They liked the way I did business, never squawking when I had to take one on the chin. Most gambling houses were run on an injunction against police interference, and since the gamblers found my parlor a convenient place in which to relax, they okayed me with the cops. As a matter of fact, my apartment became a hangout for the police themselves. On many an evening I should have had a green light out in front as well as the red one which tradition says should be there. Sometimes the law-enforcers gave me more trouble than my rowdiest clients, but there was nothing I could do about it except hang on to my temper and keep telling myself every business has its drawbacks.

My skyrocket rise to popularity had not passed unnoticed by my competitors, most of whom were old hands at the game while I was a comparative newcomer. Naturally enough the other madams resented me and were jealous of the money I was making, and they gave me a rough time of it for a while. When they could devise nothing else to annoy me, they resorted to such childish tricks as sending hearses to my address, so that—just when things were going full swing—a couple of lugubrious characters would appear at the door with the announcement that they had come for the body.

Friendly cops kept me informed of the number of complaints turned in at the Commissioner's office at my rivals' instigation. It was on the cops' advice that I kept moving in order to close out each complaint as it was filed, and for a few months there I was hopping around like a flea. Some apartments I was in hardly long enough to powder my nose. (No doubt it was this frenetic period of my life which gave rise to the legend that I "changed my residence every twenty-four hours"—a tidbit I gleaned from the tabloids some years later.) Aside from the obvious inconvenience to me, it wasn't good business to lead a nomad's life just when I'd gotten my address fixed in peoples' minds, and I saw I'd have to take steps to correct the situation.

After pondering the matter I decided to carry the battle

into the enemy's camp. So I arrayed myself in my mink, threw a saddle on the Buick, and set out to call on three ladies—Mesdames X, Y and Z—who were, like myself, prominent in the executive end of the whorehouse business.

My first stop was on Riverside Drive. I gave my name to the uniformed maid—whose take, as I announced myself, was something to behold—and, while I was awaiting Madam X, made a quick inspection of her parlor. I had to admit it was a pretty good layout, furniture expensive, comfortable and conservative, and not littered up with those dust-catching little gimcracks which are always getting smashed.

Madam X was a woman getting on in years, gray-blonde, chunky, hard-eyed, with an incisive manner. When I explained who I was (as if she didn't know), she was extremely gracious and offered me tea or sherry, being careful to let drop that the sherry was the kind to be found in the cellars of King Alfonso XIII.

When the amenities had been observed, I got down to business. There was, I said, enough money and enough men for all of us. Why should we waste time and energy cutting each other's throats? What hurt one, hurt all. In the words of Ben Franklin, we must all hang together, or we'd hang separately. So instead of spending her time scheming to make it tough for me, why didn't Madam X do something constructive? Why didn't she get her fat bottom out and spend money around town the way I did?

"You have to spend money," I told her, "if you want to make it."

She agreed to take the matter under advisement.

My calls on Madam Y and Madam Z followed the same pattern. In both cases their reception of me paralleled that of Madam X. Both attempted to put on the Ritz. One of them told me I might borrow her Cadillac limousine any time

I wanted it, and the other introduced me to her husband
with an air of saying, "This is something I've got that you
haven't." But the only thing I wanted from them was to be
let alone. And, apparently, confronting them as I did was
the right strategy, for I no longer had any trouble from this
quarter.

As my business continued to grow by leaps and bounds, I
rented a larger apartment in the fifties near Seventh Avenue, and since I thought I could count on staying there for a
time—now that the ladies had ceased molesting me—I had
it done up in style. Always before this I had selected the furnishings for my places myself, but I had been impressed by
Madam X's establishment and I felt like splurging, so I engaged an interior decorator.

Mostly the décor was period French—Louis Quinze and
Louis Seize, which is sort of traditional for a house—and I
acquired some really valuable antiques, cabinets and tables,
a Sèvres dinner service and a Gobelin tapestry depicting Vulcan and Venus having a tender moment while Eros took
over Vulcan's smithy and forged a set of arrows. The bar
was supposed to be Egyptian in style—King Tut's tomb had
been opened just the year before and there had been a lot of
publicity about it—and there was also a Chinese room, as
mah-jongg was all the vogue.

Now, of course, such a mixture of styles seems laughable,
but in those early Twenties to us in America the whole
world seemed a big toy shop, and in our travels abroad we
helped ourselves at random to all the glittering odd things
that took our fancy. (It was about this time that Mencken
and Nathan pointedly observed that Americans played the
game of Chinese coolies, drank the beverages of French
peasants, wore on state occasions the garb of English clerks,
had a melodic taste for the music of African Negroes, and

ate in alligator pears the food of Costa Rican billy goats!)
Anyway, it was a nice spacious apartment with room for four
girls to live in. In addition each night from five to ten show
girls would drop by, including some of Ziegfeld's and Earl
Carroll's kids. They were always sure of picking up the price
of a Madam Frances gown.

I now employed a domestic staff of three: a cook, a house-
cleaner and my own personal maid, a tiny, trim, colored
woman of about forty. Despite her small size—she was an
inch shorter than I—and her frail physique, there was no job
too big for her to tackle and no one on earth—be it a six-foot-
three cop or a pistol-packing drunken hoodlum—whom she
feared to face. In fact, she was, as one of the customers said,
a regular female Richard the Lion-Hearted, and this sobri-
quet soon was shortened to Lion—the name by which we all
called her. During my years as a madam I had literally
scores of maids, many of whom were loyal and efficient, but
there was never another one to compare to my Lion. She
had a fiery temper and a sharp tongue, but once she took
you into her heart, her devotion was absolute, you could do
no wrong, and she would lay down her life for you.

I first encountered Lion in 1923 when I still had the
shop. She worked in the ladies' room of a restaurant I often
went to, and one day when I happened to be there she had
just gotten word that her only daughter had been terribly
burned in a fire in Camden, South Carolina. She told me
about it, the tears rolling down her face, and though she
tried to keep control of herself I could see she was nearly
crazy with anxiety. She did not have the price of a ticket to
Camden, so I loaned her thirty-eight dollars which was all I
had on me. That was in May, and though I never expected
to see either the money or her again, one evening in July
when I left the shop, there she was waiting for me. She

couldn't pay anything back yet, she said, because she was still paying off her daughter's burial expenses, but she hoped maybe I would let her come and do my laundry and mending on her day off. When I said it wasn't necessary, she insisted. I was her "folks" now, she said.

The following year, when I could afford a maid, she came to work for me full time and was with me until shortly before her death in 1929. Besides being one hell of a good maid, Lion was my champion and protector, my confidante and my comforter, and, in my absence, a trustworthy assistant manager. What's more, she was a good personal press agent. Often I heard her assure new customers, "Oh, you'll like my little madam! You'll be right at home with her."

It helped that she could hold the fort while I went out and did a little drum-beating. Already my girls were known to be the best-looking, best-dressed and best—well, best all-around in New York. And since it would help business, I myself wanted to be tagged as a character. I wanted my name to be a byword and the expression "going to Polly's" a euphemism for the world's most popular indoor sport.

If you're going to become known to the public, you have to make public appearances, and with Lion in charge I was able to take a night off now and then to attend night-club openings. When I'd walk in, surrounded by my loveliest girls, it was always a show-stopper. Soon there was a whole file of Polly Adler jokes which the emcees would haul out and dust off when we made our center-door fancy entrances, so along with goggling at the girls, the customers would be giggling at quips about me. Although the tabs were never less than five hundred, I felt our evenings out were a good investment. The clubs were a display window for the girls. I'd make a column or two; the latest Polly Adler gag would start the rounds, and no matter where we happened to go, some of the club patrons would follow after us and end the evening at the house.

As a result of all this publicity (plus a good word-of-mouth from satisfied customers), business got better and better, which meant a correspondingly large increase in my hand-outs to the cops and a decrease in the amount of time I could devote to my private affairs. In fact, I had almost no life of my own, or—more accurately—the house was my life. It absorbed all my energy and was the focus of all my thoughts. Once, perhaps because of my having to go it alone almost from scratch, I had yearned for love and affection, and I had been willing to go considerably more than halfway to respond to it. But now business came first and personal relationships were second by a country mile.

This change in my outlook was reflected when I ran into Ernie Levin one day at the Chelsea Bank. It was the first time I had seen him since his marriage four years before. He said he had just put his wife on the train for Cincinnati and asked me to have dinner with him at the Pelham Heath Inn. After we had cut up a few touches about old times, he asked what I was doing now. When I replied that I ran a house, he didn't bat an eye. Instead he was in hopes we could take up where we had left off. But whatever Ernie once had had for me, now was gone. I used to admire everything about him. Now I saw that his nose, which I had once thought distinguished, was like a parrot's beak, he dressed like a muzhik, and his line of conversation was corny and provincial. He called me daily for some time, and I must admit I was tempted to go out with him just to sabotage his marriage and make him as miserable as he had made me. But I was doing a good business and had no time for revenge.

I had no time for fun either. Although it was part of being "the notorious Polly Adler" always to keep up a smiling front, always to be the devil-may-care party woman, I never forgot that I was in business. Sometimes the nicer men among my clients would invite me to the theater or a night club, but such evenings were never very successful. Even when Lion was in charge I still felt I must check with the house seven or eight times a night. I never knew but what the place might be raided. Also, if a good drinking crowd dropped in, it was better for me to be there. So even on my so-called nights off I was spending most of my time in the telephone booth, and all too often would get an S O S which meant I had to apologize to my host and depart. I remember one occasion when I called the house during intermission at the theater and, hearing a customer had gone slightly berserk, flew out of the phone booth and into a taxicab without even a wave of farewell to my beau.

I couldn't behave like other women—the house was forever uppermost in my mind. And no man wants to take out a woman who can't keep her mind on the date, who remains a business machine even off duty and even when in an ostensibly hilarious mood. So I decided the best thing I could do was put me as a private citizen in cold storage and, so long as I was a madam, "temporarily disconnect" my personal life. I was only twenty-four and, like other women, I wanted a home and a husband, but that part of my life would have to wait. I would do nothing but work until I had saved enough money to quit the whorehouse and find myself a decent man.

That was in 1924 and twenty years later I was still a madam.

Chapter 3

Holiday from Thinking

> Among the very young the impression pre-
> vails that the so-called Jazz Age was marked
> by a collapse of morals, public and private. . . .
> It is true that the enactment of prohibition had
> the unexpected, but logical, effect of converting
> public drunkenness from a disgrace into a dis-
> tinction. . . . It is true also that the operations
> of the Ohio gang debauched the public service
> on the highest levels to the point at which we
> saw a former officer of the Cabinet in a prison
> cell for taking bribes while in office—a disgrace
> that had never befallen the United States up to
> that time. It is true that fashion hiked women's
> skirts up to such an altitude that the lingerie
> shops were filled with knickers meant to be
> admired by the public. It is true that popular
> novelists began to write out plainly details
> of amorous experience that they had hitherto
> modestly—and obscenely—indicated by a row
> of asterisks. . . . (But) the great sin of the
> Jazz Age was not drunkenness, nor lechery, nor
> plunder, but a vast, a criminal irresponsibility.
> . . . The average man took a holiday from
> thinking.
>
> *Gerald W. Johnson*   INCREDIBLE TALE

I

By New Year's, 1925, the national gravy train really was beginning to roll, and, as more and more passengers squeezed

aboard, the temper of the times began to reveal itself in the din, the flamboyance and the headlong pace of life which characterized the Roaring Twenties. In Manhattan, where the fleshpots were cooking on the front burner, speakeasies and theaters, night clubs and bordellos swarmed with the boys who had it and were busting to throw it around. Every other guy was a Champagne Charlie, a Diamond Jim, a Bender the Spender, ready to shoot the wad on such necessities as Corona-Coronas, Veuve Clicquot, Cartier knickknacks, Cadillacs, yachts and fancy ladies.

Such famous pleasure domes as Rector's, Delmonico's and Reisenweber's had vanished from the scene (when America went dry, they went too), but speakeasies and clubs popped up overnight like mushrooms. Although they were operated on the sneak, almost anyone could obtain the password to any oasis in the city, providing he had dough in his jeans. There were raids, of course, and places would be padlocked, but the government's attempts at enforcement only underlined the futility of passing such a law in the first place.

Two of the best-known prohibition agents were Izzy Einstein and Moe Smith, whose habit of going around dressed up like Tugboat Annie and Charlie's Aunt enabled them to spy out and knock off hundreds of blind pigs and distilleries. In five years they made 4,392 arrests, ninety-five per cent of which resulted in convictions, but they might as well have been trying to dry up the Atlantic with a post-office blotter. Liquor had never been more plentiful. From coast to coast the land was awash with rum "right off the boat" and bathtub gin and whisky aged with the electric needle.

Since the demand for liquor could not be supplied legitimately, the bootlegger became a familiar figure on the American scene. He was the local distributor, the middle man, behind whom stood the kings of gangland, the organizers and enforcers—like Al Capone and, in New York, Joe (The Boss) Masseria and Owney Madden and Dutch Schultz—whose henchmen extinguished encroachments on their domain with sprays of machine-gun bullets, and who sold "protection" to everyone from the proprietors of the neighborhood delicatessens to the owners of the town's plushiest clubs. Politicians and preachers sounded off continually about the depredations of mobsters, but the thirsty citizenry, instead of rising up in righteous wrath and casting the hoodlums out, invited them right into the parlor.

Prohibition did much to knock the props out from under the existing social structure, and the drama of the Roaring Twenties was played out by an astonishingly heterogeneous cast. At popular night spots, you saw bankers and safe-crackers, lawyers and boosters, publicists and con men, politicians and beer barons, artists and brokers, film stars and jockeys, dowagers and kept women, butter-and-egg men and pimps, exiled royalty and out-of-work chorines, millionaire playboys and penniless gigolos—and always, of course, visiting firemen of varying degrees of sophistication and prominence and prosperity. In that colorful, boisterous, constantly changing crowd, the Four Hundred, as such, got lost in the shuffle, and though its doings were still reported by Maury Paul (alias Cholly Knickerbocker), the true court chronicler of the age was Walter Winchell, whose column was then appearing in the first of the tabloids, the New York *Graphic*.

Inevitably, this intermingling of inhabitants of the top drawer, the demi-monde and the underworld left its impress on the speech and manners of the day, and it quickly became apparent that Emily Post was fighting a losing battle. As one writer put it, "The deportment and language of the gangsters and their 'molls' was aped . . . by the 'swells,' and the patois of prison-yard and call-house became the *lingua franca* of society." It was the saloon, not the salon, which set the tone. And presiding as Master of the Revels was not some self-appointed stooge to the Astors and the Vanderbilts, a Harry Lehr or a Ward McAllister, but the "Night Mayor" himself, the Honorable James J. Walker, who in 1925 succeeded Mayor Hylan at City Hall.

Some of the swankiest saloons and night clubs were owned by gangsters. Jack (Legs) Diamond had the Hotsy-Totsy, Dutch Schultz the Embassy, and Larry Fay, the kingpin of the milk and taxicab rackets, opened the most famous of them all, El Fey Club, where Texas Guinan was the star and hostess. When Texas waved an arm coated with diamond bracelets, gave that wise grin of hers and cried, "Hello, sucker!" the public ate it up and hollered for more. Tex was a hep girl all right, and wasn't above exchanging cracks with me now and then. There was no difference between her business and mine, Tex said once, except that she could have her name up in lights. Another famous hostess was Belle Livingston, who was at The Mansion, which was sometimes known as the Fifty-Eighth Street Country Club, where guests shelled out heavy sugar for the privilege of doing their boozing on the floor, Japanese-style. A man could get hurt, said Livingston-san, falling off a bar stool.

I was living on Fifty-fourth Street then, and on the same street over east, was the House of Morgan where the incomparable Helen held forth, enthroned on her piano, half-sobbing, half-singing the great torch songs of the Twenties. "Can't Help Loving That Man," which was always to be associated with her name, might well have been the theme song of Helen's life. (I remember vividly one time finding her helplessly drunk and crying her heart out in the ladies' room of a speak. When I tried to get her to pull herself together she wailed, "I'm in love with that bastard at the bar, and he

doesn't want me." I peeked out at the guy, and I must say
the epithet was deserved. Poor Helen! She was always going
overboard for some jerk and then hitting the bottle to try to
forget him.) Helen's club was never on the sneak. When the
boys with the fat bankrolls went barreling around town on
a spree, they always found its doors wide open.

Sometimes after leaving the House of Morgan, the
spenders found their way up the street to the House of Polly.
(The comedian, Joe Frisco, always got a yak from his audiences when he commented, "At Polly Adler's p-p-place it's
the m-m-man who pays, but at Helen M-m-morgan's everybody p-p-pays!") Or perhaps the boys tooled up to Harlem
to one of the rent parties at which jazz musicians helped their
friends collect the dough for the month's nut. And maybe
they kept on rolling until they landed in the hands of
"Money," a little hunchback who was one of Harlem's best-
known characters. Money really cleaned up steering white
customers on what they called "slumming tours," which usually ended up at a dive run by a girl called Sewing Machine
Bertha. There they would be shown lewd pictures as a pre-
view to the performance of the same tableaux by live actors, white and colored. Money also supplied reefers and cocaine and morphine so that the "upper clawsses" could have
themselves a real low-down time.

Viewed in retrospect, after the sobering years which have
intervened, the dead-pan thrill-seeking of the self-styled "lost
generation," the senseless cavortings of "flaming youth," the
determined squandering and guzzling and wenching of the
newly rich, combine to form a lurid picture of a race of mon-
sters outrageously at play. But hindsight seldom gives you
the same picture you get when you are in the thick of things,
and, more than that, you take for granted the world you live
in—at least I think most people do. Certainly *I* didn't know

there was anything unusual about the times, any more than I realized that conditions then were peculiarly well suited to promoting a career like mine. In fact, if I had had all history to choose from, I could hardly have picked a better age in which to be a madam.

In the world of the Twenties, as I saw it, the only unforgivable sin was to be poor. Money was what counted, money was the magic word. Everywhere I went people talked about ways of making it and ways of spending it, lived by standards and on a scale based on having plenty of it, grabbed for more with one hand and tossed it away with the other. Everybody had an angle, everybody was raking in the chips, there was no excuse *not* to have money—and, along with everybody else, I was right in there, my front feet planted firmly in the trough.

To have money and to have fun—these were the great goals of life, and having fun usually included having a love affair. Movie stars, in particular Rudolph Valentino, were the reigning heart throbs of the day, but in the mid-Twenties band leaders were beginning to be regarded as romantic figures too and—right in style—I fell for one.

My hero, whom I'll call Casey Booth, was not nationally known like Paul Whiteman and Vincent Lopez and Brooke Johns, but his band was very popular in New York. When I first knew him he was playing at the Salamander Club and I met him, unromantically enough, in my professional capacity. He came to the house with a group of his pals and proceeded to pass out in one of the girls' rooms. As he was too stiff to leave when the night was over, we had to haul him into my room and I had to doss down on the couch in the living room. I always parked the pass-outs in my bed (sometimes it held as many as three at once) because the girls needed their sleep. But then, so did I, and I was muttering irritably to myself as we tucked Mr. Booth into the feathers.

I called him about noon the next day, and it must have been quite a shock to wake up and find himself gazing into my funny face instead of that of the dream girl he'd last been with. I gave him a dose of Eno's salts and a cup of black coffee, and sent him on his hungover way with a warning not to get so stinko again.

That night when Casey phoned and asked me to join him for dinner I was really surprised. I had thought he was the type who went for strictly ornamental females. Maybe he was looking for novelty, I don't know, but whatever he was looking for he must have found it in me. After that first date we saw each other every night for weeks. As Casey worked until four or five A.M. his schedule fitted in perfectly with mine, and when we had finished our respective chores, we used to meet in some after-hours spot, like the Club Durant.

Casey was tall and dark but not handsome—he was too thin for that. However, he had an air about him, and when he strolled down the avenue, looking as spruce as if he'd just stepped out of a bandbox, a cornflower in his buttonhole and jauntily swinging a cane, there were plenty of doll-babies giving him the eye. Why some guys should send you and others leave you cold is a question to which, I suspect, there are as many answers as there are women. In any case when you're in love you don't stop to analyze the combination that adds up to the winning number. But I suppose it is mutuality of interest and how many experiences you can share which, in the end, determine the amount of sympathy and understanding you give and get. And, since our lives were lived in the same after-dark Broadway world, we were able to share a great deal.

As I look back, I see Casey embodying all the virtues and

faults of the man-about-town of the Twenties. He was generous and gay and easygoing and considerate. He never forgot birthdays or the anniversaries of small personal occasions. He was the first to reach for the check and the first to laugh at the joke. He never failed to notice a new dress and come up with a compliment, and if, as sometimes happened, he thought an outfit didn't suit me, he would tell me later. Never would he spoil the moment when I made an entrance. He had what might be called the easy virtues, the ones that are easily recognized and acknowledged, and that make it easy for people to like you and for you to like yourself. But they are the virtues that, by extension, can louse you up. Everybody said Casey was a prince, and on Broadway a prince is a guy whom the drinks are on, a prince is a soft touch.

Although Casey was earning very good money playing at the club and doubling in theaters, he drank heavily, he liked to drink in company, and he never knew when the party was over. So, as a result, both his health and his bank account took an awful beating, and many a golden opportunity went by because he wasn't in shape to grab it. I tried to point out to him that he was jeopardizing his whole future—and for what, except backslapping from a bunch of freeloaders?— but it was a waste of breath. "Who wants to live forever?" was his stock answer to any suggestion that he slow down.

As he came to mean more and more to me, I got ambitious for him. I gave parties for big wheels in the advertising business, hoping to land Casey a sponsored radio show. But invariably he would get pie-eyed and insult the very guys who could do him good. This would cause me to blow my top. I'd accuse him of ingratitude, and he'd tell me to run my house and let him run his own affairs. For several days after such quarrels we'd try to get along without each other, but always he'd come back or I'd break down and call him.

Our romance was the talk of Broadway and—unbeknownst to me—Casey was taking a lot of needling because of it. Night after night when he was on the bandstand some wise guy with a snootful would dance by and call out, "Not bad, Casey, ol' boy, not bad! You're dragging down heavy jack waving a stick here, and now we're on our way to your whorehouse to spend some more." If he lost his temper and started a fight it would hurt us both and accomplish nothing, so Casey would just have to stand up there and take it. But he never said a word about it to me. I got the story from his manager, Dave Norris.

It was fresh in my mind one night when we met as usual at the Club Durant. (This was the place run by Lou Clayton, Eddie Jackson and Jimmy Durante—perhaps the most screwball establishment of all time.) I was in the midst of telling Casey that I had heard from Norris about the needling he was getting, when the band struck up a wedding march and over to our table came a waiter carrying a big wedding cake. He presented it with a flourish and, going along with the gag, Casey and I led the other customers in a grand march around the club. Then Casey bought champagne for the house and everybody cheered and toasted the "happy couple."

After people had gone back to their tables, Casey said, "How about it, Polly? Shall we get married?"

Thinking he was kidding, I said "Oh, sure"—and who did he have in mind for the best man, John S. Sumner? (Sumner was the guiding spirit of the Society for the Suppression of Vice.)

"No, I mean it. We could drive up to Greenwich this morning. What do you say?"

Frankly, I was more irritated than flattered. I loved Casey more than I had ever loved anyone, but I knew that our marriage was out of the question. And it seemed to me, whether he was aware of it or not, he was counting on me to be the practical one. He could credit himself with making a grand gesture and leave to me the thankless task of being "realistic" and hard-hearted.

"Casey, stop talking like a fool," I said. "You can't marry a madam. Think what people would say."

"To hell with people!"

"You know what they're saying now. How would you like hearing remarks about your *wife*, Madam Booth, and her whorehouse?"

"Then get out of the business."

"That wouldn't stop the cracks. Even if I got rid of the house, you'd still be labeled as the pimp orchestra leader who married a madam for her money. So don't let's have any more of this silly talk. You've got to think of your future."

"To hell with my future!"

Suddenly I lost my temper. "To hell with this! To hell with that! That's been your attitude as long as I've known you. Even if I weren't a madam I'd think twice before marrying you. What future would there be for me, married to a guy who doesn't give a damn about anything but kicking the gong around and having enough liquor to carry him from payday to payday?" Naturally Casey didn't relish this kind of talk, so one word led to another, and we were still at it hammer and tongs when the yawning waiters swept us out.

Out on the sidewalk, there in the bright sunlight with people hurrying by on their way to work, Casey pulled me to him. "I love you," he said, "but I guess that's not enough for you." He pushed me away and walked off.

So far our romance had followed the classic Hollywood pattern of boy-meets-girl, boy-loses-girl. The difference was that I stayed lost. I heard that Casey was on the town with a vengeance, running around with one woman after another, showing me, I guess, that I must have been nuts not to snap him up. But, even though I was determined to write him off, I missed him terribly and many times it took all my will power to keep from calling him. When he was scheduled to broadcast, I used to shut myself up in my room to listen, and when Dick, the band vocalist, sang "Charmaine" I'd bawl like a lovesick schoolgirl.

It was on my return from a vacation in New Orleans that I next saw Casey. His manager, Norris, called and asked me to go to him. He said Casey was ill and needed help. I hurried over to the Park Central Hotel and found him flat on his back and obviously a very sick man. Norris had said that he was broke. Yet his room was crowded with the usual gang of free-loaders—booking agents and song-pluggers and stooges—and there was a steady stream of waiters and bell-hops flowing in and out supplying them drinks. But though they were soaking up booze and charging it to his unpaid bill, no one had a thought for the host, lying there coughing into a blood-stained handkerchief.

I wasted no time getting rid of those leeches. But when I expressed my indignation to Casey, he gave me that charming grin of his and said, "Well, anyway, now I won't have to have a wake. This was it."

A specialist confirmed that he had tuberculosis and said he must leave for a sanitorium immediately. He recommended Saranac Lake Sanitorium, and as Casey was unable to travel alone I went along with him. A few of his so-called buddies called to say good-bye and wish him luck, but most of the tin-horns from Tin Pan Alley didn't bother; now that he was no longer fronting a band, he was no use to them.

When we got to Saranac, I stayed until he was settled, and

arranged with the doctor to take care of all expenses. Casey had never before accepted money from me. If he needed quick cash, he would borrow it from Arnold Rothstein or some other Broadway usurer. But now I refused to discuss finances with him. Whenever he brought up the subject I would tell him to shut up and get well. I visited him as often as I could, and as soon as he was on the mend suggested that he be transferred to the N.V.A. Sanitorium where he could be with other people in show business.

He was discharged from there a year later, and I staked him while he was getting a band together. He opened with his new outfit at one of Billy Rose's clubs, but the siege of t.b. had weakened him and he had a relapse. What Casey needed was a woman willing to devote her life to taking care of him, and he finally found her in Jane H. She was deeply in love with Casey, and she undertook to nurse him back to health. When he recovered they were married, and they are still together.

So my big romance had a happy ending after all—even though I wasn't in on it.

II

The year 1926 saw prohibition gangsters, racketeers and bootleggers enjoying just about their palmiest days. Quite often on their spending sprees they made my place a hangout, but it wasn't because I encouraged them to come back. Too frequently, they wrecked not only the house, but my nervous system.

One such episode began calmly enough with a phone call from a friend who ran a night club. He said to have a couple of cases of champagne chilled as he was bringing up seven or

eight very important people. This was good news to my girls
and me. It had been a slow night, and the prospect of a party
with a flock of big shots cheered us all up. But what a shock
I got when I opened the door on a group of the town's tough-
est boys headed by George McManus, Mike Best and Eddie
Diamond—Legs' brother.

All were very drunk and McManus was drunker than all
the others put together. He had been one of the gamblers
who helped me buy my first mink coat, and on previous visits
always had behaved like a gentleman, but now he shouldered
his way past me without speaking.

I said, "Hello, George. It's nice to see you again."

"Who the hell are you?" he growled, staring blindly at me
from under his hat brim. "I never saw you before in my
life."

"Quit your kidding," I said. "I'm Polly."

"Oh, you're Polly, are you?" He whipped out his gun and
waved it back and forth under my nose. "If you're Polly,
prove it. Go look out the window."

If I obeyed, it meant I would have my back to him. I
didn't move.

Suddenly he laughed. "Okay, okay," he said and staggered
against me. "I was just gonna give you a little scare."

I said, "Georgie, remember when I first started running a
house, you used to check your gun with me? How about letting me take care of it now?"

He thought this over, then slammed the gun in my hand
and walked away.

I hid the gun in the bathroom hamper and hurried out to
mingle with the rest of these troublemakers and try to keep
things under control. As I came into the room, I overheard a
character known as "Playful Joe" saying to one of my girls,
"Why do you work for this Jew-bastard?"

"Because I like her and she's fair to us," the girl said.

Apparently this answer annoyed Joe for he quickly jerked off his belt and began to beat her. The belt had a metal buckle and when it bit into her flesh, the girl shrieked. I got across the room in a hurry and grabbed Joe's arm. He shook me off and when I came back and fastened myself on him again, he gave me a shove that slammed me up against the wall. I was a little stunned because my head had banged into the wall so hard, and, like a wild woman, I ran around the room begging everyone to make him stop, but they laughed at me.

The girl was sobbing and I couldn't stand it. I ran back to Joe. "Leave her alone!" I screamed. "She hasn't done anything to you! I'm the one that's wrong. I deserve the beating for letting you bums up here!"

"That's okay with me," said Joe. "Since you deserve it, you'll get it." He turned and the belt cracked down across my back. The steel buckle ripped through my dress.

My friend from the night club tried to interfere. "What's the matter with you guys?" he shouted. "Have you all turned sadists?"

Two of them whipped off their belts and started for him, and when he saw them coming he turned and ran out of the apartment.

Somebody fired a shot, creating even more confusion. The bullet shattered the French doors leading to the bedroom which Mike and Catherine were occupying, and everyone rushed in to see if there had been any casualties.

"Jeez, Mike," somebody said. "I'm sorry. You okay?" (The hell with Catherine. She didn't matter, dead or alive.)

While they were all pushing and milling around the bedroom, I got the girls out of the apartment, dressed or undressed. I told them to hide in a friend's apartment across the street, and they cleared out in a hurry. This was one time I prayed that the cops would arrive, and hoped against hope that somebody had reported the shot.

When the gang trooped back again, George asked for a girl whom he had met at my place some years before. I explained that she was a motion picture star now and no longer on my call list.

"Then get others," he said, giving me a shove. "Get lots of them."

"I can't—not at this time of night."

"Okay then, Polly," he said, "we'll all sleep with you."

"Over my dead body," I said, and I meant it.

"Okay," one of them staggered toward me, "if that's the way you want it, that's easy."

He grabbed me by the throat and started choking me, laughing as I twisted and kicked and tried to claw away those hands that were crushing my windpipe. I would have screamed, but there was no air in my lungs. No one would have heard me anyway. Finally he dropped me to the floor.

"She's not dead yet," one of them said when I sucked in a painful breath.

I knew it would be smarter to stay where I was, but the rage in me was so strong I staggered to my feet and stood there swaying, facing the whole pack of them.

"You dirty, yellow rats," I gasped in a whisper, which was all the voice I had left, "you wouldn't have done this to me before, when I was a green kid, because you'd have been scared I'd call the cops. But you can do it now because you know I won't squeal on you. You know what you are, you dirty sons of bitches?" As I began telling them, one of them really let me have it. His fist crashed into my right temple and I went down as though I'd been struck by lightning.

That about concluded the evening's fun. They rifled the apartment, helping themselves to seven hundred and fifty dollars, and then, as they were leaving, some humorist unscrewed a light bulb and threw it down onto the sidewalk. It made a noise like a pistol shot, and apparently this killed them, for they exited laughing merrily.

I was in bed a week with a swollen face, a raw throat, and a back that looked like hash from the whipping. But what made me feel sicker than anything was the knowledge that there was no way in which I could retaliate. However, several of my friends bawled out the man who had unloaded the gang on me, and he made the excuse that they were in a troublesome mood and he didn't want them shooting up his place. I sent word to him kindly in future to refrain from doing me any more such favors.

The seven hundred and fifty dollars was returned to me by messenger, and I heard that the gang had used part of it to buy a couple of bushels of straw hats. Then they had gone to a saloon on Eighth Avenue and had themselves a ball punching their fists through the skimmers. I thought it was too damn bad their heads weren't in them at the time.

For a long while after, whenever I saw any of the pranksters, they would practically break their necks to avoid meeting my eye. Finally, one night I all but collided with George McManus, and he apologized for what had happened, offering me a large sum of money in compensation. It gave me some satisfaction to tell him what he could do with it.

There was a curious postscript to this episode with the hoodlums. Several years later Arnold Rothstein was shot in Room 349 at the Park Central—George McManus's room. When McManus was held for the murder I got a phone call from one of the gang, who asked if the District Attorney had sent for me. It seemed that one of my girls had talked about that night at the apartment and had said it was George who fired the shot through the French doors. If the D.A. could prove that George went around shooting up places just for his own amusement, it would certainly strengthen the case against him, and my informant had heard I was going to be questioned. Since I was the only one who could back up George's statement that he had turned over his gun to me before the shooting occurred, this placed me in a rather ticklish spot. I assured the caller that my girls would do no more talking. Luckily, I was never called and George was acquitted without my having to testify.

III

When you get your education from people, instead of books, what you learn about is pretty much determined by what interests them. And so, as most of my customers were sports' fans, I found myself hearing a lot about the exploits of Red Grange and Babe Ruth and other idols of the gridiron and the diamond. But I was more interested in prize fighting and racing—maybe because you don't have to learn a whole new vocabulary to be able to converse about them. One wealthy American League club owner used to bring his whole team up to my house whenever they beat the Yankees (which was not often enough for me to learn much about baseball), and my ignorance of how the game was played used to give the boys a lot of laughs. It got to be a standard gag that if one of them had stolen a base in the game that day, I would buy him a drink on the house—because I once had said it must take a lot of nerve to steal anything before a whole stadium full of people.

Another idol ·of the day was the Toy Bulldog, Mickey Walker, who was welterweight champion until 1926 when —as he had gotten too heavy to fight in that division—he took the middleweight title from Tiger Flowers. Mickey came around to my house every now and then, and I got to be very fond of him. I still am. However, on his first visit he must have been under a misapprehension about the duties of a madam, for he kept insisting that I go to bed with him. In the group accompanying Mickey that night was one of his handlers, and taking this man aside I told him either to explain to Mickey that I was not available for that kind of entertainment or else take the kid home.

The handler became extremely indignant. "You should be honored," he said. "That kid is the champ."

"Fine," I said. "He's your champ. You sleep with him."

When Mickey went out on the town, he usually made quite a production of it. One time he and Swifty Morgan started out with twenty-one thousand dollars between them, twenty of which Mickey said he would hang on to. By six A.M. they had blown the odd grand and headed for my place. As I already had shut up shop, I only let them in on condition they would leave after one drink. At this point Swifty asked Mickey for the twenty grand, which he duly handed over but asked for a few bucks back for cab fare. This precipitated a long-drawn-out drunken argument during the course of which I managed to ease them out of the apartment. But they didn't go very far. One of Mickey's entourage, who knew the boys were loaded with dough, had been out looking for them, and he found them sound asleep propped up against the fire hydrant outside my house. The twenty grand was still intact.

But it was horse racing I liked best, and when the season

opened at Saratoga, I decided to go up for it. Many New York celebrities would be there, and as I was still not getting the play I wanted from the socialites and theatrical crowd, I thought this might be my chance to make a bid for their patronage. So, combining business with pleasure, I took a house near the track and, as soon as I had concluded arrangements, sent for ten of my most beautiful girls.

We had a table reserved daily at the clubhouse and caused a sensation every time we made an entrance. The girls were gorgeous and exquisitely dressed, and the men made a circle around us as soon as we were seated. "How is your Rancocas stable today?" someone would always ask. The Rancocas stable, belonging to Harry Sinclair, was considered the leading stable of thoroughbreds, and my "fillies" were the best in our business.

I had been open only two nights when my house was surrounded by police. I was amazed. I had paid a packet to the right people for protection and was sure it was safe for me to operate. On this particular night, I had a full house, and among those present was Moe Smith, of the team of Moe and Izzy, the famous prohibition agents.

The chief of police strode in. "Who owns this place?" he demanded.

"Why, I have no idea," I said modestly.

"Well, I have," he said. "We're taking you to the station house."

I sighed. "Get your hats and coats, girls," I called up the stairs. "We're going for a little drive."

Just then the exploring cops found the plump prohibition agent hiding his curves behind the dining room door. Moe emerged sheepishly and he and the chief of police withdrew for a quiet talk. What passed between them I don't know, but we didn't go to jail that night, and the chief said I could keep open for a week in order to recoup my investment. Then I must get out of town.

One night during the week I had a little trouble with a guest who squawked about the size of his bill. My bills were high, but this was hardly a secret and I had no patience with him.

"Look," I said, "my prices are the same for everyone. If you don't like them, stay away."

"I'm an upright, tax-paying citizen of this town," he shouted.

"If you're so upright, what are you doing here?"

This infuriated him. He slammed his money down, saying as he did so, "This is going to cost you plenty!"

The little skunk went right from my house to the police and reported that he had been robbed of sixteen hundred dollars. So next morning I was called in by the commissioner. I told him exactly what had happened, and gave as character references the men who controlled the biggest gambling houses in Saratoga. They knew I operated on the square. The commissioner then asked me why I had set up my house in one of Saratoga's finest residential districts. I answered him truthfully that I had never been in Saratoga before and I didn't know one neighborhood from another. I was only interested in locating near the race track. Either because he was impressed by my frankness or because of the intervention of Moe Smith, the commissioner gave me permission to remain at the same location till the end of the racing season.

Saratoga was heaven for my girls. They all went jock-crazy. I just couldn't control them. After the house was closed for the night, they'd sneak downstairs and raid the wine cellar, then open the door to their little friends. When I came down in the morning, I'd find jockeys curled up asleep in every corner—stable boys too. In fact, it wouldn't have surprised me to find the ponies themselves. I worried because I knew that if the owners found out their riders were carousing all night at my place I'd probably be closed. I used to lecture the boys, warning them they couldn't drink all night and turn in a good ride the next day. But nobody paid the slightest attention to me. The girls thought the jocks were cute. The jocks thought the girls were gorgeous. And the free liquor was fine.

Kid Speed, one of Colonel Bradley's leading riders, was spending all his time running around with a very beautiful girl of mine named Lila, and I cornered him one evening and tried to talk some sense into him. "Kid," I said, "you're at the peak of your career, you've a chance to be the top jockey of the season, but these nightly drinking bouts are going to ruin you. And Lila's not helping you any either. Get smart and leave her alone."

"The hell I will," he snapped. "I'm taking her out of your joint tonight."

I shrugged my shoulders. "Have it your way. Just don't come back again, either of you."

Not long after, Bradley suspended him and I heard that he developed into an habitual drunkard. I saw Lila once, years later. I was coming home from Madison Square Garden, where the bicycle races were being held, and I noticed a grotesque-looking creature in a black ill-fitting dress, white stockings, heavy make-up and a mop of red hair flying all over Eighth Avenue. I remarked to my companion on her pitiful appearance, then I stopped short as I realized it was Lila. I was so shocked all I could think of to say was, "Lila, have your teeth fixed." She put her hand over her mouth and scuttled away while I just stood there stupidly. When I snapped out of my trance and started to run after her, she had disappeared in the night.

Finally, the girls got so out of hand that I sent them back to New York with Lion and turned my establishment into a speakeasy. It was just as profitable as running the house, and at the end of the season (as the gamblers say) I "won"—that is, I broke even. For though I usually finished ahead at the races, in paying complimentary visits to the houses of chance I picked too many wrong numbers at the roulette wheels and my throwing hand wasn't too gifted at the crap tables, especially when my come-out point was a ten or a four and I had side-bets that I'd make it the hard way. But in my biggest gamble I had succeeded. At last I'd made contact with the clientele I'd been shooting for, my address book was crammed with new names, and I knew Saratoga would pay off for me in New York.

IV

My next establishment was to become a rendezvous for many celebrities and members of the Social Register, but in the beginning it certainly looked as if we were off to a flying standstill. The building at Fifty-ninth and Madison into which I had moved was a very old one. The floors creaked with every step and the walls were so thin that the ringing of the phone could be heard three doors away. And so, being afraid the other tenants might complain, I took the precaution of putting down double carpeting and muffling the telephone bell with cotton.

Shortly after I had opened for business there was an important fight at the Garden, which meant a big night for us.

So the girls got themselves all primped up and we sat around the radio listening to the fight and killing time till the guests arrived. But hour after hour passed and to our intense dismay not once did the phone ring. Finally, at five A.M. we decided to call it a night and went glumly to bed.

Next day I ran into a friend of mine at Reuben's, which was then on Madison, just down the street. "Polly," my friend said, "Where in hell were you last night? Waxey Gordon made a killing at the fights and was all set to throw a champagne party at your place. We tried to get you a dozen times but couldn't raise a soul. You missed out on a thousand or more."

I rushed back to the apartment, gnashing my teeth all the way, and on checking the telephone found we had done such an efficient muffling job as to silence the bell completely. While I was still brooding over this, one of the girls came in with the news that all my precautionary measures had been unnecessary. The other tenants in the building merely rented office space, and at night there wasn't a soul on hand to be disturbed!

So we took the cotton out of the telephone and let it ring its fool head off—which, to my relief, it did with hardly a letup. However, the comedy of errors was not quite finished. I still had a thing or two to learn about my new aristocratic clientele—for one thing to know them when I saw them.

Late one night a Mr. Tom H. and a Mr. O. S. were announced. Now I knew their names (as who didn't?), but only through reading Cholly Knickerbocker's column, and I couldn't quite believe my fame had spread to such exalted quarters. Figuring it was a hoax of some sort—probably a police dodge to gain admittance—I sent the girls out the back way before I opened the door to my callers, both of whom were in top hats and tails.

"What can I do for you, gentlemen?" I asked, on edge.

They laughed self-consciously. "Charlie Mullens said we could find some pretty girls here."

"You've been misinformed," I said severely. "You can see for yourself there's no one here."

They looked around the apartment. Everything was so quiet they became a little unsure of themselves. "Aren't you Polly Adler?"

"I'm Miss Pearl Davis," I said, giving one of my aliases. "I must ask you to leave."

Rather dejectedly, the two young men departed. Still thinking they were police in disguise (I should have known better—top hats and tails yet!) I smiled smugly, much pleased with the way I had handled things.

Charlie Mullens had a speakeasy about a block away, so I decided to stroll over and check up on the callers. Besides I was curious to see Charlie's place. It was located in a mansion that might have belonged to a millionaire—in fact, probably once had—and I'd been told that you had to be in Who's Who to get in. After ringing the bell, I waited while I was scrutinized through a mirror reflector, then the door opened and I was ushered into a large foyer. I asked to see Mr. Mullens and was taken upstairs to his private office which, like the rest of the house, was richly and tastefully furnished.

Charlie, whom I was meeting for the first time, was tall and distinguished, and the gray at his temples made him look more like a banker or an ambassador than a glorified saloon-keeper. But despite his imposing presence and all the grandeur surrounding him, I was not intimidated. I felt that we were on the same team. He, too, was breaking the law; he, too, lived in fear of the cops and had to cater to the whims of a different clientele.

His cordial greeting put me completely at ease and soon we were chatting like old friends. Finally, recalling the purpose of my visit, I told him of the two phonies who had used his name.

"But that *was* Tom H.," he said. "That *was* O. S."

"You mean they were the McCoy?"

At my shocked expression Charlie burst out laughing. "In the flesh," he said.

"Give me a gun, let me shoot myself! How could I be such a schnook! Just think—me, Polly Adler—giving the bum's rush to the Blue Book. I'll never live it down!"

Charlie explained that the two boys patronized his place with the knowledge and approval of their parents, who knew it was strictly reserved for the upper classes. All the young chaps called him "Pop" and often came to him with their problems. And because of my reputation for running a clean house, Charlie said, he would like to send me some of his younger customers. He knew they would be far safer there than if they picked up girls on the streets. I gave him a code to use when phoning me, and from then on, thanks to Charlie, I entertained many young men from Harvard, Yale, Cornell and other Ivy League universities.

Contrary to rumors I heard of their behavior at my competitors' establishments, they always behaved very well. The only time I found them a little unruly was during football season. But unlike my competitors I had strict rules for the younger set. No one was allowed to have more than two drinks and at no time would I allow off-color conversation or the practice of unnatural sex by any of my girls.

I grew very fond of these boys, who nicknamed me "Polly-Pal," and before long they began seeking my advice as they did Charlie's. Probably this was because their own parents were too busy marrying and divorcing, or traveling around, to be close to their children. In most cases, the boys had been reared by nursemaids and servants who were kind to them, but with whom they were embarrassed to discuss their intimate problems. And so these poor little rich kids turned to a speakeasy owner and a madam.

Thanks to the contacts I had made in Saratoga, I was now in a position to eliminate many undesirables, and more and more restricted my clientele to the upper brackets of the social, financial, literary and theatrical worlds. As a result, my house began to take on the special atmosphere which was to make it unique among contemporary bordellos. It became a gathering place for intellectuals and business tycoons and men with high positions in the government as well as playboys and scions of inherited wealth.

Studying these people, learning their likes and dislikes, listening to them and watching them, I found myself absorbing all kinds of new and fascinating information. It was untabulated, it was added helter-skelter, but I was beginning to build up a little stockpile of knowledge about music and literature and art and history. And I began to catch glimpses of another "Goldine Madina" which I might one day explore. One thing I knew for sure—I was never going to run out of things to learn. I didn't even know the meaning of many of the words I was now hearing (and using!), and it's probably just as well I hadn't yet learned how to look things up in a dictionary. It would have left me no time to run a house. But I knew that my use and misuse of the new words I was picking up amused my customers, and many of them respected me for my eagerness to learn.

At least, I could hold my own in discussions of the news of the day, for in the middle years of the Twenties the big stories were not of the kind to put a strain on anybody's in-

tellect (unless maybe you were a member of a national lu-
nacy commission). It was in this "era of wonderful nonsense"
that a wealthy real estate man named Edward F. Browning
put an ad in the *Herald-Tribune* announcing his wish to
adopt a "pretty, refined fourteen-year-old," and the subsequent trials and tribulations of "Daddy," Mary Louise
Spas (who turned out to be twenty-one, so was thrown back)
and "Peaches" (whose winning candidacy was announced,
appropriately enough, on April first) kept the papers in
headlines for months. Also signalizing 1926 were such banner occurrences as Earl Carroll's bathtub party at which a
Miss Joyce Hawley was laved in a tub of champagne, the host
genially instructing the several hundred guests who wished
to assist her at her ablutions that "the line forms to the
right." This was good for God only knows how many tons of
newsprint since the party was in honor of the Countess of
Cathcart (who had been detained at Ellis Island on charges
of moral turpitude; she had been gadding about Africa with
the Earl of Craven), and since Earl Carroll subsequently was
sent up for perjury—he had said under oath the wine was
water. There were lively doings on the West Coast too,
where Aimee Semple McPherson, the famed Evangelist, ostensibly was drowned off Santa Monica Beach, but turned up
in Mexicali a couple of weeks later with the filmiest of tales
about having been kidnaped. Despite allegations that she
had been seen in Carmel with a male companion, her faithful followers stoutly maintained she had "spent seventeen
days and nights walking on water." So quite a few sticks of
type were used up during the unraveling of the various
yarns.

In the absence of sensational stories like these, there were
the great sporting events like the first Dempsey-Tunney fight
down in Philadelphia, where they were having a sesquicen-

tennial celebration ("sesquicentennial" was one of my new words). And of course Queen Marie's triumphal tour supplied headline fodder for months. As a matter of fact, I always thought the queen's reception in New York was more of a triumph for Mayor Walker. Certainly it was a tribute of some kind when, as Her Majesty and His Honor were riding up Broadway in the welcoming parade, one of the onlookers cried, "What's the matter, Jimmy? Haven't you made her yet?". . . . So you see the topics of the day were right down my alley. (Of course in Germany Hitler was writing *Mein Kampf,* and Stalin had succeeded Lenin in Russia, and Mussolini's black shirts were darkening the landscape in Italy, but this was back-page stuff, if it made the papers at all.)

Aside from the personal satisfaction I derived from cultivating my mind, it was good business to be able to converse intelligently with my clients as it helped promote the sale of drinks. My new customers did not always come to my house for sex. "Polly's" also was a place to meet friends, play cards, arrange a dinner party, kill time—a sort of combination club and speakeasy with a harem conveniently handy. Many a big business deal was clinched at my bar over a Scotch and soda. Men often brought prospective clients there when they were having a hard time making a sale, for my brand of hospitality had been known to soften them up when all else had failed. In fact, a number of important executives regularly sought my advice on how to entertain visiting firemen, and this didn't necessarily mean how to entertain them at my house. They relied on me because they knew that I was usually successful in sizing up men quickly and figuring out what would appeal to them.

I was regarded as an expert on human relations too, and frequently played the part of "Mrs. Anthony" to men who wished my advice on intimate domestic problems—matters which they were too proud or too shy to discuss with their closest friends. They knew they could count on my discretion and sincerity, and they were grateful for an impersonal opinion. More than once, I was instrumental in preventing a messy divorce case, and always, I think, the men felt better for having aired their difficulties.

My closest friends among my clients at this time were a writer and a chain-store magnate, a member of one of the "sixty families." Mr. Chain-Store used to drop in at all hours to drink a glass of wine and tell me his troubles—of which he had more than about anybody I have ever listened to. He also had more millions than Heinz has pickles, but he was constantly making the point that money didn't bring happiness. (However, I don't think he had anything against being rich.) Sometimes it got tiresome listening to him bellyaching about nothing, but he had a good sense of humor and was generous. If one of my girls strolled into the room on the chance that he might want to engage her, he would always rise, bow courteously, and present her with a hundred-dollar bill. He came for conversation only—maybe that's why he was usually so low in his mind.

But Bob, the writer, was quite another story. Instead of telling you his troubles, he'd urge you to spill yours. Lion worshiped the ground he walked on. You could always tell when he was in the house just from the increased candle power of her smile, and she never would let any of the other maids serve him.

Every so often, Bob would arrive and inquire if I had a room to spare—an empty one. He would say that he was in need of a good night's sleep before tackling a magazine piece. Sometimes, when he had a deadline to meet, he'd stay right there to do his writing. He claimed his best articles were written in my homey atmosphere. "The Waldorf just isn't in it with you when it comes to service, Polly," he'd tell me. "Lion never fails to have my suit pressed and my shirt and socks and drawers laundered. What a valet! By golly, she even has a light hand with a razor. And then that terrific smile at breakfast—why, it lights up a room like the sun!" Certainly Bob lighted up my life like the sun, and sunny was the word for his whole nature. Of all the friends I made during my years as a madam, I think his was the friendship I valued most. I have never known a finer man.

Bob always was egging me on to tell some of the funny experiences I'd had in the business, and one of his favorite stories concerned a practical joke which was inspired by Queen Marie's visit and the ensuing mania to "shake hands with royalty."

One evening three of my socialite customers came by for cocktails and mentioned they were expecting some friends from San Francisco. Apparently none of them was looking forward to the visit and all were bored at the thought of having to entertain them.

"It's one of those dreary combinations," said Charlie. "You know the kind I mean, Poll—the wife has pots of money and the husband is just good-looking."

"And to make it even drearier," said Bill, "they're the most appalling social climbers. To hear them talk you'd think this tour of Queen Marie's was on a par with the Second Coming."

I asked if their friends had met the queen and this gave Charlie an idea. "Why not make 'em happy?" he said. "Even if we can't produce the queen, there's no reason why they shouldn't meet her dear friend and former lady-in-waiting, the Baroness von Wiener." He looked at me. "How about it,

Baroness? Will you and a couple of your nieces honor us with your presence at a dinner?"

So that's how it came about that a few nights later, I found myself being kow-towed to by a very awed and impressed Mr. and Mrs. Climber from San Francisco. Never a man to do things by halves, Charlie had rehearsed the girls and me the day before, had supervised our costuming, and coached my two "nieces" in speaking with a Mittel-European accent. And there was an orchestra, place cards with coronets, caviar and champagne—everything in the grand manner.

While we were served cocktails I discoursed about my castle on the Rhine and my villa on the Blue Coast, dropped blasé references to a recent dinner party at Buckingham Palace ("it was just family"), and—as the drinks started to get to me—graciously condescended to answer many questions about the private lives and personal habits of royalty. Charlie and Bill had promised to be standing by in case I got out on a limb, but before long they were laughing so hard I was afraid they would give the game away. However, everything went well until dinner was announced, and I was escorted to the place of honor while the orchestra played what Charlie claimed was the Roumanian national anthem.

As the champagne corks began to pop, the girls got more and more giggly. But they stuck gamely to their accents and there was so much *zis-ing* and *zat-ing* it sounded more like bees swarming than conversation. Finally during a lull between courses Nellie (one of my "nieces") rose, hiccuping slightly, and said, "Auntie dear, where is ze—how you say?— ladies room—la toilet?" Mrs. Climber looked at me horrified, and I registered blank. Quickly Bill got up and showed Nellie to the bathroom upstairs.

On his return, dinner was resumed and Mrs. Climber was

talking busily across the table to me when all of a sudden she broke off, a frozen expression on her face. I turned to look, as did everyone, and even I did a double-take. For there stood Nellie, naked as a needle. For a moment it was so quiet you could have heard a jaw drop, and then, apparently sensing some explanation might be required, Mademoiselle Nellie spoke up.

"I peed on my dress," she said matter-of-factly. "The butler is drying it."

Of course there was nothing to be said after that—at least not with an accent. But to my surprise Mrs. Climber was a much better sport than her husband. He was all set to leave in a huff, but she insisted on staying. "I've had just enough to drink to enjoy this kind of thing," she declared. "Now if that phony Baroness will come down off her high horse and admit who she is, maybe this party can get going."

So I told her she could just call me madam.

V

Up until 1927 my publicity had consisted chiefly of what theater people call "word-of-mouth," but as of July twenty-second of that year, I crashed the headlines in no uncertain terms. The twenty-first of July was the date of the Dempsey-Sharkey fight, and as a sequel to it came my first big raid. Needless to state, I had been raided before, but this was a four-star, five-alarm, full-dress affair in gorgeous technicolor.

After the fight, a very prominent gentleman—who had bet on Dempsey to win by a kayo in the seventh and had thereby garnered himself seventy thousand iron men—brought a party of friends over to the house to celebrate. And the joint was operating under a full head of steam—corks popping right and left, champagne being sipped out of slippers and other even more exotic receptacles, rose-garlanded dancing girls fighting their way out of pies (at least that's how a literary gentleman of my acquaintance used to tell it)—when tramp, tramp, tramp, the bulls came thundering in and blew the whistle on us. My friend who had made the seventy G killing beckoned to the arresting officers (one of whom later was flopped and sent to jail during the Seabury Investigation), and offered two thousand dollars if they'd go out the way they'd come in, closing the door after them. But the boys weren't having any that night, which meant that seven of the girls and I were hauled out and stuffed into the pie-wagon.

However, not even the Bastille could have held us that night. Our customers bailed us out almost before we were booked, and when we came out of the station house a great wave of cheers went up from several carloads of gentlemen who were waiting at the curb to escort us back to the house. We kept things rolling until nine the next morning, at which time we were scheduled to appear in court.

Our entrance into the courtroom caused quite a stir among the court officials, for there were my girls, tall and beautiful, gliding down the aisle like swans on a mirrored lake, with me bustling along after them like Donald Duck.

A member of the D.A.'s staff was grinning from ear to ear. "Reduce your prices, Polly," he said, "and every man here will be your client."

The case was dismissed that same morning.

Dempsey's victory over Sharkey was only a prelude to one of the most sensational fights in history—his rematch with Tunney, which took place at Soldier Field in Chicago and drew a two-million-six-hundred-and-fifty-thousand-dollar gate, the largest ever. Although not much of a fight fan, I saw this one and since I had bet five bucks (big deal!) on Dempsey, I screamed my head off when Tunney went down for the historic long count. But I screamed just as hard when Tunney was proclaimed winner. I was on a vacation and didn't really care who won—just so somebody did.

More memorable than the fight (at least to me) was the party thrown by Al Capone at the Metropole Hotel. It lasted a solid week, during all of which time the champagne and every other kind of liquor flowed like Niagara. Capone was certainly a grand host—Lucullus and those old Roman boys could have taken lessons from him—and his guests, among whom were legal lights, politicians and mobsters, from all over the country, made the most of his lavish hospitality.

I know that society takes a dim view of Al Capone. But I make a habit of judging people only in their relationship to me, and such times as I happened to run into Al he was always very pleasant. I first met him in the early Twenties. We were introduced by Francesco Castaglia who, some twenty-five years later, was to make quite a stir on television under the name of Frank Costello.

Chapter 4

Just Lucky
I Guess

It's pretty difficult to prove that a girl from
a milltown who comes to a city brothel didn't
know perfectly well what it was all about and
wasn't to some extent a willing conniver at her
own shame. Likewise it has been pretty
thoroughly demonstrated that what keeps a
girl in the life is, as a rule, debt or illness or
lack of vitality or sheer weakness of the will-to-
do-otherwise. Seldom, if ever, is she held by
actual iron bars across a window or shackles
bolted to the floor. "White Slaves" are enslaved
quite as much by themselves and their own
poverty and neuroses as they are by the
madams, panders and cadets.

Ernest Jerome Hopkins   Article in New York
MIRROR

I

Sooner or later everyone who came to my house would ask
me about the daily life of my girls. "What do they do with
themselves? Do they ever read? How do they get along
together? Are there any dope fiends among them? Any Lesbians? What do they do with their money?" and so on. Usually, unless the questioner happened to be a personal friend,
I'd wink and reply, "Those are the secrets of a whorehouse."
I figured it just wasn't any of their damn business, and I re-

sented their assumption that the girls were a separate breed, like Ubangis or Hottentots. Many of my customers never seemed to realize that a prostitute is just as much a product of our so-called culture as is a college professor or a boot-black, and, as with them, her choice of occupation has been dictated by environmental and personality factors. No woman is born a whore and any woman may become one. But even some of the men who were longest on book-learning completely failed to appreciate what Kipling meant when he wrote that the Colonel's Lady and Judy O'Grady are sisters under the skin.

This curiosity about the girls and what goes on behind the scenes is not limited to the patrons of houses. It is universal and age-old. The literature of all countries teems with novels and stories and plays about prostitution, and the prostitute as a character has fascinated the men with the noblest minds, the giants of letters, no less than the hacks and the pornographers. But the great to-the-life portraits in the gallery of "fallen women"—the Nanas and Sonyas and Sadie Thompsons—are as few and far between as the Zolas and Dostoievskis and Maughams who created them. The overwhelming proportion of writing on this subject—both fiction and what purports to be factual—is cheaply sensational, or distorted by prejudice, or uninformed, often all three. In this kind of writing, the prostitute comes in two standard models. Either she is presented as a brazen hussy who arrived in the world equipped with marabou-trimmed garters, black silk stockings and a sexy leer (heart of gold optional), or as an innocent victim, a babe in the woods, seduced and abandoned by a city slicker, or maybe shanghaied by a white slaver while on her way from choir practice. And, depending in which category she belongs, her life, when there's no company in the parlor, appears to consist entirely of (a) sitting around in a dirty kimono drinking gin, or (b) weeping and wailing and hammering her fists against the door until someone shuts her up with a smack on the chops.

Now, like all stereotyped conceptions, these have some basis in fact. There have been and there are prostitutes who are slovens and drunkards, just as there have been and may still be (though I very much doubt it) cases of innocent girls being lured into houses and held captive there. Certainly it is true that many girls are forced to ply their trade in the most degrading surroundings under conditions ruinous both to their physical and mental health. But just as the owner of an exclusive Fifth Avenue gown shop operates on an entirely different level than a Lower East Side pushcart peddler, so did the kind of a house I ran compare with the ordinary bordello. Far from having to lure girls there, I was forced to turn away thirty or forty for every one I was able to accommodate.

The routine of life in my house varied only if some customer on a binge took it over for a nonstop party. Our "business day" was, of course, night, and after it was over, the girls usually took a long walk and then had breakfast before retiring. Breakfast was a hearty meal and always included waffles or hotcakes and sausages, or bacon and eggs. It was the only time we would all be together, and the conversation consisted mostly of what might be called "shop talk." The girls would relate their experiences with the men they had entertained that night and compare notes about the quirks of their customers. Sometimes the episodes reported seemed to us very funny, and we all laughed long and loud—perhaps because the tension of the night was over, and it was a relief to let go. But many times the stories were anything but amusing, and then the girls would yawn and look at their plates, sympathetic but not really wanting to hear and be reminded of humiliating or painful experiences which they themselves had gone through.

I was kept busy at breakfast watching and correcting the girls' table manners. At that time of day, it almost might seem I was running a finishing school, for I made a point of training my girls so that when a man took them out to dinner, they would not embarrass or disillusion him with gauche, unattractive table manners. For example, one of my girls had a habit of taking a whole slice of bread, laying it out on her palm to butter, and then doubling it up and stuffing it into her mouth. I scolded her constantly about this and eventually the etiquette lessons must have sunk in. She told me that once, when she was dining at a very posh hotel and started to give a piece of bread her customary treatment, it seemed to her she heard my voice right in her ear— "Millie! How many times must I tell you? *Don't fold your bread!*"—and it startled her so, she dropped the bread like a hotcake.

However, some of the girls—the Duchess for instance—had beautiful manners. The Duchess never talked much about her beginnings, but it was obvious she had been well educated and she spoke several languages. She was a tall willowy blonde with a straight aristocratic nose (on which she wore a pince-nez) and a haughty manner. When she first came to me, it was only because she was broke and on her uppers that I took her in, for even though she had previously worked at a West Coast house, I could not believe that this staid and proper-looking young lady would have any appeal for my customers. I was so wrong! As they got to know her and were no longer intimidated by her regal air, the Duchess became extremely popular.

In spite of her standoffish manner, she was one of the few girls I have known who really loved her work with a nymphomaniac's devotion. At five thirty one morning, after she had finished her chores for the night, I saw her getting fixed up to go out. "Where are you going?" I asked her. "Where do you think?" she said. "Out to get myself a little sex." But as I have said, the Duchess was an extremist. At the opposite extreme were the girls who hated their job, every moment of it, and who, while lavishing smiles on their customers, thoroughly detested them.

After breakfast the girls would make plans for the day. I would marvel at their persisting to do this when, day after day, the plans came to nothing because most of them slept until dinnertime. Occasionally an early appointment meant a girl would have to welcome a gentleman caller almost before she had time to get the sleep out of her eyes, and her dinner would be postponed until she was free—which rarely was before midnight. When at last she got to the table she would be served a wholesome but not fancy meal—usually minus dessert—for the girls had to watch their figures.

The cook was given full charge of the kitchen, planning the menus, purchasing provisions and preparing the meals in her own style. The only time I might suggest a menu would be at the request of a customer who was having a private party. Otherwise she was on her own, and the girls were forbidden to interfere with her schedule in any way. However, if, as now and then happened, a girl requested a favorite dish, she always obliged.

The girls were liberal with the maids, although sometimes their tips were more in the nature of bribes not to tell me of certain things they had done. For example, if a man complained to a maid that a girl gave him the rush act—tried to wink him in—which was not permitted at my house, the girl would slip her five or ten not to tell me. Also, when reefers became fashionable among call girls, they would bribe the maids to hide them. (If a girl's bag containing reefers should be picked up during a raid, I would have been held for possession of drugs, so when I suspected a girl of using marijuana I searched her bag before letting her in the house.) One girl bribed the cook to hide her supply in the icebox among the lettuce leaves—a deed for which the cook received plenty of "cabbage." I didn't find out about this during all the time the girl worked for me. In those days, luckily, I didn't like lettuce or I'd have wound up with a reefer salad.

Most of my girls were of at least average intelligence and I don't think a one of them, in her right mind, ever had any intention of staying on in the business. They knew that it was a short-lived career and that, like baseball players, they had to be young to stay in the game. Therefore, the smart ones either saved their money against the day they would have to retire, or learned a trade, or worked out ways and means of snagging a rich husband.

Unfortunately, however, the majority weren't smart. It worried me to see so many of them making no preparations for the future, and I used to nag and prod the girls to read good books and make something of themselves. Marching into the living room, I would inquire of one of the lazy ladies lolling on the sofa what she expected to do for a living when she was thirty-five, and all too often the only answer was a bored sigh. Or perhaps one of them might say, "Oh, don't worry about me, Polly. I won't wind up in the poorhouse. Just as soon as I lay my hands on enough money, I'm going to open a shop. I'm quite creative, you know; I took a correspondence course in designing. As a matter of fact, I could go to work in a dress house tomorrow."

"Then why don't you?"

"Because I'm ambitious. I don't want to work for somebody else. Doing this I can make some quick dough and then start out right." Ten years later, she would still be hustling, her ideas and ambitions gone, and not even a bank account to her name.

Few of the girls had any sense of values. They never planned their wardrobes, they would buy anything in sight. Childishly, they would think that blowing their money gave them an excuse to continue in the life. They would have to make more in order to blow it—the old vicious-circle pitch.

Some of my girls were talented—actresses who couldn't get that first break, singers or dancers who had run out of dough before they clicked solidly, show girls between jobs. When they weren't working for me, they were dancing in night clubs or going to drama school, and some even took secretarial courses. But most of the girls spent their days in not too purposeful a fashion. They went to the beauty parlor, washed out stockings and undies (if they couldn't con the maids into doing it for them), took in a movie, played cards or went on an afternoon date. Few of them bothered to keep up with current events, except what was happening on Broadway, and their reading was mostly confined to the pulps. Still, they led pretty strenuous lives, and perhaps it was natural that they preferred relaxing over copies of *True Confessions* and *Modern Romances* to fighting their way through books which they couldn't understand without expending mental effort.

Nearly always they got along quite well together. Occasionally one girl would get jealous of another, thinking she was getting more money, and sometimes one of them would deliberately make a play for a man who was talking with another girl—which was not considered cricket. Now and then there were petty quarrels over a pair of stockings, or who

swiped whose hairpins—things like that. But in general the
girls got along as well as, or better than, a group of chorus
girls sharing the same dressing room. Inevitably I had a few
Lesbians, some of them troublemakers, some very peaceful
souls. It's often been said that a prostitute becomes so tired
of being mauled by men that she turns to a woman for ten-
derness. Maybe so. I have no figures on the incidence of female homosexuality, but it's my observation that it occurs
in every walk of life.

In the evenings, waiting for calls, the girls most often
played cards. Their favorite game was Hearts, and there was
always an outburst of squeals when Dirty Dora (the Queen
of Spades) was passed to somebody. Sometimes a big argument would follow, and if the other players felt a girl was
being a bad sport they would gang up on the squawker and
slip her Dirty Dora at every opportunity. They just played
for fun, but from the way they carried on you'd have
thought a fortune was riding on every hand. Suddenly everything would become quiet. "Hurry, Lion, answer the phone
—the business phone!" They knew it was the business phone
because it had a shriller ring than the other one.

During a lull between calls, I would try to relax in one of
the back bedrooms—read or listen to the radio—but there
was never quiet in the house for very long. The constant
ringing of the telephone was in itself enough to get on anyone's nerves. And for the girls there was the added strain of
knowing they always had to be ready with a bright smile and
a big hello, no matter what the hour. Sometimes when a late
call came and a girl had just retired, I wouldn't have the
heart to disturb her and would arrange for an outside girl
to keep the date. But the next day, if the girl found out, I'd
be raked over the coals because an outsider had gotten the
money. They were go-getters, my kids.

Every fall some of them would announce that they planned to spend the winter in Florida and talked expansively of the wonderful vacation awaiting them. But they never made hotel reservations. The minute they got off the train in Miami, they headed straight for one of the better whorehouses. Which probably explains why they came home in the spring with no sign of Florida suntan. Some vacation!

It is traditional that prostitutes are a sentimental lot and, in the main, this is true. Times I would take the girls to a club, they never failed to bombard the entertainers with requests for the kind of songs that had a sob in them. Their favorite entertainer was Tommy Lyman, and their favorite songs were such numbers as "Rings on Your Fingers," "Heartaches Inside," "Oh, How I Miss You Tonight," "Melancholy Baby," and "Broadway Rose." When the lights were turned down, all except for the spot on the young man with the megaphone (those were the days of crooners), the girls would seize the opportunity to shed a few tears, and often I could hardly hear the singer owing to the chorus of muffled sobs around me. But then who am I to talk? If anyone sang "Charmaine" I'd get misty-eyed myself, for I could never hear it without thinking of Casey.

As with the girls in any job, there would be times when they would get fed up with the same routine, the same grind, night in, night out. Usually, when a girl was in this fed-up mood, she would wait until she had a late call at a hotel and then just forget to come home for a day or two. I used to beg the girls to telephone me—otherwise I'd worry my head off, not knowing if they were in jail or just taking a breather. (It would have been useless to try and check with the man at the hotel—the one the girl had kept the date with. Nine times out of ten, he'd have left a "Do not disturb" order with the operator, fearing a check-up call from his wife or mistress. A smart woman could hear the guilt in his voice, whereas not being able to reach him she would assume he was "tied up in business.")

I never questioned or scolded the girls about their holiday escapades. I only asked that they call to let me know they were all right. Then they could go ahead and have their fun, providing they behaved themselves in public. This was one thing I never stopped harping on—that in public places they must always act like ladies. Sometimes, of course, a girl would get a snootful, in which case her conduct often would leave something to be desired. When she sobered up, I would call her on the carpet, and there would be tears and promises never to do such a thing again. Naturally the promises weren't always kept, but on the whole my girls' batting average for ladylike behavior was pretty high.

The girls loved to go to night clubs. They would get just as excited about making an entrance as any débutante and were usually, I might add, much better behaved. This is not just prejudice on my part. My girls were taken out by some of the most attractive and eligible men in New York—men whom I had seen pictured in the society pages with the season's most glamorous débutantes. I often asked these chaps why they took out my girls, whose company they had to pay for, in preference to the buds from the Social Register. I always got an answer something like this, "Who wouldn't rather be with one of your girls than some spoiled, smart-alecky deb who combs her hair at the table, who can't talk about anything but herself, and who has nothing on her mind but whether or not the restaurant photographer will snap a candid shot of her for the paper? Your girls make better drinking companions and never behave like tramps."

Also, my girls never affected the blasé, world-weary air which many of the debs seemed to think was as necessary as lipstick. If they were bored, they knew better than to reveal it.

A weekly event to which all the girls looked forward was the visit of Wally Pierre. He was a well-known and extremely talented hairdresser, regarded by my girls as the ultimate authority on matters of appearance, taste, style and grooming. He came to do their coiffures, just as a manicurist checked in every week to do manicures and pedicures. But Wally was more to the girls than a hairdresser, and his word on clothes was law. He loved to dish with them and whiled away many a long hour when business was slow, talking girl-talk.

Sometimes when he arrived, he would have a gown over his arm. He would swish importantly over to one of the girls and hold it out to her. "Mary," he'd say, gazing at her mystically, *"this* is for *you*. I knew the moment I saw it you'd look *perfectly* divine in it." Then he would take it back. "But *darling!*" he'd scream. "First we've got to *do* something with you. Your eye shadow is simply all wrong, *wrong* as it can be. Come on, girl, I'll get you fixed up."

Hours would be spent dressing her hair and changing her make-up, with Wally prancing back and forth showing her how to "walk the dress," like a model. Then, when at last his artist's soul was satisfied, he would lead her out to the others to be admired and applauded. Nobody dared question his taste. Everybody sang out praises and Wally was all smiles as he took his bow.

I used to think that he was the only real friend the girls had. Other girls in the same business were, after all, competitors. Men were clients. I was strictly business—I had to be. It was only with Wally that they could let down their hair. They told him all their secrets, and he listened and compared notes. Everybody trusted him and enjoyed him, and I'm sure that, popular as he was with his friends, nowhere did Wally get the reception he got at my house.

II

I often have been asked what yardstick I used in selecting my girls, what traits and qualifications I looked for or required. Well, naturally, beauty or at least comeliness was practically a must. And I never employed a novice. Although I was a madam, I never wished to have it on my conscience that I had inducted a girl into the life. So I always engaged girls with enough experience behind them to make them interesting to my customers. And then, of course, their health and personal habits were big factors.

In interviewing a girl who wished to get on my call list, I always asked the candidate to undress so that I could make certain her underwear was fresh and her armpits free from hair. If she passed inspection in these departments, I could feel reasonably confident about her personal cleanliness, and that it would not be necessary to coax her into taking a weekly examination. (When I found that my girls did not like to go out for the examination, I retained a doctor to come to the house and put them through the routine which meant safety and protection for my patrons.)

No girl ever made the grade who attempted to apologize for her careless appearance by telling me she hadn't found time to get to the beauty shop. This would infuriate me. "Do you think a model or a secretary would be hired if she applied for a job and appeared untidy? Of course she wouldn't! Then how do you expect to be a successful prostitute when your looks are your stock in trade and making a good first impression is all-important?" Usually I would add, "If you want to be a prostitute, be a good one."

Those experts on white slavery, the holders of a Sunday-supplement degree in sociology, will be disappointed to learn it, but often I have tried to talk girls out of prostituting themselves. Sometimes I was successful, many times I failed. It depended on the girl. Most of them were in it for money, a few for kicks. Some didn't know when to quit; others wouldn't try to do anything else. In any case, I can say definitely that the great majority of them came into the business with their eyes open, knowing the risks.

Every so often, however, I bumped into a woman who had been so sheltered from the sordid side of life, or who had been so taken in by trashy novels glamorizing whoring, that she thought prostituting herself was "nice work if you could get it." One such deluded dame was none other than a cousin of my friend, Mr. Chain-Store, although I guess the millions ran out before they got to her branch of the family, as she worked for a living.

One evening she came up to the apartment, using Mr. Chain-Store's name to gain admission. After she had introduced herself, she wasted no time getting to the point. "Miss Adler, I would like to work for you."

"What for?" I asked, sure she was kidding.

"Every job I've ever had," she said, "the boss always tries to make me, and I'm getting sick and tired of being chased around the desk. The way I look at it, if I have to sleep with some guy to hold a job, I might as well be a whore."

As some customers were scheduled to arrive—and also because I wanted to make sure this babe wasn't pulling my leg —I told her to call me the following day. It was apparent she had had quite a bit to drink, and in any case I felt that if she really knew what she was letting herself in for, being chased around a desk would seem a lark by comparison. Although she thought her life had been tough, she had never been either hungry or homeless—there was no real economic necessity for her to hustle—and I knew that one day she would thank me for dissuading her.

So when she called the next day, I really let her have it. "You suppose," I said, "that a harlot's life is full of thrills and excitement and easy money. But why do you think the girls only last in the business a few short years? Why do you think so many of them are addicted to drugs and alcohol? And if *they* can't take this life without a crutch of some kind, without something to numb their misery and wretchedness, what makes you think you can? Believe me, whoring is just a slow form of self-destruction!" Then in the bluntest possible language I told her some of the shocking things I had known to happen to girls—the abuse they took from some of the customers, the degrading acts they sometimes were compelled to perform—and I really laid it on. I wound up by telling her to mull over what I had said for a couple of days, and then, if she still felt like entering a house, "Take my advice and shoot yourself—you'll be better off dead!"

My harangue scared her off all right. She never called me again. I often thought about this girl and was relieved to read of her marriage to a nice young chap a year or so later. I couldn't help wondering what Mr. Chain-Store's reaction would have been if I had told him his cousin had applied for a job. Very likely, if I have him sized up correctly, he would have howled and said, "Gad, Polly, do you think she'd qualify?"

To qualify as one of my girls, a candidate either had to know how to dress and behave like a lady or be willing to learn. I stressed to them that the man who paid a couple of hundred to take a girl out for the evening didn't care to be seen with a painted slut. I insisted that on such occasions they dress quietly and use a minimum of make-up. The days of the flagrantly dressed, flagrantly "refined" tarts, who tossed down their snorts of rotgut with the little finger well out, were long past. In fact, ironically enough, in the town's most fashionable restaurants the way to spot a prostitute was to look for the woman who looked least like one. . . . As for the girls' conduct in the house, the rule was: Be a lady in the parlor and a whore in the bedroom.

I tried not to play favorites among the girls, but of course there were some that I liked better than others. One of my particular favorites was Gigi, who was as well educated as the Duchess and had a far more attractive and better-balanced personality. Gigi was one of the few who enjoyed reading, and she made a point of keeping up with the best-sellers and subscribing to the class magazines. My brighter clients found her especially good company. She had an alert mind, was witty and gay, and could swap repartees and opinions with the best of them. She had the good sense and the character to get out of the business while she was still young enough to make another life for herself, and while working at a hotel behind a jewelry counter, met the man she later married.

Not so long ago, after losing track of Gigi for many years, I encountered her in New York and she invited me to her home for cocktails. Oliver, her husband, made quite an impression on me—tall, gray-haired, distinguished-looking. But after we had been introduced his first remark knocked me right off my perch. "You must admit, Polly," he said, "I married one of your best girls." Gigi came to my rescue. "Relax, Polly. Oliver knows all about my past." Later she told me that when she first knew Oliver he was engaged to another woman, but he became ill and had to spend several months in the hospital. His fiancée neglected him, whereas Gigi visited him daily and later looked after him at home. "I guess he just got used to having me around," she said. "Anyway, when he popped the question, I said yes with no regrets, and we've been very happy."

But Gigi was many cuts above most of the girls whom I had in my house, and my reunions with "alumnae" were not always so felicitous. For example, there was my experience with Sybil. She was a college graduate and a beauty, a girl with a solid upper-middle-class background. Why she was a prostitute I never knew, and, although I tried to understand her, she would not let me. Sybil was a cold fish, reserved and calculating—just how calculating I discovered after she left my employ. She tried to blackmail me.

Perhaps the strangest girl I ever employed was a demure, tidy little creature named Fran. She was the delight of my patrons for some time, especially one literary gentleman of whom I was very fond. He never failed to ask about her, always with a slow grin spreading across his big good-natured face, until at last he had to shake his head and laugh out loud.

"How's the schoolgirl?" he'd ask.

For that's what Fran was. She was about twenty-two, and I don't know how she had got started in the business. When she came to me and asked for work, she explained that she was a student of journalism at Columbia and intended to continue her studies. She would come to work after school and remain on call until eleven o'clock. Every afternoon she would arrive after her classes, carrying her schoolbooks, wearing the short skirts, oxfords and beret that were the thing among the coeds, and settle down to work. She neither drank nor smoked and, when not otherwise occupied, stayed in her room and studied. She saved every cent she could, traveling to and from her dates on the subway—all the other girls went in cabs.

Fran was pleasant, smiling, and matter-of-fact about her method of earning a living, and no matter what amount of money was offered her after her deadline of eleven o'clock, her answer always was "No." I once saw her refuse a man who had offered her a thousand dollars. She explained to me that she needed her sleep if she was to get good grades and the honor degree she was after. When Fran finished "working her way through college," she disappeared from the demi-monde to emerge a well-known novelist. I have kept Fran's secret, as I have kept many secrets.

Another one of my girls, Margaret, was a Social Register-ite and pillar of the Junior League. When she phoned and told me she would like to work for me, I was convinced it was either a gagster or a snooping wife. Her voice was low and cultivated, her diction strictly finishing school. She did not sound at all like a person who would have any reason to put her sex life on a commercial basis. However, it was simple enough to check whether or not she was who she claimed to be. I asked permission to phone her back and, rather reluctantly, she gave me her number. Then I looked in the telephone book, found the number corresponded with the name she had given and that it was a Park Avenue address, then called the number and got her. Nonetheless, I was still suspicious and suggested that she stop by that evening to talk things over.

When she was announced from the lobby, I sent a maid down the back way to check on her. I wanted to know if there were cops around and if she was the spearhead of a raid. But the maid came back and reported no cops; the girl was with a boyish-looking young man. I spoke to Margaret, telling her to get rid of the man and then she might come up.

Her face matched her voice. She had that clean shiny look of the débutante, and the glossy, well-brushed hair. She was a little mousy, but no one would question her breeding. We visited together for a while and when she mentioned a number of well-known people around town—among them a famous publicist and a night-club entertainer—who knew her, I proposed that we go out and see them. I still didn't feel that she was on the level about wanting to work in the house.

The people knew her all right and she was on the square. After Margaret came to work for me, I learned that she was the wife of a very wealthy young man (the boyish one who had brought her to my place!), that he knew what she was up to and apparently didn't mind. Margaret said she was broke and needed the money, but she wore thirty-dollar shoes and clothes with fabulous labels. When I asked her about them, she said that her mother-in-law bought them for her. She herself cared nothing about clothes. I kept telling my girls to watch her and to learn from her how to act like ladies. They watched and I guess they learned, but we were all a little uncomfortable around Margaret, sensing that there was something psychopathic about her. Eventually, she became erratic and irresponsible, and I couldn't count on her keeping appointments, so I dropped her. Years later I saw her in a store and was surprised to find that I felt no impulse to speak to her. I just walked by. It wasn't that I didn't like her—I did. But I suspected she was dangerously mixed up and therefore best left alone.

I should have obeyed that impulse not to speak another time when I was in a big department store. I saw a girl who had once worked for me, named Martha, and hurried after her into the elevator.

"Hello, Martha!" I said happily. "How are you?" She was looking very well.

She stared straight ahead. I couldn't believe it when she didn't answer, for we had been great friends. I spoke again. She ignored me and got off at the next floor without a backward glance. Later I spoke about her to a mutual friend and told how Martha had cut me.

The friend laughed. "Aren't you stupid!" she said. "She was working."

"Working?"

"Sure, she must have been loaded. She was protecting you from arrest."

Then I got it. But Martha had not been a booster when she worked for me, and I didn't know she had taken up the profession. Of course, when I understood, I was grateful to her for keeping away from me.

Another time, in Saks, I saw a girl I knew and started to smile at her, but she bumped into me and spoke without moving her lips, as she had learned to do in jail.

"I'm working. Stay away."

This one was a successful pickpocket plying her trade among the shoppers. I stayed away.

One girl, Alice, who worked for me part-time turned out to have such a passion for shoplifting that after a couple of experiences I was afraid to go into a store with her. The first time I learned of Alice's proclivity I had been looking at a handbag but decided thirty-five bucks was too much to pay. We had hardly got outside the store when Alice produced the bag from under her coat. I was furious and bawled the hell out of her (but later, honesty compels me to admit, bought the item in question from her for fifteen). However, after that I was prepared and on another occasion, in a book store, I was able to forestall her. I had gone there to buy a Social Register and Alice was appalled. "I won't let you pay seven dollars and a half for a small book like that!" she said. But I quickly got hold of a clerk and steered her out of there before another larceny could take place.

Then there was Yvette. She was a troublemaker, as I discovered when my cook gave me two weeks' notice. This surprised me because I had thought she was satisfied. When I questioned her, she said she was quitting because of the girls —they were forever complaining. It turned out that the one who was fomenting the trouble and egging the others on was Yvette. As good cooks are hard to find, I told Yvette she must leave the next day. But that night I had a group of politicians as my guests, among them a noted legislator, and— boom!—it was love at first sight when he saw Yvette. I didn't blame him. She was a striking blonde with a French accent (and, although he didn't know it, a caustic tongue). He furnished a luxurious apartment for her in the Fifties and gave her a gorgeous country home. He was married, but not working at it.

I ran into Yvette years later at Bonwit Teller's. She looked marvelous—chic, well-groomed, as young as ever. She thanked me for introducing her to the legislator, saying that he had recently received his divorce and she planned on marrying him within the next few months. But shortly after this encounter the legislator died, leaving Yvette a hundred thousand dollars. Subsequently, she married a successful broker and, I am told, has lived happily ever since. Although she had not been a girl of whom I was particularly fond, I was glad for her. This kind of luck happens once in ten thousand blue moons. Most of the girls end up so tragically.

Far more typical was the fate of Muriel. I don't know

much about Muriel's background, but originally she was from the West Coast, and when she first came to New York lived with the chap who brought her there. He was studying medicine, and Muriel worked as a model. As soon as her lover graduated and began his internship he threw her over for a girl from a wealthy family, whom he later married. This almost killed Muriel. She began to drink to excess and asked a madam named Renée W. if she would get dates for her. (It was Renée who told me this part of Muriel's story.) At first she worked not so much for the money, but because she wanted to be around drinking people who would help her forget her sweetheart.

At the time I knew her, Muriel was a stunning girl—jet-black hair, rather Spanish features, about five feet five, weight one hundred and fifteen. She dressed simply but smartly, had a likable personality and none of the hardness of the average prostitute. (No, I don't have total recall—I kept a card index of the girls.) She would not accept every date, only choice ones. I used her when a man wanted a girl for the whole evening—dinner, theater, night clubs and so on—and the price for that was high. Muriel had a very profitable clientele which she had acquired on her own, but she was a square-shooter. When a man asked for her telephone number, she would tell him he'd have to get in touch with her through me.

Later she lived with an Englishman, a night-club and radio comedian. He wasn't a pimp, but his engagements were few and far between, and Muriel kept up the expenses of their apartment and occasionally helped him out financially. One time when he was playing a date in Detroit, Muriel telephoned and begged me to let her come over. When she arrived at the apartment, she was talking wildly and was clearly out of her head.

"Polly, be careful," she kept repeating. "Two cars loaded with cops followed me here. They're trying to arrest me. It's that girl's family. (The girl who had married her lover.) They're afraid I'll blackmail their son-in-law. But you know I wouldn't do a thing like that. I still love Don." She pulled me to the window. "Look! Cops! They're getting out—they're coming upstairs! Hide me!"

The poor kid was seeing things. There were no cops around. I gave her a sedative and then called her boyfriend, Cedric, in Detroit and told him Muriel was not herself and shouldn't be alone. At my suggestion, he called her back later and invited her to spend the rest of the week in Detroit. I thought if she felt somebody needed her and wanted her, it would steady her down. She seemed delighted to hear from him and agreed to take the midnight train out there.

The following Sunday at a milk farm where I was week-ending, I got a call from Renée W. Muriel had committed suicide by turning on the gas. She left several notes, including one to her parents. When Cedric arrived he telephoned them long distance to make arrangements for shipping the body. "We don't know anyone by that name," her parents said. "Our daughter died when she went to New York. Do as you like with the remains. We don't want them."

Muriel was buried on Long Island. Cedric, Renée, a few call girls and myself were the only ones who attended the funeral. As I stood there by Muriel's grave, I wanted to believe in hell so that I could think those unforgiving parents and that snide doctor-lover would one day go there and burn.

I have said that my girls were go-getters, but it wasn't only because of the money that they liked to keep busy. It was also an escape from thinking. Even the least introspective could not always avoid recognizing the precariousness of her position—and the loneliness of it. By becoming a prostitute, a girl cuts herself off not merely from her family, but from such a great part of life. She is isolated not just by social custom but by working conditions, and she has to some extent deprived herself of her rights as a citizen for she has forfeited the protection of the law. It is not syphilis which is the occupational disease of the prostitute, but loneliness. And no one yet has discovered a miracle drug to cure it.

As might be expected, the worst times for the girls were the big holidays. On Christmas Eve a man with a family stayed home, and on New Year's Eve he went out with his wife. So on those nights the house became a funeral parlor, the girls drooping around red-eyed, with not even work to help numb the painful awareness that *they* couldn't go home. Perhaps Christmas wasn't quite so bad because they had been busy making up packages and squandering every cent they had on gifts for the folks back in Dubuque or Dallas. But by New Year's Eve, not having received so much as a thank-you note, most of them would be deep down in the dumps.

For another reason, New Year's was a painful time for them, since traditionally it is then that people make resolutions and lay out plans for the future. But most prostitutes try to avoid thinking of the future and the passing of time. If they could have their way, they'd stop the clock or, better still, turn it back. Youth is their capital and at New Year's they can't help but be reminded it is dwindling away. For a whore New Year's is a season of regret for the past, rather than of hope for the future.

One New Year's Eve I happened to be in Chicago. I had no real friends there and nothing to do, and I was homesick and morose. In an effort to snap out of it—what's the percentage in singing the blues all by yourself?—I telephoned all the madams I knew and told them I was throwing a party, and to bring along any of their girls who were feeling low.

The invitations were received with cheers, and my thirty guests (all women) really had themselves a rip-roaring time. We all had things we wanted to forget, and there was plenty of champagne on hand to help us drown our memories. One aged madam, who wore heavy steel-rimmed spectacles and got around with the aid of a cane, at first kept a hawklike eye on everyone as though making notes on the girls for future employment. But after a while she forgot business and settled down to telling the story of her life to another madam, who finally dozed off sitting bolt upright in her chair. At intervals the old lady would turn to me and inquire why I hadn't called her place for girls. (Hers was a check-in-and-out system. None of the girls stayed with her or received callers there. All she did was keep their dates straight, and they checked with her when they were available for the next date.) I explained that I wasn't in business in Chicago, but every half hour or so she'd start the routine all over again.

Another madam, who was also more than a little woozy, kept pleading with me to serve sauterne instead of champagne. No one, she assured me, was in any condition to know the difference. "Relax, Ruth," I told her, knowing what was worrying her. "I'm giving this party and I promise you won't get a bill on the way out."

Finally, just as at an office party, the girls overcame their awe of the madams and began to say what was really on their minds. One little creature announced between hiccups that she wouldn't be a madam for anything. "I'd rather be a prostitute," she said. "Madams don't have the fun we girls do. We're the ones that get to sleep with the men!" For girls like this perhaps the appellation "daughter of joy" is not such a misnomer, but nymphomaniacs are rare among prostitutes, and the others soon shouted her down with remarks impossible to quote here.

When they said good night a number of the girls told me that the evening had been particularly enjoyable just because there had been no men present. I did not point out to them that the unseen guest of honor was a man called Father Time.

III

Inevitably, there is one question which every customer puts to a prostitute—what might be called the sixty-four-dollar question: "How did you get into this business?" As a rule men ask it, expecting to hear a tale of woe, but the sort of answer they would prefer to hear is implicit in a well-known joke. According to this story a man sleeps with a beautiful girl who, though a prostitute, is rich, well-bred, well-educated, and intelligent. Amazed that a girl with all these endowments and advantages should stoop to whoring, he asks how she got into the business. "Oh, I don't know," the tart answer. "I'm just lucky, I guess."

Men particularly relish this joke because it feeds their egos, and also because it would lessen their pleasure to think that a girl was submitting to them strictly from necessity. Actually, of course, despite all the feigned transports of ecstasy (for purposes of increasing the tip), to ninety-nine out of a hundred girls going to bed with a customer is a joyless, even distasteful, experience. Nothing could be farther from the truth than the "just lucky" explanation—unless the girl meant bad luck.

No girl, as a social worker once said, sets out to be a prostitute. Such stupidity would be incredible. Who wants to be a pariah, a social outcast—treated with contempt, jailed, beaten, robbed and finally kicked into the gutter when she is no longer salable? A prostitute can count on no more than ten money-making years. Then she is through—if not dead or diseased, so broken by drugs, alcohol and the steady abuse of her body that no one will hire her again. And since the sordid and pitiful fate of the prostitute is far from being a secret, no wonder people ask what propels a girl into this short and unhappy life.

No doubt there are as many answers to this question as there as sociologists, psychiatrists, philosophers and doctors of divinity. But in my opinion the greatest single factor—and the common denominator in an overwhelming majority of cases—is poverty. It is true that, though many girls are poor, only a small percentage of them take to hustling. But there is more than one kind of poverty—there is emotional poverty and intellectual poverty and poverty of spirit. As well as material lacks, there can be a lack of love, a lack of education, a lack of hope. And out of such impoverishment the prostitute is bred.

When a fifteen-year-old girl looks around her with the new awareness of adolescence and sees only poverty and ugliness, the groundwork is laid. She doesn't want to wind up like her mother, wornout from too much childbearing, slopping around in an old ragged dress, beaten by a drunken stupid husband every Saturday night. She wants a chance at the kind of life she's seen in the movies, with becoming frocks to wear and handsome men to pay her court, a house on a pretty street, clean, smiling children. . . . And suddenly she sees that she might not get all this, nor even any part of it, that in fact she does not even know how to go about getting it.

But she's heard that wishing will make it so, and she keeps on hoping that someday Jimmy Stewart or Dana Andrews will come through town and see her. And she does her hair the way Rita Hayworth does, and walks with a strut the way Lana Turner does, and she wears a tight sweater designed to emphasize she's a woman. And maybe she begins to get a bad name in the neighborhood because she makes such a parade of her nubility, and one of the guys outside the drugstore tells his pals he's had her and he'll line her up for them some night. And the story gets back to her parents and they call her a bum and she sasses them back, and after that there's a new defiance and don't-careness in her manner.

Then one day she meets Jimmy Stewart. Well, not exactly Jimmy Stewart, but a guy with a new convertible and sharp clothes and a snap-brim hat and a fast, easy line. And he wants to know what a pretty kid like her is doing without a boyfriend. He tells her she's beautiful, and he can see she's got too many brains to stay in this little tank town, and how would she like to take a trip? So why not? He says he loves her—and anyway what's she got to go home to? So she goes away with him in his shiny car, and he buys her some flashy clothes, and she thinks the pretty house on the pretty street comes next.

He has told her he's a salesman, but before long she finds that his line is selling underwear and junk jewelry to girls who work in joints. When she's gotten used to that idea, she meets some of the girls and the madams, and it seems that he's kind of in love with one of the girls in one joint. When she questions him, he tells her he owes a lot to Dolores. She's helping him get the money together to buy a shop of his own so he can settle down. Soon she understands that he would love her more if she helped him, too.

He takes her to the madam and she goes to work. She

stays there all week, and at the end of the week he comes and collects the money she's made. She gets a card, which she wears fastened inside her working dress (with a zipper down the front, easy to get out of, which is important since no man can spend more than fifteen minutes with her, according to house rules), and every time she takes a customer, she opens the door and holds out her card so it can be punched. When it looks like a lace curtain, she's made her quota.

At first she's a little offended that the men don't even take off their shoes, but pretty soon she stops noticing those things. When the girls kid her about her "sister-in-law," she learns that they mean Dolores, and that other girls working for pimps have their "sisters-in-law," too. She makes about a hundred and fifty dollars a week, at two dollars a customer. She's glad when her period intervenes to keep her from working, and she can spend the time with her sweetheart.

She loves him. He's all she's got to love. The other girls are competition, and the madam is a slave driver. She does without everything—new clothes, underwear—to get the money faster. She lives for that week with him. Only, after a while, he tells her he knows a way she can work that week, too. When she cries, he tells her to forget about it. But she learns that her sister-in-law does it, so, since she can't lose him to her sister-in-law, she agrees to work the full month, and then he loves her again. When they're raided and she's thrown in jail, he gets her out. When she has to move on because they're tired of her in that house, he gets her in another. When she gets pregnant, he pays the doctor who takes care of it. She can't do without him.

But one day she rebels. She screams and yells and flies out at him because suddenly she's gotten a vision of how it really is and what's really happening to her. She threatens to turn him in to the cops for transporting her across the state line, and he quiets her down with a needle. And then for the first time since she was a kid (now she's seventeen), she's happy.

The time goes by and she isn't shocked any more at what she's doing. She almost forgets that there's any other way of living, and when she remembers, there's always the needle and the immediate happiness she can get from it—and from him. But now he says she's got to work harder. On the dope she costs him more, and he withholds the dose, won't give her that, won't give her anything, tells her she's an old bag he's ashamed of, that he can't sell her in the houses any more, and she can get out and walk the pavements for the money to pay for her stuff.

So she hits the small hotels, the beer gardens, the street corners, learns how to stand in the shadow so the man won't see her too clearly. After a while she can't kid herself any more, she knows she's sick. She has pains that shoot up from the groin so sharply that she staggers and people stare at her as if she were drunk. One day on her beat she walks up a dirty stairway to the doctor's office, afraid all the time that her sweetheart will find out she's spending the money on this, or that the doctor will say she has something that will keep her from working. And the doctor does say that. He tells her she must have an operation or she'll die, and she says it's got to be some other way—she can't take the time. Only there's no other way.

She's almost calm when she stumbles down the wooden stairs. Now she doesn't have to worry any more because tomorrow (and she knows when she's charged it'll be easy to go through with it) she's going to step into the East River. She likes the idea of death by water. There won't be any blood or noise or pain, and the river will feel cool and it will be dark and solemn as death should be. But first there is tonight, and maybe tonight he'll be nice to her.

Does this sound like a throwback to the days of the ten-twent-thirt?—a recitation to be delivered to the accompaniment of "Hearts and Flowers" with the professor bearing down heavily on the G-string? But the story I have outlined here is one with which social workers in every big city are bitterly familiar.

I had two great enemies all the time I was in business. (I had many enemies, of course, but my years as a madam were years of war against two particular evils.) One was drugs, the other was pimps. On occasion I have taken drug addicts into my house, always with a stipulation that the girls must take the cure. But I never would take a girl if I knew she had a Good Man Friday, more commonly known as a pimp. If a girl acquired one after she came to work for me, I gave her an ultimatum: Get rid of him or get out.

The case of Susan provides a good example of how a pimp operates. The year was 1928 and I was then living on West Sixty-ninth Street. Early one morning I answered the telephone and a voice quivering with urgency asked, "Is this Miss Adler's residence?"

"It is," I answered drowsily.

"My name is Susan. Olive referred me to you. Have you an opening for a position?"

"You have the wrong number. This is not an employment agency."

"I know what it is. May I come to see you?"

It sounded to me like trouble. No prostitute would refer to her profession as a position, any more than she would be looking for work at quarter of nine in the morning. And the name Olive meant nothing to me, though of course the girls change their names as often as they change the color of their hair. But mysterious calls always left me uneasy, and, anxious to clear up the matter, I agreed to meet her later that afternoon.

Susan turned out to be an angelic-looking child whose cute Southern drawl made it unnecessary to ask where she hailed from. She said she had run away from home and gotten a job at a club in New Orleans as a cigarette girl. It was there she met Olive whom, it turned out, I had known under the name of Jackie. Susan had been anxious to leave New Orleans, never knowing when someone from her home town might come into the club, and so when she had got together enough for a bus ticket she had made a beeline for New York. She had arrived only that morning, and I was the only person she knew.

When I learned that she had never worked in a house, I tried to dissuade her from taking the step and offered to pay her fare home.

"I can't go home," she said.

She didn't have to explain. Times without number girls had said to me, "I can't go home" or "I have no home." Nevertheless, I told Susan that I was sure she could find other work, jobs were plentiful then, and she had a high-school education. I provided her with enough money so that she could pay room rent and keep eating if it was a while until she found work, but she found a job fast enough —a job streetwalking. The very same day of our conversation she was picked up by a pimp called Leo, who also was a hophead, and he put her right out on the streets.

I learned this six months later when Susan called on me again, so bedraggled and down-at-the-heels I hardly recognized her. She asked me to reconsider employing her and this time I consented, but only if she would pledge her word never to see Leo again.

After she moved in her few belongings, I took her to Antoine's beauty salon where she was given the works, and then to Wilma's dress shop for a complete outfit. After a few days of good food and rest, she got back her angelic beauty and soon became the most popular girl in my establishment. "Pretty Susie," as everyone called her, commanded top money, and I advised her the smartest move she could make would be to start a savings account. She appeared flattered by my taking an interest, and said she had a little sister back home and would start saving to send her to college.

The mayor of a city in New Jersey fell hard for Susan and asked her to become his mistress, offering her an apartment, an allowance, charge accounts, and a Cadillac. Surprisingly she turned him down, despite my urging her to grab this chance to get out of the business. And then one evening when she was dining out with one of my patrons, she met a top-flight picture producer. (She was introduced to him as a model.) Mac, the producer, was so impressed that, as early as their second meeting, he offered her a film contract. It was not a gag, he was genuinely interested, and saw her for cocktails or dinner every day while he was in New York. Naturally I was elated that such an opportunity should come her way, and was completely nonplussed when she informed me that she had decided not to sign the contract.

"But why on earth not?" I demanded.

"Because Mac has asked me to go to bed with him," she said primly. "And I don't like him that much."

I was rocked. Here was a girl who earned her living saying "yes" to all comers, saying 'no" to a man who was waving a picture contract at her. She simply did not make sense.

That night Leo the pimp slithered into my living room.

Though he was considered to be strikingly handsome, his glassy eyes and quivering hands stamped him plainly as a dope addict and this made him repulsive to me. By what right, he wanted to know, was I interfering with his livelihood, encouraging his girl to go off to Hollywood. He continued to harangue me for several minutes, but between my anger at Susan for lying and at myself for being so gullible, I was too incensed to listen. So this was why Susan had brushed off the mayor, Cadillac and all. For this she had rejected a film contract! And all the time I had supposed she was socking away money in a savings bank, this dreadful leech had been sniffing and smoking her earnings. . . . I saw to it that she left my house that night.

I knew it would be only a matter of time until Leo coerced her into using drugs, so that if love lost its potency he would have this other hold on her. But though I warned Susan, I might as well have saved my breath. . . . As she was so well known, I was able to keep track of her and a year or so later learned that her pimp was booking her into one joint after another. But her looks were fading so fast that soon not even the cheap joints would take her, and she was forced to peddle herself to the fifth rate hotel trade with the help of bellhops. Her sister, who never saw the money Susan was supposed to have saved for her, came to New York and she, too, fell under Leo's spell. He had the two of them working for him, supplying him with money for his, and their, craving for drugs.

I happened to visit an after-hours club in Harlem one night, and the first person I saw, dancing with a Negro, was Susan. I don't know how I knew it was she. There was no shred of beauty left to recall her to me. I started toward her, but she left her partner and slunk out the back exit.

Not long after this, it was rumored that Susan was dead. Her sister went to live with a Negro in Harlem, a pimp by the name of Brownie. He was sent to Sing Sing for a stickup job and what finally became of Susan's sister I never knew.

Perhaps the most terrible thing about the story of "Pretty Susie" is that it is such a commonplace one. The degree to which a pimp, if he's clever, can confuse and delude a prostitute is very nearly unlimited. Take, for example, the case of Violet. Unlike Susan, she played fair with me. When she learned that giving up her pimp was an entrance requirement, she said that rather than do so she would go back to the cheap house in another state where she had been working.

She had become a whore, Violet told me, because her family had talked her into marrying the wrong man. She had been madly in love with a boy she'd gone to school with. But it was another three years till he would get his law degree and her family kept working on her until finally she consented to marry their candidate who was rich but, in her own words, "a blubbery, bulgy, baldheaded stuffy old man." During the year she lived with him, she continued to meet secretly with the boy she loved, and then gossip started and finally word got back to her husband. He talked with Violet's parents and they ordered her to leave town before she disgraced them any further.

"I was glad to go," she said. "I went to Chicago and had a wonderful time till my money ran out. But by that time I knew Henry, and he's been looking out for me ever since."

I knew of Henry. He never had less than five or six girls working for him and would play them off against each other, promising the one who brought in the most money that she would be the Queen of the Harem. But not even this could disenchant Violet. She bragged to me of how Henry had taught her the ropes and how carefully he looked out for her, always reminding her when she went to work in a new house that she must be watchful and have an exit or hiding place picked out in case of a raid.

"Without Henry," she told me, "I'd be nowhere."

"And where do you think you are now?" I asked her. "You and your sisters-in-law?"

"Oh, I won't have competition very long," she said seriously. "In another few months Henry and I will have enough money saved to buy a butchershop, and then he says I can leave this business behind. And he's promised it will be me that will live with him. Those other girls are just tramps."

But of course Henry continued to maintain his string of girls right up to the day the FBI caught up with him. After his conviction Violet came to see me again. She looked ghastly and said she had been ill for some time, but hadn't wanted to worry Henry by telling him about it. Besides, "It would have been imposing to ask him for money for a doctor when he had all those lawyers to pay. But will you do me a favor, Polly? Will you let me sit in the parlor with some of your drinking men, the ones who aren't here for sex, so I can earn some money in tips?"

I took her to my doctor that day. He told me she had an inoperable cancer and could not last more than a few months. At that time I had a little weekend place up at Peekskill, so I suggested to Violet that perhaps she would like to live up there as a sort of housekeeper until she "got better." But I think she sensed what was the matter with her, for she thanked me and told me she would let me know. I asked her if she did not want to come back to the house till she made up her mind, and she said she would do so, but first there was some business she had to tend to for Henry. The "business" was writing him a good-bye letter. That night she threw herself under a subway train.

To outsiders, it may seem a bit of hypocritical hairsplitting for a madam to make a distinction between herself and a pimp. "What's the difference between them?" people might ask. "Both of them peddle flesh, make money on girls' bodies, employ and exploit them." Well, in the first place, when a girl came to my house she was no wide-eyed innocent. She was a full-fledged whore committed to the game. I considered it my job to protect her from the police, to cure her of drug-taking if she had the habit, to provide a doctor's care if she needed it, to defend her from abusive customers, to aid her in getting out of the life if she had the opportunity, and to do all I could to persuade her to save money and provide for the future.

But a pimp seeks out a girl and seduces her into the life. Far from weaning her away from drugs, it is he who teaches her the habit. He makes no attempt to protect her from customers (since, for the pimp, the customer is always right). He does everything in his power to keep her a prostitute, for if she quit the racket, it would reduce his income. And, instead of helping her to save her money, he takes every cent she's got and beats her into making more.

I do not mean to imply that I was a fairy godmother to whores, or that any madam is. But I made an equitable business arrangement with the girls which gave them their fair share. I provided the capital, set up the business and ran the greatest risks so far as the law was concerned. I invested the money, the time and the work. The girl invested her person. If she was with a pimp, there would be no return on her investment.

One might argue that if there were no madams operating houses, there would be no pimps to supply them with girls. But this is nonsense; not all girls are booked into houses.

Many of them—the less fortunate ones—walk the streets at the command of their pimps. In fact, according to statistics, there are fewer girls working in houses than there are hustling on the streets. Moreover, only the ones arrested are listed as streetwalkers. Cagier or luckier girls who have not been caught are not included in the records.

I cannot deny that I mortally hate pimps. Still, in the long run, they also are victims—though not so obviously or so pitifully—along with the girls they exploit. Most of them come from poverty-stricken homes, and they acquire their education in the streets and in the pool halls, first out front, then in the back room. Their only talent seems to be that they have a way with women, and they find this out hanging around the dance hall chippies, the drugstore waitresses and the high-school sweater girls who flaunt their sex and ask for attention.

The pimp doesn't feel that he's doing wrong in putting his girls to work. He and the girls are in it together to trim the suckers. He thinks of himself as a smart operator, and sees nothing shameful in exploiting women and living on their earnings. (To his mind, all men exploit women to some degree.) He regards himself as an employer or a property owner, not as a criminal or a parasite. He considers that in taking over certain responsibilities for his girls, managing them, booking them into houses, getting them out of jail, teaching them the ropes, he earns the money the girls give him. He dins it into each girl that if she wants to survive she must give him unquestioning obedience. In return for the money she makes (which he teaches her she could not earn without him) he listens to her complaints and is kind to her, when he has the patience and when she has earned enough to satisfy him. Since these girls almost never find other men who care for them—what man wants to love a prostitute?—their relationship with the pimp constitutes the only important human tie they have.

Just as the prostitute never, until the very end, is able to perceive that she is a victim, so the pimp never regards himself as exploited. He would be thunderstruck if it were pointed out to him that he lives a miserable life, despised by other men, by the madams he meets and deals with, by the underworld and by society. He thinks he is a very clever character, a sharp guy, able to make a buck and put up a front.

Among pimps as among prostitutes there is the one per cent variant, the exception, the success. I knew of one who was maintained in luxury by a madam named Cupie. She had a house in an open town, run openly, and managed to make money only by the volume of her business. She gave it all to her man, whose name was Jo-Jo (as in the song, "Good-for-nothing Joe"). Jo-Jo lived in style, was a Beau Brummel and a gourmet, and traveled to Europe every year. Cupie could never afford to take even a few days' vacation, and finally from overwork and her unhealthy life contracted t.b. Jo-Jo moved her to a shack in the country and within two days of her departure took up with one of the girls in the house. Cupie learned of it, and knowing she was going to die anyway and not caring to lie there in the shanty with only her thoughts for company, put a bullet in her head. Jo-Jo was her heir. He sold the house and headed west, alone. Of course he didn't take the girl. What would he want with a prostitute now? He bought a ranch and settled down to a life of comfortable respectability.

There are a few others I know of who made it—actors, agents and businessmen who took all the money they could lay their hands on and got out. But the average pimp becomes an alcoholic and/or drug addict, and in his last days a panhandler.

Periodically, the FBI stages a roundup and puts away a swarm of the boys who have made themselves federal offenders by violating the Mann Act. (This is the so-called "White Slave Act," passed by Congress in 1910, which forbids aiding, causing or inducing the transportation in interstate commerce of any woman or girl for immoral purposes.) Since pimps go out and look for girls, they frequently are guilty of transporting them from state to state, and this makes them eligible for the attention of the federal men.

An arrest by the FBI is the McCoy. When they put the finger on you, you're as good as found guilty because they never crack down unless they have you cold. Unlike many local law officers, they don't go in for frames or raids to pacify their superiors. They are an intelligent, honest body of men and—with reason—the terror of the underworld.

As no pimp ever had entrée to my house, or ever could place a girl there, and since I never engaged in any activities in violation of the interstate commerce law, I never got involved in a Mann Act case. But of course I was always under scrutiny by the federal men, as is every madam, and several madams I've known—who did not mind their p's and q's (for pimps and queers)—have been caught in roundups and done time along with their Good Men Fridays.

Chapter 5

Everybody Ought To Be Rich

> A man with a million dollars used to be considered rich, but so many people have at least that much in these days . . . that a millionaire does not cause any comment. . . . Ten thousand dollars invested ten years ago in the common stock of General Motors would now be worth more than a million and a half dollars. . . . It may be said that this is a phenomenal increase and that conditions are going to be different in the next ten years. That prophecy may be true, but it is not founded on experience . . . I think that we have scarcely started. . . . I am firm in my belief that anyone not only can be rich but ought to be rich. . . . [But] no one can become rich merely by saving. Mere saving is closely akin to the socialist policy of dividing and likewise runs up against the same objection that there is not enough around to save.
>
> *John J. Raskob*, quoted in an interview, "Everybody Ought To Be Rich," appearing in the LADIES' HOME JOURNAL, August, 1929

I

Almost everybody, I guess, would find it easy to understand why I loathed pimps and drug peddlers, but the average law-abiding citizen would hardly go along with me in my detestation of cops unless he, too, at some time or another, had locked horns with a crooked bull. I didn't resent the honest cop, and I was able to stay in business because of the dishonest variety. But the members of gendarmerie who really started my adrenalin flowing like wine were the boys who believed in playing it both ways, and who wouldn't have turned a hair if their own mother happened to be the one caught in the middle.

It can't be denied, however, that the boys were right in step with the times. It was becoming increasingly fashionable to make money any way you could—except by working for it. And it wasn't only angle-shooters and corner-cutters and big-city sharpies who were on the "get-rich-quick" kick. Such magicians as Ivar Kreuger and Samuel Insull were working their wands overtime for the edification of the "little people," and captains of industry like John J. Raskob were urging everybody to get in on the act. So—having been assured that "the old precepts contrasting the immorality of speculation with the morality of sound investment have no basis in fact"—all over the land, in order to participate in the national pastime of playing the market on margin, farmers' wives were emptying the egg money out of the teapot, schoolmarms were drawing out their life savings, and white-collar workers were cashing the bonds put aside for Junior's college education. After all, "saving is not to be regarded as a financial plan: the way to wealth is to get into the profit end of wealth production," and if you could just get your hands on a little dough, then you could sit back and let it work for you.

As far as the boys in blue were concerned, bleeding me and the other madams was the handiest of shortcuts on "the way to wealth." Picking on women didn't worry them—it was not a notably chivalrous age. Even so popular a figure as Belle Livingston had drawn a thirty-day sentence for running a night club, and Mae West spent ten days on the Island for appearing in a play called *Sex*. And, in 1927, Ruth Snyder had been the first woman to die in the chair at Sing Sing—a news item which one tabloid considered so tasty that it whetted the public's appetite with the announcement that she was "to cook, *and sizzle,* AND FRY!"

However, even though I was resigned to the shakedowns, I was *not* resigned to including a jolly laugh and a party on the house in the pay-off—particularly when all I got for my pains was a close-up view of the hindside of the eightball. But what could I do? The double-dealers who were sitting in on the game were officers of the law, and they were to keep right on raking in the pots until Judge Seabury yanked their chairs out from under them.

It was early on a May morning in 1928 that what was to be one of my most unfavorite days began with a call from a cop whose palm I'd oiled so often it was a wonder the phone didn't slip right out of his hand.

"Hi, Polly," he said. "This is Bill. One of the boys at headquarters is being promoted to a lieutenancy, and we want to throw a shindig at your place tonight. No outsiders, understand?"

"I understand," I replied.

"Jenny the Factory or Sadie the Chink would be tickled to death if we'd chosen their place," he went on, "but since you got the nod we know you'll see to it everything's Park Avenue style. Nothing but the best, see? Tom is a swell guy, and he's going to be boss in the location you're operating from, so if you're smart you'll turn yourself inside out to give us boys an evening."

"How many in your party?" I asked, wishing to God they'd go to Jenny's or Sadie's.

"Ten of us. See you at eight."

I dragged myself out of bed, reluctant to begin preparations for the entertainment of unwelcome, nonpaying guests. Cops and cuffo both begin with C, and I hated to think how many C-notes this evening would set me back. Something told me that before the festivities were over, I would be wringing my hands and echoing that classic summation of the sentiments of the weeper-over-spilt-milk: I should of stood in bed.

At eight sharp the party barged in—fifteen strong instead of ten—and soon made it apparent that they were trying to see how fast they could change civilized living quarters into a reasonable facsimile of a pigsty. One particularly drunk and obnoxious slop yanked me over in a corner and in a portentous manner announced that his name was Johnny. I repressed the impulse to remark that no doubt he had been named after the plumbing fixture, and merely said that it was an easy name to remember.

"Yeah, well, you ain't going to get a chance to forget it," he told me. "I just been transferred to the Fourth Division, and now it looks like I'm gonna achieve my life's ambition."

"More power to you," I said. "What is this ambition?"

He smiled a big, greasy smile. "Why, what do you think? To raid Polly Adler's, that's what's my ambition."

"Oh, go on, Johnny," I said, playing along while I tried to figure out what line to take. "I'm not *that* bad. Don't you like me?"

"That's got nothin' to do with it," he said. "The thing is you're newspaper copy, sister. When Adler's is raided, that's headlines, see? And my boss goes for headlines, and he goes to bat for the boys that grab 'em off for him. So when I'm lookin' at you, Polly, I'm lookin' at a promotion."

This charming tête-à-tête was just a foretaste of the eve-

ning's delights. As the party gained headway, it progressed—
or degenerated—from rough to rowdy, from vulgar to revolt-
ing. One of the boys had broken into the liquor closet, and,
having hauled forth a case of champagne, was opening bottles two at a time. With a stiff smile on my face, I had to stand
by and watch them slopping their drinks about on the furniture, trampling cigarette ends and cigar butts into the carpet,
burning and marring and staining what they did not smash.

About midnight I was called to the telephone, and my
legs buckled under me when I heard my cousin's voice saying that my parents and four brothers had just arrived from
Russia. Then my mother came on the phone. The only coherent sentence to emerge from that emotion-charged exchange was my promise to leave for Brooklyn immediately.

The shock of my family's unexpected arrival made me feel
dizzy and sick at my stomach and, standing there by the
phone, I began to sob. As soon as I could pull myself together, I asked the maids to take over, but as I got into my
hat and coat, someone sang out, "Hey, Poll, come in here."
Which was followed, as soon as they saw how I was dressed,
by, "Where the hell do you think you're going?"

"Listen, boys," I said, "my family has just come here from
Russia. I haven't seen my mother in fifteen years."

"So what?" one drunk yelled. "You get that goddamned
coat off and give us some fun!"

If I disobeyed their majesties' command it would mean
one raid after another, complaints, constantly being on the
move, the dreary round of appeasing, palm-oiling and bigger
and better shakedowns.

"Just let me make one call," I said, taking off my coat.

The party broke up at six A.M. and I showered and put
pads on my eyes to take out the lines of fatigue I knew must

be there. I dreaded the thought of putting my arms around my mother and having to look in her eyes. It was a beautiful morning, but all the way out to Brooklyn I was weighed down by the question of how I could keep my profession a secret. I'd been smart enough to keep out of jail, to rise high in my profession—but would I be able to keep a mother from learning the facts of her daughter's life? I knew that from now on I would have to lie like hell to cover up.

When the cab pulled up in front of my cousin's house, they all came running out to greet me. There were Mom, Pop and four little brothers, two of whom I had never seen. My mother embraced me and cried and called me her little girl. Pop kissed my cheek, and my little brothers grinned awkwardly and shook hands.

All morning long I sat with the family at the round kitchen table, nodding in the sunlight. The talk was of their journey and of Yanow, and I was glad that they did not inquire too much about me. I was too tired to make up lies. Later, I had a nap and waked to find that Lena and Yossell had taken my parents apartment-hunting, so I collected the boys and took them over to Pitkin Avenue and bought them some new clothes. They were very pleased and kept saying, "Now we look just like Americans!" To top the afternoon off, we went to a drugstore and I ordered us all chocolate sodas. But when the sodas were put in front of them, the boys had no idea how to proceed. Leon even sniffed at the straw to see if he was supposed to eat that part too. I remember vividly how puzzled they looked that this should be considered a treat. None of them liked the fizzy sodas, but they felt for politeness' sake they had to finish them.

My parents found a six-room apartment, and I stayed on in Brooklyn to help them pick out furniture and get settled. Though this involved considerable expenditure, mother did not seem surprised at my prosperity. Is not America the Golden Land? After four days they were all moved in, and I thought it was high time I was getting back to my house.

When I phoned to say that I would be in the following day, a man answered, and I asked who it was.

"It's the police. Is this Polly?"

"Who are you?"

"It's Johnny, that name you ain't gonna forget—remember?"

"You shouldn't give me a scare like that, Johnny. I thought you were some cop I didn't know."

"Today I *am* some cop you don't know. I'm here on business. But it might so happen I could change my mind if you get here fast."

I said I'd be there at once. Making hasty excuses to my parents, I promised to return in a few days and grabbed a cab. All the way back to New York, I kept thinking: Johnny's kidding—he probably just needs a few extra hundred. He couldn't be such a louse as to turn me in.

When I put my key in the lock, Johnny opened the door, his face one big smirk. I followed him into the living room where three of my girls were sitting with a couple of cops. "Here she is, boys," Johnny said, waving his arm at me. "The Queen herself." Then he turned to me. "It's a good thing you didn't horse around getting here. Without you, the pinch wouldn't be glamorous."

I still couldn't believe it was a pinch. "What a kidder you are," I said, and gave a weak laugh.

"Who's kidding?"

"Surely you're not going to frame me! You've been sitting here for hours. You've seen no crime committed, and there have been no men around."

"So what?" Johnny said, shifting his chewing gum against

his back teeth. "We'll pull a John Doe out of our little hats."

He walked over to the bar and poured himself a drink. Turning, he saw the look on my face—it must have been pure, undiluted hatred.

"Your Highness," he said, bowing, "how would you like your ride? In a patrol wagon? Or in our car?"

We were taken to the precinct station and booked, and I was charged with procuring girls for immoral purposes. It didn't matter that I was not even there when the cops entered the premises. A frame is as good for a pinch as the real thing—at least in the beginning and sometimes all the way down the line. And it didn't matter who the boys hauled in, so long as they filled their quota of arrests for the month. (Three years later the Seabury Report was to have this to say about just such frame-ups: "The diligency and efficiency of the members of the Vice Squad were judged by the number of arrests they made and the convictions they procured each month. The testimony shows that when the end of a month approached and the record of arrests and convictions was low, the officers would arrest women indiscriminately and frame up cases against them until the number so arrested was sufficient to bring the officers' record up to the desired number.")

The case dragged on for a week, and although finally it was dismissed for lack of evidence, I was mad enough at my "friend" Johnny to tear him apart. Accepting my money, enjoying my hospitality and then paying me off with a phony raid! But I wasn't a squealer and I just had to take it.

As soon as I could get free, I hurried back to Brooklyn and the other half of my "double life." All that summer, whenever I could, I spent time with my family, but I began to dread these visits more and more. Since I always had to be on my guard, had to monitor every word and thought, being with my parents was a great strain. I had to suspend being my real self—leave it, so to speak, on the doorstep—the way Moslems leave their slippers outside a mosque. I loved my parents, but there was no longer any real communication between us. There couldn't be.

The only way I could express my feelings was by showering them with gifts and money. Whenever I purchased household supplies, I always made an additional purchase for them. But I had to remember to remove the price tags, for my mother was certain I had no idea of the value of money, and even thought Macy's overcharged me deliberately! Of course I couldn't help wondering if she would accept anything from me if she knew how I had earned the money. But what was there to be gained by confessing? I knew I wasn't going to give up my house until I'd made enough to retire on, and with the way my bank balance was building up as a result of the many market tips I received, I didn't think that day would be too far off. . . . No, telling my parents would only mean sorrow for them. Not honesty, but silence was the best policy.

II

At this time, I was playing the market constantly and investing my profits in "gilt-edged" stocks (or so I thought then). One of my good friends was a Vice Squad officer whom I will call Irwin O'Brien, and I used to buy stocks for him, with his money, later transferring the stocks to his account. All these transactions were to come under intensive scrutiny three years later during the Seabury investigation and with dire results for poor Irwin, even though he was guilty of nothing but following my advice.

Indirectly my friendship with Irwin could be traced back to Joan Smith, for it was Joan who had introduced a girl named Mae Duffy to me, and it was because of Mae that I became friendly with Irwin. Mae had first worked for me years before, but when she started going with Tommy Pennochio and became a drug addict, I ordered her out of the house. (Pennochio was one of the men convicted during the Lucky Luciano trial and is now serving a thirty-year stretch.) I had thought that was the end of Mae, at least so far as I was concerned, but she turned up three years later, claiming she was cured. I was not at all sure she was telling the truth, but she was pale and thin and so pathetic-looking that I couldn't turn her away.

At that time, I had a very pretty little thing named Marcia working for me. She was a Ziegfeld girl, but needed the extra money because she was supporting a blind mother. (Honestly! I met her mother one day and found the old lady completely helpless.) I admired Marcia with all my heart. Plenty of other show girls had worked for me, but she was the first who had a motive other than merely to earn money for finery. Marcia and Mae became very chummy, much to my annoyance, for I felt Marcia was too new and inexperienced in the game to be palling around with Mae. One evening Marcia failed to show up after the theater, and Mae, who had gone out around eleven supposedly to get a soda, did not come back that night either.

Three nights later, when finally the culprits returned, Mae was charged to the gills while Marcia looked as if she'd been at the bottle the entire time. They were accompanied by a colored waiter who said that the girls owed him seventy-five dollars, and after I had paid him off, what I didn't tell those girls isn't worth mentioning.

I was particularly upset about Marcia, whom I had almost placed on a pedestal. I told her she must leave because I couldn't take the responsibility of her acquiring the dope habit through association with a girl in my house. "You've done all these things for your mother," I said. "Are you going to throw everything away now? You say you haven't taken any dope yet, but you will if you continue along this path. One of the girls will take you home now, and I don't want you ever to come back or ever try to contact Mae. Try to get your Follies job back, if you've been fired for staying away these three days—but whatever you do, keep away from this business and everyone connected with it."

As soon as she was gone, I turned to my other problem child, but my feeling toward her was anything but sympathetic. Mae was glassy-eyed and silly, and I felt like walloping the daylights out of her. She giggled constantly all the while I upbraided her.

"They were chasing us and chasing us," she said between giggles. "We tried to get away, but they chased us."

"Who chased you?"

"They did. They kept asking where you lived and we wouldn't tell. We saved you, we saved you, we saved you——"

Someone was knocking at the door. I grabbed Mae's shoulders and shook her till her teeth rattled. "Who chased you? Who asked you? Tell me!"

Her head lolled on her neck. She grinned foolishly. "Cops," she giggled.

They were striding into the parlor right then, six of them.

It was the usual business—a quota raid—and they would not take money for an answer. Although no customers were in the house at the time, seven girls, two maids and I all went to the station and were booked. I posted bond and that was that. I was worried about Mae, not knowing what she might do or say, but she kept quiet till we got home again.

"Thank God," she burst out, "thank God the cops didn't find what I hid." She staggered over to the bar, reached behind it and brought out a thick white paper packet. I grabbed it out of her hands and tore it open. A sugary-white powder dusted my carpet. I knew it was dope, and I knew Mae must have concealed it when the police came. I was beside myself with rage.

"Do you know what you could have done to me?" I yelled at her. "I could have taken a serious rap for being in possession of narcotics! Who would have believed you brought it in? Who would have believed I didn't know it was here?"

I walked up and down, excoriating her. The thought that I might have gone to jail for years so frightened me that I scarcely knew what I was saying, and the trip to the station house had sobered Mae enough so that my words penetrated. She could not stop crying. She lay on the sofa, still wearing her coat, tears flooding down her white face.

"Get out of my house," I yelled at the end.

"But where will I go? Where can I go?"

She got to her feet, swayed crazily and fell to her knees, pressing her face into my skirt. Now that her voice was muffled by the cloth and husky with tears, she sounded like Joan. My eyes filled with tears, too. When Mae was not hopped up, she had a certain pride in her bearing, a certain arrogance. I couldn't stand to see her humbled like this. It all reminded me so painfully of Joan, awakening my old sense of guilt and helplessness toward her.

I said, "All right. You can stay, but you're taking the cure. Right here, right now."

"Make me take it," she said, her voice wild and high. "Oh, you don't know how I hate the monkey on my back. I'll do what you say, Polly, honest to God I will."

Mae said she'd prefer to get the agony over with as quickly as possible so I might as well give her the Cold Turkey cure. This meant that there'd be no tapering off. All drugs would be withdrawn at once, and, if the patient lived, she would be cured in five days. I didn't know about the "if," or I wouldn't have done it that way. But Mae would not go to a sanitarium, and anyway, in most of them, it was possible for a smart junky to get drugs.

The first step was to give Mae a laxative. When the time came for her shot, the cure proper would be begun. I settled her in my bedroom. She smiled at me and said, "Better clear the sharp things out of here." It was the last time she smiled.

She was due for a shot at four P.M. I sat with her, working at my desk, while she lay on the bed staring at the ceiling. Glancing at her now and then, I observed that she kept looking toward the clock on my vanity table. As the hand crossed four o'clock and crept slowly down to the four thirty mark, she kept twisting her fingers, cracking her knuckles. She tossed back and forth on the bed and finally got up and wandered to a chair. But she did not stay there long. Next she went and stood by the window, then began to pace aimlessly, running her hands through her long mane of red hair and biting her lips. She kept going the rounds, wandering from bed to chair to window and back again.

About six, she yawned and stretched. For the next two hours she yawned almost steadily, great gasping yawns which shook her entire body. I found it hard to stay in the room with her, because yawning is catching and soon my jaws ached from imitating her. Then she began to shiver violently and complained that it was cold.

The nightmare closed in on us now. Mae could not stay still a moment. First, she would roll herself up in a tight cocoon of blankets and lie on her stomach, pushing her head as hard as she could under the mound of pillows. Then she would jerk upright, throw herself the length of the bed, moaning and gasping, and begin to plead incoherently, dragging herself up from the bed to pace back and forth, trailing the blankets like some crazy queen in her royal robes. She walked with her head lowered, her shoulders hunched. Her lips were drawn back tightly, exposing her teeth, and she looked like a ravening animal. She would hurry to the radiator and hold her hands over it, complaining irritably of the cold, only to beg me a moment later to open the window—she was stifling.

I was even more frightened when Mae began to breathe in a funny way, sucking air into her lungs hungrily like someone who had been running. Toward dawn, she broke out with such goose flesh as I have never seen. Her skin, ordinarily soft and creamy, turned blue. Presently little bumps appeared and swelled into weals. It did look like the flesh of a turkey, which is how the cure got its name.

Mae said she couldn't breathe through her nose, and in two hours used two boxes of handkerchiefs, blowing her nose harshly, loudly and constantly, as though she had a very bad cold. Then, all at once, to my intense relief she fell into a deep sleep, lying perfectly still and breathing naturally. I lay down on the chaise longue. I was tired out, but I imagined Mae would be better when she awoke.

Instead, I had a shrieking madwoman on my hands. She grabbed her throat and swore she was suffocating, called on God to help her, sneezed, cried, sobbed, threw herself out of bed onto the floor and screamed and jumped up again. I dragged the mattress off the bed and hauled it over beside the radiator (she was freezing! freezing! she yelled at me) and put her there. She had a great bruise on her forehead where she had struck the floor. But in a moment she got up and charged at me, her fists flailing, then clawed at my face. She tried to force open the window and throw herself out, and when I called for one of the maids to help, she fought her off so ferociously that no one would come into the room after that.

She developed diarrhea, vomited almost constantly and screamed that her appendix was ruptured. Really frightened, I examined her abdomen, knowing that if her appendix were inflamed the muscle over it would be more rigid than on the other side. Then I saw that she had a scar there— her appendix had been removed years before.

Attacked by violent cramps in the muscles of her abdomen and legs, she shrieked so loudly I was sure that someone would come to investigate. When she banged her head on the floor, crawled along to the wall and began banging her head against that, I feared I could no longer control her, and went to see if I could find someone reliable to help.

From among the people in the living room, I singled out a stalwart chap who I knew was a cop, although I didn't know his name. I called him out into the hall, and he introduced himself as Irwin O'Brien.

I said, "Mr. O'Brien, I'm in trouble. I have a girl here I'm trying to cure of drug addiction. Can you help me with her?"

He looked at me thoughtfully. "Cold Turkey?" I nodded. "That's taking kind of a chance, isn't it?"

I listened a moment—it was ominously quiet in the bedroom. I said, "I can't stand here talking to you. She's alone

in there," and started back to Mae. I was relieved when he
followed me. Though he hadn't said so, I had a feeling he
would help.

No sooner had I unlocked and opened the door than Mae
made a lunge at me. O'Brien caught her in his arms and let
her fight him. He stood holding her until her strength was
spent, then laid her down carefully on the mattress and pulled
up the blankets. His eyes were kind as he knelt there, watching her, and Mae must have sensed this for she took his hand
and held it.

The maids refused to enter the room for any reason whatsoever. They were frightened and disgusted, and I couldn't
blame them, for Mae had become so weak that she was completely incontinent. I regretted that I had ever gotten involved in such a thing, but I couldn't quit now or all we already had gone through would have gone for nothing.

Perspiration welled from every pore of Mae's wasted body,
soaking her night clothes and the sheets. I was constantly
changing the linen, and when she had to be bathed O'Brien
would carry her to and from the bathroom. When Mae would
have destroyed herself, O'Brien held her, letting her pound
the solid bulk of his shoulders, catching her when she would
have pitched herself against the wall.

By the end of the fourth day, I feared that she would not
live. Her cheeks were sunken, her eyelids swollen and blue,
her lips purple and her mouth shriveled to a small O. Her
eyes were half open, with just the white showing. She would
take no food, only water, and this only from O'Brien. The
day before, it had been necessary to place cardboard between
her teeth to keep her from biting her lips to pieces. Now
she lay absolutely still. Throughout the day she remained
quiet, never moving, scarcely breathing. I sat beside her bed
that night, afraid of the very shadows in the room, leaning

forward now and then to check her respiration. Toward dawn, I slumped over in my chair and fell sound asleep. I could not have stayed awake for anything; I had run through all my reserve strength.

When I opened my eyes, sunlight lay across the bed, blazing whitely on Mae's thin hands. I raised my eyes to her wan face.

"Thanks, Polly," she said in the faintest of whispers.

It was over.

I went for a walk—my first time out of the house in four days and four nights. When I returned, I changed Mae's bed linen and gave her a sponge bath, powdered her and brushed her long red hair. I tied it back with a blue hair ribbon, and she looked like a sick child.

I said, "If you knew what you've just been through, you would never touch drugs again as long as you live."

"I know. I'm cured." Her tongue was still thick and swollen. "I can feel the difference. I don't know how to say thank you."

I took a piece of paper folded like the packet of drugs which Mae had hidden from the police, and set it down on the night table within her reach. "I believe you," I told her, "and I'm leaving this beside you to prove it."

"Quit kidding me," she said. "I'm off the stuff forever." She managed to smile. "Could I have a drink of water? My throat is so dry."

"Sure," I said. I went out of the room, but once outside I tiptoed back and stood watching through the open door as Mae's trembling hand crept slowly across the tabletop to the folded paper. I came back into the room, took the paper and slapped her across the face.

"I was only kidding," she cried. "I knew all the time you

were watching. I wouldn't have taken it for anything in the world."

After the lift it had given me to believe Mae was cured, the letdown was terrible. I felt I had been a fool to waste my time on a junky. However, I sent her to the country and although I expected the worst, she did stay off the dope. Instead, as many addicts do after they have had the cure, she started drinking to excess and eventually became an alcoholic.

Having gone through this ordeal together, Irwin O'Brien and I became good friends. Since he was as discreet as he was kind, he was an ideal person to have around when I wanted to air my troubles, and I can pay him no higher compliment than to say that when we were together, I forgot he was a cop. Although he had been in the department for quite some time and had a family of four, he had remained a playboy and was chronically short of money, so I began passing on to him market tips I got from my big-shot customers. I also insisted he start a savings account. My only wish was to repay his kindness and see him get ahead, but because of his association with me Irwin was to be dismissed from the force in disgrace.

III

As 1929 dawned, although I was making plenty of money, my luck seemed to have changed. Nothing went smoothly. There were constant small annoyances. Partly, of course, this was because my Lion was no longer with me. In 1928 her health had failed alarmingly, and finally, over her violent protests, I took her to my doctor. He told me that for several years she must have been suffering from sickle-cell anemia, and the disease was in its terminal stages. I could not tell Lion this, but I explained to her that she was seriously ill and must take a long rest. I thought perhaps she might like to go back to Carolina, but when she refused I arranged for a niece to come North to look after her. She died in the spring, after six months' illness. . . . In some ways I think I owe Lion more than anyone I have ever known. She gave me faith not only in myself, but in other human beings.

Along with my worry over Lion, late in 1928 came the Rothstein murder and, as I have told, from the time of George McManus's arrest until his acquittal I was on tenterhooks, fearing I might have to be a witness. An additional headache at this time was that two of my girls were the mistresses of cops, and if either found things at the house not to her liking, a word to her lover would shutter my place and land me in pokey.

On February fifteenth occurred the "Valentine's Day Massacre"—the gang-shooting of seven hoodlums in a Chicago garage—which caused an eruption of headlines all over the nation. And on March thirty-first occurred the "Easter Sunday Sabotaging," which also was an intramural affair, but caused no stir whatsoever for the excellent reason that it was never reported to the police or anyone else.

On Easter Sunday I always gave the girls and maids the day off and closed up the house. This year I had planned to spend the holiday in Brooklyn with my family. But when two new girls, Bobbie and Jane, asked me up to their flat for dinner, using my favorite dish, lobster with Italian sauce, as bait, I accepted. I was tired and tense, my nerves were in knots, and I knew that at least with Bobbie and Jane I could relax and be myself. I would not have to leave "Madam Polly" outside on the doorstep.

I should have. I had a hunch something was wrong when

I met the two boyfriends. They were sitting side by side on the sofa as I came in, and neither of them rose. The dark young man, called Gypsy, was tall and good-looking, the magazine type of romantic hero. His black brows were straight over sleepy black eyes, his hair had a patent-leather sheen. I thought perhaps he was a pimp. But the other one, Ed, reassured me. He seemed a nice boy. He was young-looking, wore glasses and had a certain shy charm. He looked like a post-graduate student which, in a way, he was.

After dinner Ed and Gypsy disappeared. Bobbie said they had gone for cigarettes. When they came back two hours later, they explained they'd stopped at a bar. Jane sat at the piano, running her fingers over the keys. "Gypsy," she said, "I won't be mad at you for staying away, if you'll sing for us."

He stood beside her and sang "When Day Is Done." When he finished, Bobbie made a peculiar comment.

"I'm glad," she said.

On my return to my apartment, I was taken aback to find it all dark. Then I remembered that it was Easter Sunday and no one was home. I went in, tripped over something, and fell full length on the floor. When I got the lights on, I saw that I had stumbled on some loose books which had been ripped from the bookcase. Tables were overturned, draperies pulled from their poles, pictures flung on the floor, upholstery slashed and stuffing strewn over the rugs. In my bedroom, drawers were jerked from dressers, their contents spilled across the floor. The closet was nearly bare, dresses were balled up and thrown anywhere. Then I saw that my Russian broadtail jacket was missing. So were my sables. I raced to the dining room. The silver was gone. All pawnable bric-a-brac was missing. I had been cleaned out.

I knew this robbery was an inside job. The locks had not been tampered with, and the elevator man could not recall seeing any strange or suspicious characters around. I sat down in the midst of the mess and tried to figure out how it had been managed. I remembered a maid whom I had fired some weeks before—she had had a key to the flat. On the telephone she said she had given the key to Bobbie to return to me.

I called Bobbie and asked her why she had not given me my key.

She laughed. She put her hand over the mouthpiece and I could hear her repeat the remarks I had made. Then I heard Jane laugh.

"You can figure it out, can't you?" she said.

I could. I raged at her.

She laughed off my anger. She said, "Sure, Polly, you're right. We were laying for you, waiting until the house would be deserted." Then she spoke very slowly. "Polly, what do you intend to do about it? Call the cops?"

With that she hung up. Enraged as I was, I couldn't call the police and she knew it. I set to work fixing the place, and after a couple of hours' work, it didn't look so bad. As my spirits rose, I began to hum to myself cheerfully until I became aware that I was singing "When Day Is Done." Then I got furious all over again. "When the job is done" was what Gypsy had meant.

One evening later in the week I passed Bobbie on the street. She was wearing my Russian broadtail.

Although gang warfare continued to rage unchecked in the United States, the international scene could hardly have been more peaceful. In the summer of 1929, the Great Engineer, who had taken over the throttle from Coolidge, proclaimed that the Kellogg-Briand Anti-War pact was in effect, and this was taken to mean that the sixty-two signatory nations would never fight again. (But I guess if you read the small print there were plenty of loopholes.) Anyway, it seemed to me now would be a good time to start seeing the world, and I planned a three months' tour which would take me to Niagara Falls, Montreal and Quebec, and then on to Europe.

I arrived in Montreal the last week in October, but instead of seeing the sights I spent the days in a brokerage office, bent over a hot ticker unable to believe my eyes. Abandoning all thoughts of continuing the trip, I hurried back to New York and found my apartment snowed under with telegrams from my broker, calling for margin. Everything I had was tied up in stocks and, like so many others, I could not liquidate my holdings. Too numb even to take off my hat and coat, I sat there in that empty apartment for hours, trying to get a fix on the situation. After working and planning for all these years, one turn of the wheel and I was staring straight at double-O—goose eggs again. And now, I thought grimly, I have the family to take care of.

All over the country people were sitting in stunned bewilderment just as I was, trying to understand what had happened to all that money. One minute you were kinging it on top of the world and the next you were flat on your behind in the street, and that "world" you had been on top of was a collapsed balloon. The Roaring Twenties were tamed all right. In the space of a few weeks they became the Whining Twenties as people hobbled around, licking their wounds.

I had thought that my business would fall off, but it was just the opposite—I had almost more customers than I could take care of. Men wanted to go out and forget their troubles, blot out, at least temporarily, those headlines which each day told of more bankruptcies and suicides. The easiest escape, of course, was alcohol, and in the months immediately after the crash I had my biggest profits at the bar. Champagne at thirty dollars a bottle sold like soda pop, but even on the less fancy drinks I did well. The maids used to shake a bottle of beer until it was foamy and in this way stretch it to yield three glasses instead of two. The beer cost me twelve cents a bottle, and I charged a buck a glass. On a case of twenty-four bottles, costing me less than three dollars, I netted nearly seventy.

Some men who had been terrific womanizers now came to the house solely to drink, and no longer showed the slightest interest in my girls. Others who had been separated from their wives for years, or steadily unfaithful to them, stayed home and turned into model husbands. And still others, who had been casual customers, now came in nightly and behaved like satyrs. The atmosphere, at times, was more that of an insane asylum than a bordello. One man kept repeating over and over again: "I used to control Wall Street. Now I don't know how I'm going to pay next month's rent." Another one told me that he came there night after night because, "A whore house is the only place I can cry without being ashamed."

A man whom I had always liked and considered a gentleman appeared one evening, requested the company of a certain girl and then proceeded to practice the most vile, cruel and inhuman acts until the girl was a physical wreck. The following morning the man went to his office and shot himself.

IV

Although it's convenient in the history books to say that after the Wall Street crash came the depression—as if it started right the next day—actually, of course, there was an inɔetween period when people were trying to figure out what nad hit them and estimating the extent of the damage. Writing of this period, Gerald W. Johnson says that "to the average American in 1929 the panic was even more incredible than the First World War had been. His feeling was that you just couldn't do that to American business" and it took "three sickening years . . . [until] he was ready to admit you *could*."

During the first of these years of progressive demoralization, the public reacted—at least in New York—like a man with a terrible hangover. First they buried their heads in the pillows (or reached for a hair of the dog), and then when the moment no longer could be postponed, tottered up and faced the new day, red-eyed and irritable, their shoulders bristling with chips. They wanted somebody to be mad at and though Hoover was the obvious candidate, they couldn't do anything about *him* until election year. As it happened, however, there were plenty of other targets for their wrath conveniently at hand. They had been there, some of them, for quite a while, but when the whole nation was living high off the hog, John Q. Public didn't give a damn how the Tammany boys were getting theirs. But now it was a different story.

Although Mayor Walker had defeated Fiorello H. LaGuardia in 1929 by a plurality of nearly a half-million votes, the Little Flower had done some finger-pointing in the direction of the magistrates' bench, and six months later— maybe because by then the public, minus its shirt, was convinced "there ain't no justice"—the law-givers really began to get it in the neck. In September, 1929, LaGuardia had accused Magistrate Albert H. Vitale of accepting a twenty-thousand-dollar loan from Arnold Rothstein shortly before Rothstein was killed, and had told how Vitale, a month later, was guest of honor at a dinner at the Roman Gardens where he fraternized with seven prominent hoodlums including "The Artichoke King," Ciro Terranova. In mid-March, 1930, after being questioned by the Appellate Division, Vitale was removed from the bench. And so began that airing of soiled linen which was to overtax the clothes lines in every one of the five boroughs, and which culminated in the Seabury investigation.

Among other things, it was learned that several judges had used their official positions to advance stock-promotion schemes, and that enterprising citizens had been able to buy their seats on the bench at prices ranging from ten grand for a magistrate's robe to sixty to a hundred thousand for a General Sessions judgeship. On May seventh, Judge W. Bernard Vause was indicted and later convicted of using the mails to defraud in a pier-leasing scandal; on August fifth, Magistrate George F. Ewald was questioned about the ten thousand dollars his wife paid to a Tammany district leader on the day of his appointment; and on August sixth, Judge Joseph Force Crater, apparently overmastered by a disinclination to stand up and be counted, walked out of a restaurant on West Forty-fifth Street, hopped into a cab, and has never been seen since.

The bully boys down on Spring Street were none too happy either. There had been considerable dissatisfaction with their handling of the Rothstein case. Police Commissioner Warren had resigned and, in the election campaign of '29, an eager beaver named Crain had promised he would solve the murder within two weeks of taking office as District Attorney. (More than two decades later it is still unsolved.) As I have told elsewhere, George McManus was a suspect, but he was not brought to trial till a month after election, and on December sixth, Judge Nott directed that he be

acquitted. Subsequently, Grover Whalen was Police Commissioner. In May, he resigned and Edward P. Mulrooney
took over. But, in the light of future events, probably the
uneasiest and unhappiest boys during that summer of 1930
were the members of the 19th Division and the other two
branches of the Vice Squad.

Ten days after Judge Crater's disappearance, in response
to prodding from the newspapers and at the urgent request
of the New York bar association, Governor Franklin D. Roosevelt asked the Appellate Division to investigate the magis-
strates' courts of New York and Bronx Counties, and on
August twenty-sixth, the Court named Samuel Seabury as
referee. A month later the investigation was under way.

As details of judicial bribe-taking and the corrupt practices of the Vice Squad filled the papers, some of my friends
began to kid me. "You'll be getting a little *billet doux* from
Judge Seabury any day now, Poll," they said. "He'll be
wanting you to whisper to him about all your friends at
court." I laughed with the kidders, but, after all, though I
had been arrested a number of times, the cases always had
been dismissed, and it might well be that this would strike
some investigator as peculiar.

It did. One evening in the middle of November, just as I
was finishing dinner, I was called to the telephone. The moment I picked up the receiver and even before I could say
hello, a man's voice blurted, "Hurry, Polly, get out of your
house. They're on their way to serve you with a subpoena."

"Who is this?"

"Never mind who it is. Get out fast!"

I have never found out who called me.

At that time, I didn't stop to speculate. I threw some
clothes into a bag, raced out of the apartment and hailed a

taxi. And none too soon either, for as we pulled away a car drew up and out piled four husky guys—quite a few to hand a piece of paper to a one-hundred-and-sixteen-pound, five-foot female. I spent a restless night in a hotel pacing the floor and chain smoking. I had a feeling this investigation, unlike so many others, wasn't just a flash in the pan, and I wasn't surprised when I got a message to leave town and stay lost until I got the green light to return.

I left at once for Newark and checked in at a hotel there. Personally, I had nothing to fear from Judge Seabury. This time the heat was on the law-givers and law-enforcers, not the law-breakers. The investigators were interested in me only because they knew I had entertained many members of the magistrates' court and Vice Squad and numerous other city officials, and because I had paid out thousands of dollars in bribes to keep my house running smoothly and my girls and myself out of jail. But I had to get out of town because I wasn't going to talk. In the first place, I am not an informer. In the second place, even though *I* knew I wasn't going to squeal, if I accepted service of a subpoena a lot of people might be dubious about my ability to keep clammed up and decide to insure my silence in ways I didn't care to dwell on. I would gain nothing by letting Seabury's battery of lawyers grill me, and despite the fact that it would do my heart good to see some of those double-crossing cops shown up, I wasn't going to be the one to name names and tell tales. I had become a naturalized citizen on May 20, 1929, and I knew that I was failing in my civic duty in not coming forward. But I didn't feel I was indispensable to the success of the investigation, and I also knew that every day all over the country many respected citizens (who had no fear of reprisals) were ducking their obligations by avoiding jury duty or failing to report accidents they had witnessed. (Hollering, "You're another!" doesn't prove anything, but it does shut people up and also quiets your conscience.)

I had thought I would go nuts waiting around in the New York hotel, but New Jersey was the topper. I didn't know where to get a drink, and I was afraid to talk to anyone for fear I'd be recognized. Every day the papers carried stories speculating about where I was hiding out, and before long I got in such a state I thought every passer-by was going to turn me in. Finally, I just stayed in my room, my only visitor a stool pigeon sent over by my cop friends to keep me abreast of the score.

Just when it seemed I could take the four walls of a hotel no longer, I read in the paper that my former sweetheart Casey Booth and his band were in Pittsburgh, and I could not resist calling him long distance. He said why didn't I come out there and spend some of my "exile" with him, and in a little less time than it takes to drop a hat, I was on my way.

Now it was Casey's turn to lend a helping hand, and he spent all his free time with me. At first I stayed close to the hotel and saw only him, but one night I was so fed up I agreed to go out with some friends of his. What a time we had! I felt as if the bars of a cage had been lifted. I don't know which made me higher, Scotch or freedom.

After we had made about five spots, my companions told me we were due at a birthday party.

"A birthday party?" I said. "At six in the morning?"

"Sure," said one of them. "The birthday kid is a rich eccentric. You'll be nuts about her."

I assumed that the elderly woman who greeted us was the mother of our hostess and went gaily on into the big living room. But I had hardly set foot over the threshold when I snapped to attention. No matter how much I've had to drink, I have always been able to sober up in a flash when an emergency arises, and though this was not an emergency, I realized I'd been framed. But it was a comedy frame-up, and I burst out laughing as I looked at the six or eight girls lounging around the parlor in shorts and negligées.

"Why, you so-and-sos!" I cried. "You've brought me to a house of ill repute!"

The guys were doubled up with laughter, but the madam and the girls were looking a little stuffy, as people do when they're not included in a joke. "My friends are treating me like a postman on a vacation," I said. "They're taking me for a walk. I'm Polly Adler from New York."

At this, all the girls smiled and giggled, and the madam introduced herself. She was Nettie Gordon, famous in Pittsburgh where she had run a first-class house for years. Nettie was about sixty, and I had heard that she was married to a former police captain and owned a beautiful estate in the suburbs of the city.

After an hour or so of conversation, I asked, "Why do you stay in business? Since you and your husband have a lovely home and plenty of money, why do you stay with this?"

Nettie frowned and looked away from me. "Sure, we got a home and we got money," she said. "But who wants to sit in a house and die of loneliness? Who'd come to visit Nettie Gordon? There's not many people would risk their reputations walking up our drive, with everyone knowing they're coming to see the ex-madam of a whorehouse! Pa and I don't want to sit around and watch each other grow older. We want life and youth around us. I'm still a madam because I like having these girls around me. Every night is a party, and

that's the way old Nettie's goin' out—with a lot of fun goin'
on around her."

A number of years later, when Nettie died, I heard about
her funeral and the crowd which attended it. There were
the poor people whom she had befriended and the repre-
sentatives of the many charities to which she had donated so
generously. There were the merchants she had patronized
throughout the years. There were the friends who remembered Nettie's kindness. There were the prostitutes and former customers from all over Pittsburgh. So Nettie Gordon,
who was afraid of being left alone in her huge house, had a
host of people around her right up to the last.

After this night's spree, I had to go back into hibernation
as I had developed a severe cold. The doctor who checked
me over told me I was badly in need of a rest, suffering from
acute nervous tension as well as the cold, and he advised
Miami. I liked the thought of relaxing in the sun, and
knew without being told that my nerves needed a vacation,
so I headed south.

I checked into a hotel in Miami under an assumed name
and settled down to wait out my time and pull myself together, but I wasn't well enough to see much of the life, and
I soon found that I had exchanged one hotel room for another. My only recreation was reading four or five New York
newspapers every day, which was not the best way to take my
mind off my troubles. Since I wasn't available for questioning, the investigators were trying to get the lowdown on me
from others and I learned that

Managers of some fifteen of New York's best known and most respected
hotels and clubs have been summoned to the Seabury Vice inquiry in an
effort to trace telephone calls to the notorious Polly Adler. Among those
subpoenaed are the officials of the Princeton Club, the Ritz-Carlton, Vanderbilt, Biltmore, Delmonico, Commodore and Elysée Hotels.

Meanwhile, my absence was no handicap to the gentlemen of the press. Whether or not it made their hearts grow fonder, it certainly made their tales grow taller. From being just "the demi-monde Queen of the May," I soon evolved into "one of the most dangerous women the city has ever known" and "a woman so powerful that she was able to make or break members of the Vice Squad." Out of sight, out of mind, so the saying goes, but in my case it worked the other way. I was twice as exciting because I was missing. After first declaring that my whereabouts were unknown, the boys were free to play guessing games, and for a while there I was all over the map like confetti. (I used to wonder why, if they really wanted to locate me, they didn't inquire of Judge Seabury or at the District Attorney's office. I'm quite sure the authorities were keeping tabs on me. But so long as I stayed out of New York State, I could not be subpoenaed, nor, since I was wanted only as a witness, could I be extradited.) Finally, when all possible changes had been rung on the madam-on-the-lam theme, the press decided to wind up the story by allowing me to make a getaway. So the headlines announced: POLLY ADLER SAFE IN HAVANA. And I had to restrain myself from wiring, "Close, but no cigar."

But just when the papers were beginning to lay off me, the Vivian Gordon murder splashed across the front pages. On February twenty-sixth, only a day or so after she had visited Seabury's headquarters and agreed to testify, Vivian was found strangled in Van Cortlandt Park—and my name and phone number were in her address book. The newspapers described her as "a misled woman who followed the tinsel path" and as "a blackmailer who associated with the most dangerous and powerful denizens of the underworld." But I knew her only as an attractive brunette in the same business as I, out to feather her nest quickly. There was nothing unusual in her having my address since we operated in the same circles, yet even though our acquaintance was of the slightest, the papers alleged that she had worked for me and that there had been a hair-pulling contest between us, and much bad feeling.

At any other time Viv's killing would have roused only routine interest, but now it was linked with the Seabury investigation, and the papers insisted that she had been killed because she could give damaging testimony. When her sixteen-year-old daughter, Benita Bischoff, committed suicide, there was an even greater uproar, and it was said that the lurid newspaper stories about her mother's "five hundred sugar daddies" had shamed and shocked the young girl into taking her own life.

Police Commissioner Mulrooney stated that until the murder was solved there would be "a stain on the shield of every policeman in New York." Many suspected that I knew who had put the finger on Vivian, and it was believed that I was less afraid of being called in on the vice inquiry than of being questioned about the killing. No one thought I had a hand in it, but they were sure I could name the killer, if I dared.

Although all I knew about the case was what I picked up from the papers, I got quite a jolt when I read:

That Vivian Gordon was murdered to seal her lips became still more apparent when it was learned that death awaits another woman of scarlet should she return to New York from her hiding place in Havana. She is the notorious Polly Adler, czarina for years of the unofficial red light apartments in the city.

I tried to laugh this off as the product of some reporter's over-active imagination, but just the same I made no plans to leave Florida in the immediate future. After all, March is a nasty month in New York—a person could easily catch cold.

Chapter 6

In a Glass-
Bottomed Boat

A reformer is a guy who rides through a sewer in a glass-bottomed boat.

James J. Walker   quoted in INSIDE U.S.A.

I

In the years since World War II, headlines containing the word PROBE or INQUIRY have become as regular a fixture in the daily papers as the weather report. Each new investigation touches off a flock of others, and it may well be that this is a chain reaction which will proceed unchecked until there is no one left to investigate. Of course ever since society got itself organized there have been inquisitorial proceedings—frequently expedited by the use of such memory-prodders as the rack and the hoist and red-hot pincers—and each age and country has developed its characteristic technique of "putting the question." Today in America the big-time probes are conducted along lines which adhere pretty closely to the classic pattern evolved by Judge Seabury twenty-odd years ago, and though later inquiries have surpassed it in scope and national significance, the Seabury investigation stands as the daddy of them all.

The Seabury technique, as analyzed by his co-workers and

reporters, was a combination of drudgery and drama. "The public," Judge Seabury told his staff, "will not be aroused by graphs and charts and reports." It was vital, he believed, to "humanize" the findings with living, breathing, in-the-flesh testimony. So first came the amassing of documentary evidence "painstakingly and implacably gathered"—for example, leads were developed by scrutinizing the bank accounts of everyone under suspicion and tracing all incongruously large deposits to their source. Then came the rounding up and questioning of witnesses behind closed doors, and from the evidence gleaned at these private hearings it was determined who would be called to take the stand at the big show —the public hearings. During the course of the magistrates' courts investigation, two hundred and ninety-nine witnesses were examined and the transcript of their testimony covers 4,596 pages.

Right from the beginning the atmosphere was, as Robert Bendiner puts it, "gamy"—and never gamier than when the extortion practices of some members of the Vice Squad were revealed. Although their function was the suppression of gambling, prostitution, and the liquor and narcotic traffic, actually—as I knew only too well—that distinguished assortment of flatfeet devoted most of their time to fostering the illegitimate businesses which gave them their victims and their profits. Perhaps if they had confined themselves to shaking down people like me, who were violating the law, public indignation would not have risen to such a pitch, but their persecution of innocent women could never be condoned, and it was the testimony of these pitiful victims of police frames —the dramatic "human evidence"—which not only proved their individual undoing, but resulted in the abolition of the Vice Squad.

Their methods, as described in the Seabury report, "featured two types of arrest—the direct and the indirect. In the direct, the officer himself was a party. He approached the victim and arrested her after she had accepted money for prostitution and was prepared to carry out her bargain. In the indirect, the stool-pigeon, the infamous 'unknown man' of the police blotters, was the customer and at a given moment the officers broke in and made the arrest. The method of the indirect arrest developed into a number of ingeniously contrived rackets. In the Doctor's racket, the stool-pigeon, posing as a patient, entered a doctor's office while the doctor was away and demanded treatment. He placed money in a conspicuous spot and, despite the protests of the nurse, began to undress. At a given moment the officers entered and placed the nurse under arrest for prostitution. All the elements were present, the state of undress of the man, and the money, in consideration for which the woman had ostensibly offered to commit an act of prostitution.

"The Landlady Racket was also popular. The stool-pigeon as a rule, after renting a room in a rooming house and paying for it with marked money, brought his supposed wife to the room. Almost immediately the police broke in and arrested the landlady for maintaining a house of prostitution. The officers thus obtained double graft. The extent of the practice of these 'rackets' is indicated by the profits resulting to the police officers involved. According to analyses of their bank accounts, five of them in a few years accumulated more than $500,000."

On October 27, 1930, just as the investigation was getting under way, Police Commissioner Mulrooney asserted that the police department never employed stool-pigeons, but *never!* Less than six weeks later Chile Acuna ("The Human Spitoona") in a public hearing pointed out a half-dozen members of the Vice Squad who had used him in frame-ups.

"It is apparent," wrote Judge Seabury, "that stool-pigeons were indispensable to the Vice Squad. Chile Acuna, the 'Dove,' Pinto, Harry the Greek, Meyer Slutsky, Chico and Harry Levey (all witnesses), were members of the brotherhood.

"The story of Acuna is characteristic of them all. Several years after this Chilean immigrant came here he met two detectives. Because of his knowledge of Spanish he was able to pick up information concerning crimes unavailable to the detectives. He was well paid for this information and worked for them until 1929, when he joined forces with the Vice Squad because there was more money in it. He worked mainly in the Spanish district of Harlem under Inspector Ryan who was in reality Lieutenant Pfeiffer of the One-hundred-and-Twenty-third-Street Station House. Pfeiffer taught him the lessons of the Vice Squad stool-pigeon: he must be prepared to give a false name or address, also for a slight beating from the police during the raid, he must never go to court, and above all, he must deny any personal knowledge of the arresting officers. Acuna was then turned over to two members of the squad, Baccaglini and Tait . . . and worked with them until he was double-crossed and sent to prison. Stool-pigeons were a costly item in the police budget. Lieutenant Pfeiffer testified that the average monthly bill submitted by each officer was thirty-five dollars. In the whole city the taxpayers paid approximately one hundred thousand dollars per year for the use of these informers.

"The picture of the Ring is complete. The stool-pigeon or the officer framed the woman, the officer arrested her, the unlicensed bondsman bailed her out at an exorbitant charge and usually recommended a lawyer, the lawyer gouged her savings and either he himself, or through the bondsman, 'fixed' the arresting officer and the District Attorney. . . .

Undoubtedly, the 'framing' of women illustrates an inhumanity more exquisite than the use of physical violence; it means a cold-blooded search for victims with money enough to make the sordid business financially profitable to everyone involved; it means, further, a thorough understanding of the potency of fear. The difficulty found in inducing women to tell their stories showed clearly how strong was the fear of publicity on which the Ring traded. . . . It is clear that after many so-called 'raids,' the innocent victims purchased freedom by the payment of money. It is impossible to estimate how many women in this city have been gouged under threat of arrest or conviction of a crime of which they were totally innocent; but enough testimony has been given on this subject to indicate that the business of framing honest women was well established and lucrative."

When some of the boys' bank accounts were analyzed, their explanations as to how they had acquired king-size nest eggs on a policeman's pay were of such a nature as to suggest that the Marx Brothers were writing their dialogue. Typical of the explanations was that offered by Robert E. Morris, who accounted for the fifty thousand dollars in his "tin box" by saying that he had won ten thousand gambling and the other forty thousand had been given to him in one-thousand-dollar bills by his Uncle George, as they were setting out to spend the day at Coney Island. Uncle George, said Morris, was like that—generous. But unfortunately the old boy was dead, and there was no way the story could be checked.

Morris often had been on the receiving end of shakedowns at my house, and it did my heart good to see him finally getting his lumps. But, much as I hated him and others like him, it would have been impossible for me to tell the investigators what I knew about them without hurting men who had done me numerous favors. However, Seabury and his staff seemed to be doing all right without me. Half a dozen police officers went to jail, and many others were broken during the inquiry. One was James J. Quinliven, who was accused of staging parties for my girls in his home, of conducting gambling games, and of sharing in the take from the distribution of confiscated liquor seized in speakeasy raids.

But the Seabury lightning bolts were not aimed only at police operatives. The removal of District Attorney Thomas Crain was recommended, two magistrates were ousted, and three resigned under fire. And of considerable personal interest to me was the admission by John C. Weston that during his eight years as a special prosecutor in Woman's Court he had accepted over twenty thousand dollars in bribes to dismiss six hundred cases. Five hundred and ninety-eight of these cases were not, apparently, newsworthy, but the other two—which were alleged to concern me—resulted in stories like this one, which appeared in the New York *World Telegram*:

WESTON CITES POLITICAL PULL OF POLLY ADLER
He Feared To Prosecute Her and "Laid Down," Ex-Prosecutor Reveals

The political power of Polly Adler is so great that a prosecutor feared he would be removed or "more than that" unless he laid down in prosecuting a charge against her, according to sworn testimony in records of the Appellate Division today.

Weston said he made no effort to show that Polly Adler, who was never convicted though arrested eleven times, had a "notorious" reputation. He said he "laid down" on the case because of the woman's influence.

"Influence with the police?" interrupted Referee Clarence J. Shearn.

"With everybody," replied Weston.

"Do you mean that you were afraid that you would be removed as prosecutor in the court?"

"More than that," replied Weston.

. . . Earlier in the day Weston, after insisting all last week that the money given to him was merely a series of "gratuities" or "tips," recanted and described the payments as "in the nature of bribes." He clung to the assertion, however, that he had done nothing to earn the "bribes" and

continued to insist that he had done everything possible to obtain conviction.

When I read that, I thought it must be even warmer in
New York than in Florida.

II

Just as a stone cast into a pond sends ripples in an ever-
widening circle, so did the investigation of the magistrates'
courts provide the impetus for a city-wide inquiry which in
the end was to force the resignation of debonair and beloved
little Jimmy Walker. A citizens' committee, headed by Rabbi
Stephen S. Wise and Reverend John Haynes Holmes, had
urged Governor Roosevelt to widen the scope of the investigation. But for political reasons he was reluctant to interfere
in the internal affairs of New York City. However, on March
23, 1931, the state legislature got him off the hook by passing a resolution calling for a further investigation, with Samuel Seabury as General Counsel of the committee, which was
headed by Senator Hofstadter.

This development, instead of increasing my headaches, actually came as a relief to me. It was now clear that the hunters
were aiming at far bigger game than corrupt jurists, cops,
bondsmen and lawyers, and I reasoned that with this shift
in the spotlight the heat would be off me too. After the
Vivian Gordon furor died down, I began to think of going
home. I needed money, I was bored with Miami, and I was
tired of living the life of a lamster. So, conning myself into
thinking Judge Seabury had lost interest in me, I took the
train north.

I arrived in New York on a beautiful evening in early May
just as the lights were coming on. I can never be blasé about

New York. Riding uptown it was as if I were seeing it for the first time, and yet there was this wonderful feeling of home-coming too. From the Hudson to Hell's Kitchen, from that rackety light-plastered arena known as Times Square to the lovely serenity of Central Park, this was my town, this was the Big Apple, this was where I had to be. Let Judge Seabury find me if he can, I thought to myself, here I am and here I stay.

At the same time the next evening I was again riding up-town, but my mood was by no means so lyrical. I had just come from investigation headquarters, and I had no eyes for the beauties of Manhattan. In my hand was an extra, still damp from the presses, which I was skimming as we bowled along.

POLLY ADLER SURRENDERS

(Thursday, May 7) . . . From court to court, from police precinct to precinct, wherever the finger of vice graft has touched in the last twenty years, it has been recognized that a few words from Polly Adler might blow the lid right off. When she was finally cornered, excitement filled the offices of the Seabury investigation. Counsel Harland B. Tibbetts could not restrain himself, and in his eagerness to tell the waiting world that Polly Adler had at last been caught, he sent for his personal friends among the reporters who have been covering the inquiry. To them he announced that with the aid of the *Daily Mirror,* his process-servers had captured Polly Adler, the most notorious woman in the history of New York vice . . . Seven process-servers covered every entrance of the apartment building when at last the woman agreed to surrender. To intimates she declared she would never be forced to tell what she knew about the vice graft of New York because "two Magistrates and a Su-preme Court Justice are on my string . . ."

Finding me had proved pie-easy for the Seabury men. Al-though I had avoided my place of business, going in-stead to an apartment I kept as a refuge from the cops and my drunken clients, on the very morning after my arrival the process-servers came knocking on my door. And to make everything just dandy I had a Vice Squad member with me! This was my friend Irwin O'Brien, who was the first person I had notified of my return, and who had stopped by early in the morning to catch me up with what had been going on. I knew that if Irwin were found there he would be cooked at headquarters, so I stalled the servers until Irwin could make his getaway via the fire escape.

While he was scampering down sixteen flights of stairs, I carried on a conversation through the door with the process-server. He pleaded with me to accept the summons, and at last I told him to hand it to me through the interviewer in the door. But when he did so, I drew back my hand because I saw a dollar bill attached to the paper. This makes the serving of a subpoena legal in New York State, but I feared that taking money from someone connected with the law might be the same as having a policeman make a direct case against me. However, a young assistant of Seabury's was along, and he assured me there would be no monkey business. So, as there had been ample time for Irwin to make his getaway, I let them in.

When they were inside the apartment and I had accepted service, I had to break down and smile. I have never seen two such tired young men; they certainly looked as if they'd had a hard night. Knowing that offering them a drink was out of the question, I invited them to sit down and join me in a cup of coffee, which they did—with thanks.

As we prepared to leave, the process-server suggested we go out by the rear door to avoid the swarm of reporters and photographers in front. (Later I learned that the Seabury staff had been instructed to knock themselves out to be courteous, and I was treated with unusual consideration so long as they thought there was a chance I might prove a co-operative witness.) But there was no shaking off the press. As we were going down a corridor at investigation headquarters on 80 Center Street, a flashbulb suddenly exploded in my face and—blinded as well as startled—I ploughed right into the camera. After that I was careful to keep my face covered. Although my mother did not read English and so never looked at the papers, I was afraid she might see my picture while passing a newsstand.

On that first day, the questioning was conducted by Harland B. Tibbetts, a mild-mannered, soft-spoken man, who recently had become a counsel for the investigation. Also present were two assistant counsels—Philip W. Haberman Jr. and the man who, I sensed, would be my real antagonist, Irving Ben Cooper. Although he never spoke during the questioning, his piercing eyes never left my face and his silence was like an attack.

This first session was mostly devoted to an examination of the docket books for the purpose of having me identify the dates of my various arrests, and the names under which I had been arrested, but of course the papers had their own ideas about what went on.

GIVE LA ADLER LEADING ROLE IN QUIZ SHOW

. . . Polly Adler, notorious vice entrepreneuse, will set off the first bomb in the city wide inquiry. She will be slapped on the witness stand at the very first open hearing. Her story will be used as a background on which Judge Seabury will attempt to paint one of the most lurid pictures of civic corruption ever presented to the public. Even now she is being groomed in secret by Seabury investigators for her "stage" appearance. They believe that she holds the key to much valuable information on the functioning of the vice ring here, and can, if she wishes, reveal the higher-ups in the corrupt organization which has reached the Police Department and into the courts.

. . . Who's who in N.Y. after the sun goes down may be told to the Legislative Investigating Committee by the notorious Polly Adler. Whether she will talk frankly and fully is another question. But at least she will be asked what connection if any exists between the police and the profession of which she is the acknowledged chatelaine, and she is also to be questioned about the eleven times she was arrested but never convicted. The committee wants to know whether her record was a matter of luck or something else.

On my next trip to Center Street I was turned over to Irving Ben Cooper. Evidently he had decided from my attitude at the first session that I was going to be anything but co-operative, so he wasted no time on the amenities and began firing questions at me the moment I came into the room. Did I know a certain man? No. Had I been at a certain place at a certain time? I didn't remember. For what seemed hours he continued to throw names at me, and I continued to deny knowing all except those who could not possibly be hurt by our acquaintanceship.

At the end of the long afternoon, Cooper glared at me out of sharp blue eyes that seemed to bite into me: "You are positive you don't know these men?"

"Positive."

"You understand, Miss Adler, that everything you say is being taken down by a court stenographer?"

You're telling me, brother, I thought to myself. But aloud I said demurely, "Yes, I understand."

Since I was not allowed to have a lawyer present, or take notes, as soon as each session ended I would rush back to the apartment and write down all the questions and answers I could remember. Then I would call a friend of mine and read off the names of the men about whom I had been questioned, together with whether I had, or had not, admitted knowing them. In this way I made sure that if any of these men should be questioned, their statements would not conflict with mine.

Other than that, about my only occupation was reading the newspaper stories about myself. I was fascinated to learn that "Polly Adler numbers among her intimates some of the wealthiest and most influential men in New York, and in all probability knows more about the trade of exploiting girls than any other in her profession." Also that my word was law "not alone in New York, but in large cities of three states," that I was a "vice overlord," and the only woman member of a combine which had an "international traffic in women and drugs."

As the interrogations continued, I realized that the investigators didn't give a damn about me personally. They were interested only in learning the names of the higher-ups to whom I had paid graft. But though I continued to impersonate a clam so successfully that Irving Ben Cooper was tearing his hair, according to the papers I was singing like a canary. At first I laughed at some of the "revelations" I was supposed to have made, but then I began to get worried. What if some of the people I was protecting started thinking these reports were the McCoy? And what else could they think after reading such headlines as POLLY ADLER BARES CITY VICE RING SECRETS, and column after column of such unmitigated malarky as

. . . it was said she began to unfold a tale of millions in graft, of gilded palaces of shame run with the connivance of the Vice Squad, of gangsters harbored in the scented boudoirs of "Polly Adler's girls." Part of the story she has to tell concerned the innermost secrets in the life of one of her girls, Vivian Gordon, who was slain by a strangler last February 26th, as she was preparing to expose those secrets in the Vice Investigation. Polly, herself, will be protected by an armed guard at all hours of the day and night . . .

. . . again and again, confronted with stories already told, she has exploded into indignant outbursts of Yiddish before grudgingly admitting the truth. She will be called upon to take the stand in a public hearing on either Wednesday or Thursday of this week—then watch for the fireworks! So far, at least two magistrates have been linked to orgies staged at Polly Adler's parties, while a high police official, four lowly vice cops and two stool-pigeons have been definitely named as partaking of her bounty. An effort to link an official high in the city government to the parties through the testimony of one of the girls has so far failed. Many of Polly's guests, informal and otherwise, will probably be named during the public hearings. Some are said to have already left town.

I had to laugh at the mention of my having an armed guard. What a joke! Aside from reporters, no one in New York came near me. All my so-called friends gave me a wide berth, no doubt fearing they might be called in for questioning or at least come in for some unpleasant publicity. Even my girls stayed away, and I thought with some bitterness probably they figured I was finished in New York and would be of no further use to them.

As it turned out, I was right about those I was protecting getting worried when they read I was "joining the stampede to tell all." Word came from some of my politician pals that if I thought things were getting too rugged, they would be glad to provide me with an attorney free of charge. I don't think it was so much that they were afraid of my squealing as that they doubted my ability to match wits with the investigating committee, but whatever their motive I declined the offer, as I did offers of loans from several members of the Vice Squad who knew my bank balance had dwindled practically to the vanishing point.

But, although I turned down help from these sources, I did know I was going to need legal advice, and I decided to engage counsel on my own hook. So that my political friends would be easy in their minds I checked with them about the attorney I planned to engage, and word immediately came back that he was an okay Tammany man in whom I could safely confide. Nevertheless, when I met Mr. Jayess I did not trust him, and in the beginning played it very close to the belt. Even after he said he knew I was scraping the bottom of the barrel and was willing to act as my advisor for the small fee of two hundred and fifty dollars, still there was something about him I did not like, and I continued to hedge.

"Look, Miss Adler," he said finally, "when you go to a doctor you expect to tell him what ails you, otherwise he can't help you. And it's the same with your attorney. I cannot advise you properly unless you give me all the details. It's not idle curiosity. I don't care who you paid off—that's not the point. But if I'm to show you what course to follow I've got to know these things."

Suddenly I was ashamed of my distrust. I told myself I was becoming neurotic to feel so suspicious of a man I had been told was dependable. Overwrought as I was from the days of cross-examining, I needed an outlet for my pent-up emotions, and so, in a moment of a weakness I have never ceased to regret, I poured out details of shakedowns and other matters pertinent to the inquiry, plus much else which I should have kept to myself.

Since then I have learned to trust my hunches about people. On my next visit, the fee jumped from two hundred and fifty dollars to twenty-five hundred and continued to go up. In just one interview, Mr. Jayess had learned how upset I was and how much I needed someone to confide in, and now that he had heard all that I had held back from the investigators, he was in a position to play on that nervousness and dependence. And he did—for years.

The first few times I was called down to investigation headquarters I was accorded many special courtesies. I was hurried in through a back entrance, thus avoiding reporters, and I was never under any circumstances kept waiting. But as time went on and even the papers got around to admitting that "Polly Adler, that mysterious figure of the vice world, has proved to be a tight-mouthed witness," I was left to sit in a stuffy waiting room through unbearably hot days, and only at the end of five or six hours would I be told to come back the next day. I was not surprised by this change in tactics. I understood that Mr. Cooper was hoping to wear down my resistance and sap my morale. There was nothing personal in it. It was just a part of the game of cops-and-robbers we were playing.

As the investigation progressed, Mr. Cooper began to delve deeper and deeper into my financial affairs. Photostatic copies of my bank and brokerage-house accounts were turned over to him, and I shook in my boots when I thought of the canceled checks and records of stock transactions which could connect me with people whom I had denied even knowing. He questioned me about deposits and withdrawals over a long period of years, and since I had played the market heavily, I was often put to it to figure out what an item might be. A deposit of ten thousand followed the next day by a withdrawal of the same amount looked like a pay-off when actually it might represent money made on a stock sale, which I had promptly reinvested in other stock. Many times I would remember just which stock, at how much, but it was impossible to recall every single transaction and of course not all withdrawals were for stock purchases.

When I became hesitant in my answers, Mr. Cooper would work me over with increased impatience. But the more impatient he became, the more deliberate I would be. My object was to say as little as possible, and to take my time about saying it—tactics which he found utterly maddening. Although we had several exchanges in which the sparks flew, I realize now that, in the circumstances, his treatment of me was a miracle of patience and self-control. I must have been the world's worst and most infuriating witness. But we were on dangerous ground—one slip of the tongue, one wrong answer, and he would have me.

On one occasion when Cooper pointed out that there were several large withdrawals I had failed to account for, I explained that frequently I would take out several thousand and stash it in a safe-deposit box where it would be readily accessible.

"How much money did you keep in your vaults?"

"Different amounts," I said slowly, "at different times."

"Twenty or thirty or fifty thousand?"

I considered. "Maybe," I said finally.

"Answer direct! Answer direct!" he snapped. "How many times must I tell you 'maybe' is an improper response?"

I apologized meekly and answered his next question with, "It might have been."

That got him. Throwing down his pencil, he shouted, "How much schooling did you have? Your mentality is low!"

I have always been sensitive about my lack of education, and I lost my temper. "If my mentality is so low," I shouted back at him, "a smart educated fellow like you should have found out all you want to know from me a month ago!"

He took a turn up and down the room, and when he next addressed me, his manner was courteous. "Now, Polly, why do you want to protect these framing cops? How much did you pay for your cases and to whom did you pay the bribes?" When I made no reply, he raised his voice again. "If you don't co-operate, I'm going to call your parents down here."

"Go ahead. Call them. They're old and they know nothing about my affairs and it would probably kill them to be dragged down here. But if that's the way you do business——"

"Why don't you tell the truth?"

"I am telling the truth."

He sighed. "I think maybe we'd better let you have a talk with Mr. Samuel Seabury."

So my next questioning was done by Judge Seabury himself—a gray-haired, fine-looking man who treated me with meticulous politeness. He began by naming over a number of Tammany bigwigs, including Mayor Walker, and asking if it was not true that they had celebrated important events at my house. I responded, of course, with noes interspersed with "I don't recalls," until suddenly the judge decided to quit horsing around.

Very politely he asked, "Is this your check?" and held it out for me to see.

It was one of Irwin O'Brien's checks. I must have turned white, and my denial was equally pallid.

"It's a policeman's paycheck, is it not, Miss Adler? And you will notice that it is endorsed with a capital 'P.' " He showed me the letter "P," but held his finger over the signature above it.

"It's not my handwriting," I said feebly.

Judge Seabury did not press me. Instead he leaned back in his chair and said, "Think it over, Miss Adler. Refresh your memory, and give me your answer tomorrow."

My memory needed no refreshing. I remembered vividly when Irwin O'Brien had given me that check in payment for some stock. I had begun to endorse it before I stopped to think how bad it would look for my name to appear on a cop's paycheck. So I had returned it to Irwin, but my initial already was on the back.

During the next month I was questioned over and over again about my dealings with Irwin and my own personal money affairs. But I kept right on denying that I knew he was a policeman, just as he later denied knowing I was a madam, saying he had heard of me only as "a woman who made her living on the stock market."

According to my notes made at the time, a typical grilling by Mr. Cooper would run something like this:

Q   *How long have you known Irwin O'Brien?*
A   *About three years. I met him in 1928.*
Q   *Where?*
A   *At a restaurant.*
Q   *Did you see him often after that?*
A   *Quite often. He would call and I would meet him at an agreed place.*
Q   *What business did you have with him?*
A   *I purchased stocks for him.*
Q   *Did he pay you by cash or check?*
A   *Cash.*
Q   *How many transactions were there?*
A   *I don't remember. I often bought stocks for him without his knowledge.*
Q   *What business is he in?*
A   *He's a Fuller brush salesman.*
Q   *I show you this letter. Did you write it?*
A   *No.*
Q   *Is it Irwin O'Brien's?*
A   *It might be. I might have asked him to write it.*
Q   *Why?*
A   *Very simple. Because I didn't want the same signature to appear at the broker's.*
Q   *Did you have the Anaconda in your possession then?*
A   *No, it was in my Irwin O'Brien account, and I had it transferred to my own account.*
Q   *I show you this check. Is this your "P" on the check?*
A   *I don't know.*
Q   *Don't you know your own writing?*
A   *It might be that I don't recall seeing this check.*
Q   *Did you ever have an Irwin O'Brien account in any other brokerage house?*

A *No.*

Q *Any other business transactions with O'Brien?*

A *Would you call making deposits for him in his bank business?*

Q *Did you?*

A *Yes.*

Q *How many times?*

A *I don't recall.*

Q *(Showing bank book) Is this your deposit?*

A *Yes. This might explain the check you showed me because this shows deposit check No. 102.*

Q *Don't you know if it is?*

A *I'm not positive. It might be and it also might be my "P" on it. I might have thought I was making a deposit for myself and then realized it was not my account.*

Q *Didn't you know this was his paycheck?*

A *I paid no attention to the check. I cashed checks for lots of people.*

Q *Irwin O'Brien's account was opened with a check for $250 drawn at the Chelsea Bank. Was it yours?*

A *I don't recall. I am not the only depositor at the Chelsea Bank.*

Q *Is Davis your legal name?*

A *No.*

Q *Why do you use that name?*

A *I have used many names.*

Q *Were you ever married?*

A *No, but I've told a lot of people that I was divorced or separated.*

Q *Did O'Brien meet anyone through you?*

A *No.*

Q *Did you entertain people?*

A *Not when he was visiting me.*

Q *Didn't you know that you were wanted for the investigation?*

A *No, except what I read in the newspapers.*

Q *How long were you in Florida?*

A *Three or four months.*

Q *Did you write O'Brien when you were coming back?*

A *I might have.*

Q *What name were you known by, Polly or Pearl?*

A *Both.*

Q *Do you know Mr. Director?*

A *No. Who is he?*

Q *He spoke to you a few weeks ago on the street.*

A *I meet a lot of people and don't remember their names.*

Q *Mr. Director was here and told us that you once called police headquarters to remove cops from the premises.*

A *I don't recall that.*

Q *Do you know the number Spring 3100?*

A *Yes, police headquarters.*

Q *How did you know that?*

A *Saw it in the book.*

Q *Did you look for it?*

A *Any child knows Spring 3100.*

Q *Didn't you call a Mr. Johnny to remove cops?*

A *No.*

Q *Who do you know at headquarters?*

A *Nobody.*

Shortly after being linked with me, Irwin was charged with "unprofessional association" and the headlines blared that SKIDS AWAITING VICE BLUECOAT. But my answers to Cooper and Irwin's testimony in court were all of a piece. We both of us had stuck to our stories, and I felt sure everything would be all right if only Irwin would keep his head.

One of the persons called in to testify was a customer's man (hereinafter designated as Zilch), who had handled one of my brokerage accounts. He was fully aware that the account which so interested the investigators belonged to Irwin and that I knew Irwin was a cop. However, when Zilch was questioned, he denied ever knowing O'Brien, and said that the account, to the best of his knowledge, was mine. This was a big thing for Zilch to do—perjuring himself—but he was under considerable obligation to me. During the months I had been away, he had used the equity in my account for his own personal investments without even a power of attorney. Of course I had no idea what he was up to as no monthly statements were forwarded while I was lying low, and when I returned the damage had been done. But before I could take any action against Zilch, I found myself neck-deep in the Seabury investigation. As it turned out, I was glad there had been no time to prosecute him, for Zilch's testimony helped build up a defense for Irwin and myself that could not be broken down by the investigators.

At long last, Cooper and the others admitted defeat, and Irwin and I were released from further questioning. In fairness to Mr. Cooper, he was merely doing his duty and afforded to me every courtesy under the circumstances.

Needless to state, I was glad to be rid of everything connected with the Seabury investigation, but it was one of those Pyrrhic victories. Emotionally, physically and financially I was on the ropes. Pal Zilch's fast-and-loose operations with my brokerage account, coupled with what I had lost in the crash, had all but cleaned me out, and on top of that there was the little matter of Mr. Jayess, my attorney, whose fee now had risen to five thousand dollars. If I refused to pay it, I felt he would double-cross me and spill some of the things I had told him about the politicians, racketeers and vice squad men with whom I'd had dealings. So there was nothing I could do but give Mr. Jayess a down payment and promise him the rest when I got back in business. This was all right with him, he said, and then added, "Oh, by the way, don't tell George what I'm charging you." George was the politician who had recommended Jayess to me, and I didn't need a knock on the head to know that a little fee-splitting was going on, with George soon due for some short-changing. What a charming character, Mr. "Honest John" Jayess!

Counting my blessings (in the absence of anything else to count), I could say that at least I had not been called to appear at any public hearings, I had protected my friends, and a number of things which might have been very embarrassing had not been touched on by Cooper and the others. But then, just as I was beginning to sit back and relax, Irwin O'Brien stuck his neck in the noose. I almost blew my top when I learned he had offered to be a character witness for one of the fourteen lawyers who were facing disbarment.

This was what Irving Ben Cooper was waiting for—a chance to take another crack at Irwin—and this time Cooper had it all his own way. One newspaper account said:

Called as a witness for the defense of William J. McAuliffe, Patrolman Irwin O'Brien, former member of the Vice Squad, was forced to admit in the face of documentary evidence, that he was, in 1929, virtually in business partnership with Polly Adler, notorious procuress and proprietor of disorderly houses.

In a cross-examination of an hour and a half, O'Brien confirmed documentary evidence showing that Polly Adler frequently deposited from $100 to $500 to his credit in his bank accounts, that she carried brokerage accounts in his name and that over a period of less than three months he deposited checks amounting to $2,050 drawn by Polly Adler against her account in one bank to his credit in another bank, and subsequently withdrew the greater part of the amount to deposit it to his credit in a savings account in Brooklyn.

O'Brien was called to testify in connection with the examination of women he had arrested on prostitution charges. As his direct examination was concluded, Irving Ben Cooper, whose presence in the courtroom had not been noted, got up and asked permission to cross-examine the witness. Mr. Cooper had a briefcase full of documents and photostatic copies of checks and letters, which he proceeded to arrange on the desk.

O'Brien was completely flabbergasted when Cooper, with the permission of the referee, began to ask him about Polly Adler.

"When did you first meet Polly Adler?"

"About two years ago," O'Brien replied after some hesitation. "I was introduced to her in a cabaret."

O'Brien admitted that they became quite friendly, and he was a frequent visitor at her two apartments, one at Sixty-Ninth and Columbus Avenue, the other at Seventy-Seventh and Amsterdam Avenue.

"Would you say you called upon her fifty times in all?"

"I don't recall," replied the witness.

O'Brien appeared amazed when Cooper asked him if he did not know of the Adler woman's notorious reputation. "Don't you know she's been arrested fourteen times?"

"No," said O'Brien.

Mr. Cooper returned to the relations between O'Brien and Polly Adler. O'Brien admitted that they were of a business nature. Confronted with a photostatic record taken from the accounts of a brokerage house, he said he bought fifteen shares of Anaconda Copper for her account on one occasion. Mr. Cooper then showed photostatic copies of letters, in what the policeman admitted was Polly Adler's handwriting, which bore his signature. They related to stock market transactions. O'Brien admitted that in the summer of 1929 he had an account in a branch of the Irving Trust Company and Polly Adler in a branch of the Chelsea Bank. He admitted the trail of checks drawn by Polly Adler on her account which were deposited to his credit in the Irving Trust Company. She turned over to him $2,050 of which he withdrew and put into a savings account $1,950.

In the face of these admissions it wasn't long until the headlines read: PURE POLICE PAL OF POLLY FIRED OFF FORCE, but it was through my protection, and constant denials, that he was saved from going to jail. No one—I repeat *no one*—went to jail because of anything I said during the Seabury investigation. Although I stuck my neck out, I kept my mouth shut.

III

To hear me tell it, you would think the whole Seabury investigation centered about Polly Adler, but of course I represented just one small angle—or maybe I should say blind alley—which had to be explored. Although I was called in again once or twice for questioning and did not receive my final subpoena till as late as October 23, 1931, my real connection with the inquiry ended in June. However, it was not until the following May that the investigation reached its climax in the duel between Judge Seabury and Mayor Walker, with the Judge winning hands down. Yet even though, according to the New York *Post*, "from a standpoint of real intelligence Walker scored a failure so deep as to make one's flesh crawl," women pelted him with roses as he stepped from the stand, and when he was introduced at a rally that night as "the best-loved man in the city," the crowd cheered him to the echo. Maybe he wasn't the world's best mayor, but he was a wonderful guy, and to the day of his death Jimmy Walker kept his hold on the hearts of New Yorkers.

Whatever else it may have accomplished, ironically enough, the Seabury investigation turned New York into a wide-open town. While the guardians of the law were busy answering questions, the law-breakers had a holiday, and they proceeded to make the most of it. Because of the odium attached to the name of the Vice Squad, many plain-clothes men begged to be put in uniform and allowed to pound a beat, and every cop on the force had to watch his step. In the old days, a policeman's unsupported word had been enough to damn a prostitute. The officer had only to stage a raid, bring in the girl, and write on the "green sheet" what suited him. The charge could be changed later if a bribe had softened him up. But now, after the revelations of the extortion victims, this vicious abuse no longer was tolerated.

Another reform instituted, of which I heartily approved, was the ordinance requiring a prostitute to undergo an examination for venereal disease before she could be released on bail. Treatment was mandatory for a diseased girl even if she should be found innocent of the prostitution charge. If she were found guilty, the probation officer would compile a full report for the judge so that sentence could be passed on the basis of former arrests and past history as well as the present law violation. A girl with a long record could receive up to two years, while a first offender might get off with a suspended sentence.

It could hardly have been what the reformers and citizens' committees and legislators had hoped to accomplish, but I found when I got back in business that the Seabury investigation had sure as hell made *my* life easier. The police no longer were a headache; there was no more kowtowing to double-crossing Vice Squad men, no more hundred-dollar handshakes, no more phony raids to up the month's quota. In fact, thanks to Judge Seabury and his not-very-merry men, I was able to operate for three years without breaking a lease.

Chapter 7

A Boy Has Never Wept

A good many things go around in the dark
besides Santa Claus.

Herbert C. Hoover in an address to the
John Marshall Republican Club

I

On July 1, 1931 the new edition of the Ziegfeld Follies
opened at the Ziegfeld Theater with all the fuss and feathers
and spectacular glitter so dear to the heart of the great Flo.
Echoing the to-hell-with-the-cost mood of the Twenties, like
all the previous Follies, it featured sumptuous girls in sumptuous settings, and for those with the urge to ignore reality
it provided the comforting illusion that nothing really had
changed. America was still The Land of Plenty More Where
That Came From.

However, current happenings were not entirely over-
looked, and such diverse topics of the day as life in Hollywood, the Seabury investigation and Al Capone's income-tax
difficulties all were neatly incorporated in the comedy hit of
the evening, a Mark Hellinger sketch inspired by the current
best-seller, *Grand Hotel.* Burlesquing the roles which later

were to be played on the screen by Lionel and John Barry-more and Greta Garbo, Jack Pearl appeared as the harassed magnate, "Cecil B. Goldwarner," my old friend Harry Rich-man as the dashing hero, "Baron Al Capone," and Helen Morgan as the moody but glamorous Russian ballerina, "Mademoiselle Polly Adlervitch."

If the Follies had opened just two weeks sooner, at least half the description of "Polly Adlervitch" would have been a hundred per cent accurate. As of June fifteenth, I was cer-tainly moody—a state which is not uncommon among those who are broke and at loose ends.

After the Seabury ordeal I wanted more than anything to get back in business again. Not only was it imperative for financial reasons, but I needed something to put my mind to —I had been out of touch with my world too long. I had been concerned only with my own personal problems, and I desperately needed people and purposeful objective activity to snap me out of the slough of despondency and self-pity in which I was wallowing. But my name still kept cropping up in the papers, and I felt it was too soon to risk opening a house. True, the town was wide open, and it nearly drove me crazy to have to stay on the side lines while all the other madams were having themselves a field day. But I knew that if, for any reason, there was a crackdown on the sin dives and a scapegoat was needed, I was a cinch to be it.

The ideal solution would have been to take a good long sea voyage until the Seabury publicity cooled off, but the state of my finances was such that even a one-way ferry ticket to Weehawken would have unbalanced the budget. Since I couldn't afford to patronize my usual haunts, I killed the days going to movies until my funds got too low even for that. After all my years of complaining about the constant ring-ing of the telephone, I now found myself staring at the instrument, trying to hypnotize it into giving one little jingle. In my self-pitying mood, I thought that everyone had forgotten me. I didn't realize that people aren't mind readers, and that my customers and girls were only waiting for me to sound the "All Clear."

One day, not knowing what else to do with myself, I went for a stroll in Central Park. I had a whole great big dime to spend on lunch, and I made the mistake of blowing it on a bag of peanuts—a mistake because in a trice it seemed that all the squirrels on Manhattan had congregated around my bench and were expecting to share my meal. Hungry as I was —I had been living mostly on bread and milk—it was impossible to go on munching away under that battery of eyes. "I'm the one who needs the handout," I told them, "but okay, you little bullies, come and get it." Which they promptly proceeded to do. In fact, one enterprising little fellow came up and took the goobers right out of my hand. It gave me a pang to see my rations disappearing so fast, but it was nice to be popular again.

While I was feeding my new pals, I heard my name spoken and looked up to see a man I finally placed as being a card-sharp who used to ply his trade on cruise ships. He was small time even in that small-time profession, and a year ago would not have dared even to speak to me, but now he plunked himself down on the bench and proceeded to gloat over my misfortunes, pointing out my mistakes and briefing me in detail on how cleverly *he* would have managed. He was a typical Broadway wiseacre, and I looked at him with contempt, not bothering to reply.

"You're finished in New York, Polly," was his parting shot as I got up and started to walk away. "You'll never be able to make another nickel here."

His words were like a slap in the face, but I should have

thanked him. I was roused out of my flabby despondency, and the old fighting spirit came surging back. *Finished, am I? I'll show that cheap little punk if Polly Adler's through before she's ready to be through!* . . . Fuming, I burned up the sidewalk on the way back to the apartment, shucked off my hat and gloves, grabbed for the telephone and dialed the first number that came in my mind.

Archie L.'s cordial greeting was just the tonic I needed. "Say, Polly, this is great! I've been trying to locate you. I have a little entertainment problem. There's a very important man coming up to my place tonight, and there'll be five or six others with him. How about it? Can you supply the talent? And can you come along too? My guest, Mr. Brown, said he'd like to meet you, and I'm sure you'll find him a profitable contact."

I hung up feeling that my luck had changed. Archie L. owned a chain of theaters, and I was certain his guests would be Hollywood big shots. When I began phoning my most beautiful girls, in every case it was the same story: "Polly! Where have you been? I've been waiting and waiting for you to call—it's just not the same working for anybody else. . . . You *know* I want to come back with you. . . . Tonight? Why, sure, Polly! I'll be there with bells on."

I was not in the habit of accompanying my girls on dates, but I felt that my first night back in business was a special occasion. The idea of a party with Hollywood people suited my mood exactly. I was starved for a little fun and excitement, and I always loved hearing inside stories about life behind the celluloid curtain. Also, the filmland tycoons were generous spenders—which, at this stage of the game, seemed to me an especially lovable characteristic.

However, when we were introduced to Archie's guests, there was no name that I recognized, and if they were from Hollywood, they certainly were not in native costume. The guest of honor, Mr. Brown, wore a gray business suit that hung about him loosely and I thought to myself he was never going to give Adolph Menjou a contest for best-dressed honors. He struck me as being rather nondescript-looking, not my idea at all of anybody important. He was of medium height, thin and sallow-faced, and his manner was abrupt and rather jumpy.

I pride myself on being able to place people pretty quickly, but Mr. Brown had me baffled. After listening to him for a while I thought he talked like a racket man, but what would Archie be doing mixed up with a racketeer? To add to the confusion, although I corrected him several times, he kept addressing me as "Peggy."

"Aren't you a good friend of Vincent Coll's, Peggy?" he said at one point.

I said I didn't know anyone by that name, but he insisted that of course I did. "I happen to know Coll sells you your liquor, Peggy," he said, "and he's shaken you down several times."

Suddenly it dawned on me that he had his madams mixed up. "Mr. Brown, I'm not Peggy Wild. I'm Polly Adler—the Polly who's been glorifying the Seabury investigation."

To my surprise he looked disappointed. For a moment he stared into his highball glass glumly, but just when I was beginning to feel a little miffed he smiled and said he was glad to meet me. "I've been reading about you, Polly. You're aces in my book."

Before long, Archie called me to the kitchen to help him set up some drinks. In quest of fresh glasses I opened a closet door—and almost keeled over. I knew Archie went duck-hunting every now and then, but you don't hunt ducks with tommy-guns, and the interior of that closet looked like an arsenal.

Archie was watching me, a big grin on his face. "What's the matter, Poll?" he said. "You're kind of pale."

"Are you in a new business? What are you doing with all these shooting irons?"

"No kidding, don't you know who those men are out there?"

I shook my head slowly, but I had a sinking feeling.

"Well," he said, "better not mention it to your girls, but that's Dutch Schultz and his outfit. You've been chinning with the Dutchman himself."

I felt like a child who'd just found out the "nice doggy" he'd been patting was a man-eating tiger. Ever since the early Twenties when he had become entrenched as a bootleg power, Dutch had been building up his underworld empire and was now said to control the slot-machine, bail-bond and policy rackets, among others. He was perhaps the most power-ful and prominent of the New York gang leaders, and to maintain him in that position his boys were constantly making use of such paraphernalia as was now parked in Archie's closet.

I remembered that one time a policeman friend, wanting to repay a favor, had offered to introduce me to Dutch. "He's a good spender," the cop had said, but I had no wish to have him spending in my house. I was anxious to avoid even the most casual association with any of the ranking public enemies. In my book mixing up in that league was a shortcut to a Chamber of Rest at Frank Campbell's. Only a couple of days before, I had read that one of the Schultz gang, Daniel Iamascia, had been shot down leaving Dutch's hideout. It was believed that Dutch himself was the target and that the killers were members of the Coll gang.

When I reported that "Mr. Brown" had asked if I were a friend of Coll's, Archie explained that Coll—better known as "Mad Dog"—had once been Schultz's trigger man, but a year or so before had quit to form a gang of his own. Since then, there had been open war between Schultz and Coll, not merely because Coll was trying to chisel in on the beer racket, but because he blamed Dutch for the killing of his brother, Pete. Apparently, Coll was in the habit of frequenting Peggy Wild's, and Dutch, thinking I was Peggy, had tried to pump me about him. However, Archie said that I had nothing to fear—that Dutch was not one of those bloodthirsty psychopaths who got gratification out of aimless violence or frightening innocent bystanders. He was more the businessman type of hoodlum.

When I went back to the living room, I tried to act normal, but I was as meek as a mouse and totally unable to be my usual gabby self. Now that I knew who these men were, all their actions seemed sinister and even though I knew their weapons were in the kitchen, every time a cork popped I jumped a foot. All I wanted to do was get out of there and get home, but it wasn't until six o'clock that the party broke up.

As I was thankfully starting for the door, "Mr. Brown" walked over and asked me for my telephone number. I stammered out an explanation about its being risky to have callers so soon after the Seabury fireworks, but Dutch brushed that off quickly.

"Don't worry," he said. "We'll handle it. . . . The number?"

There were two things I could do. I could give it to him or I could give it to him. I gave it to him.

At twelve that night my phone rang. There were no pre-liminaries. He simply said, "This is Mr. Brown. I'm coming up."

In less than five minutes he was at my door—he must have called from the corner drugstore, taking it for granted that he would not be refused admittance. Accompanying him was a tall, taciturn heavy-set man, who at once posted him-self in the foyer and stood there like a statue, his eyes glued on the door. His name, I later learned, was Lulu Rosenkrantz, and four years later he was to be shot down with Dutch in a Newark tavern.

Dutch asked me if I were alone. When I nodded, he said, "From now on, don't answer the phone or the doorbell." Then, turning to Lulu, "I'm okay here. Call for me about ten in the morning."

Without a word, Lulu left.

Dutch strolled into the living room to the couch. He bent over and removed his shoes and then leisurely lay back, fac-ing the door. He asked me for a drink.

While I fixed it and one for myself (which I may say I needed), he asked me about the Seabury investigation, what politicians I knew, and what sort of clientele I had. I refused to tell him the names of any of my customers but I tried to do it jokingly and politely so as not to anger him. "In my pro-fession," I said, "the higher you go, the more secrets you had to keep. And I'm known as a thirty-third degree mason —or maybe I should say thirty-third degree madam."

"I like a dame that keeps her mouth shut," Dutch said. "You got a lot of moxie, Poll." I had been calling him "Mr. Brown." Now he jerked his head toward me and said, "You can cut out calling me Mr. Brown. I'm Dutch Schultz." And then, watching me narrowly, "You know, at this moment Vincent Coll would part with fifty grand if he could lay hands on me."

A chill went over me. I swallowed a couple of times and finally managed to say, "What good would fifty thousand do me if I'm sitting on the bottom of the East River in a hunk of cement?"

He smiled slightly. "I'm not worried about you, Polly. I looked you up—you're thumbs up with the mob." He stretched and yawned. "From now on you'll be seeing a lot of me. You better get a larger place."

I knew an order when I heard one, but there was the little question of what to use for money. "I want to oblige you in every way," I said, "but I got flattened in the market crash, and since the investigation started I haven't been taking anything in."

He pulled a rubber band off a thick roll of bills and gave me a thousand dollars. "Here's a start. If you run into any trouble getting an apartment, let me know. I got plenty of connections with apartment-house owners."

Dutch was not the easiest man in the world to converse with. Every time the elevator stopped or there were sounds in the hall, he would leap to his feet. I pretended not to notice this and would keep on talking. But my frigidaire was unusually noisy, and he kept looking toward the kitchen. "Who's in there?" he demanded. I assured him again and again that we were alone, and begged him to relax. He was making me even more jittery than he was. Finally about five A.M. he announced that he was going to get some sleep, and without so much as an if-you-please strolled into my only bedroom.

I settled down on the couch, worn out, but sleep would not come. I found myself listening to every little noise, listening for Mad Dog Coll who would pay fifty thousand dollars to kill the man in my bedroom. . . . I realized this was just the first of many such nights. By taking Dutch's money I was on the way out of my financial hole, but in return I had put myself in bondage—from now on my life would be ruled by fear.

Nevertheless, in second-guessing the events of the past two days, I couldn't help smiling. If I hadn't let those squirrels con me out of my peanuts, I'd not have encountered the cardsharp. And if I hadn't had to listen to his spiel, I'd not have called Archie L. And if I hadn't called Archie—well, anyway, I would certainly think twice before I ever again fed a squirrel!

Now that the depression was on its way in, there were plenty of expensive apartments to be had at a reasonable rental, and I leased a furnished one on West Eighty-third Street. It was just as well that I hadn't let any grass grow under my feet. That evening Dutch came up again and brought with him two members of his gang whom I had met at Archie's party, Bo Weinberg and Swede Stockholm. Bo was a big dark-haired fellow, about forty years old. He was the brains of the outfit, and though his habitual expression was blank and stolid, he never missed a trick. Swede was pleasant and well-mannered and much easier to be around than Bo or Lulu. There was a gentleness and a boyishness about him which made him far less frightening than the silent Bo.

Dutch immediately inquired if I'd had any luck apartment hunting, and when I told him everything was arranged, he was very pleased. "I told you this gal was okay," he said to Bo. "I think we ought to have a little celebration. Polly, you're supposed to be the Ziegfeld of your profession—show us what you can do. And let's have some champagne." As I went to call the girls, he warned me that I wasn't to reveal his identity or that of any of the gang. When anyone was around, he said, I was to call him Pop.

Right after that I got a bad scare. I went out to the kitchen and the maid was sitting there reading a copy of *Time,* which she left open on the table when she went to ice the champagne. I glanced down and found myself looking at a picture of Dutch. Quickly I tore out the page and at the first opportunity flushed it down the toilet. But I noted what issue it was—June twenty-ninth—and the next day got a copy and read it when I was alone. The story was about Dutch and other leading racket men such as Owney Madden, Larry Fay, Waxey Gordon and Ciro Terranova, and told about Dutch's questioning in connection with the recent shooting of Iamascia. It said how nervous he was, practically fainting, when the cops took him in, but of course it wasn't the cops he was afraid of—it was Coll. Later, I learned from one of the mob that Dutch had seen the story and had pointed out that they had misspelled his real name, which was Arthur Flegenheimer. (But I don't think he ever wrote a letter to the editor about it.)

The "celebration" party lasted until eight in the morning, and without any sleep I set out to make arrangements to move into my new quarters. As I was not certain how much of my time Dutch and his retinue would require, I did not give my new address to any of my friends or customers. It was just as well. The apartment became the gang's headquarters, and it was like Grand Central Station, with mobsters coming and going at all hours. But neither the maids nor I were allowed to open the door for anyone until they had been okayed by Lulu and Mac, Dutch's bodyguards, who first would inspect the caller through the "interviewer" which I had especially installed.

Dutch usually received in my bedroom, where he lay propped up in the canopied bed, like Louis XIV receiving at a levee. I dared not interrupt him when a conference was in progress—not, of course, that I wanted to. As much as possible I stayed clear of that room and if I had to go in, I knocked and waited for permission, and then passed in and out as quickly as possible. My life depended on not being the recipient of confidences, even inadvertently. Only if I knew nothing and avoided hearing anything could I expect to survive.

Dutch was seldom fully dressed, and he would stay awake most of the night reading. He seemed to fear the darkness. He slept no more than four or five hours, and would instruct the maid the preceding evening to serve his breakfast in bed at noon. It was always the same menu—hot water with lemon juice, a large glass of grapefruit juice, two eggs, sunny side up, toast, marmalade and black coffee. He would smoke incessantly, strewing cigarette butts all over my rug.

He was certainly not neat in his habits around the house or in his personal appearance—his clothes were always badly in need of pressing—yet he was very clean about his person. Daily, around seven in the evening, he would take a tub bath. He always insisted that I be in the bathroom during this ritual to scrub his back. That was an excuse—he feared being left alone. While I was scrubbing, he would tell me how many to expect for dinner. It was always ordered for eight thirty, but we seldom sat down to eat before midnight, much to the displeasure of my maids and the girls.

Many things about Dutch got on my nerves, but I tried to hold on to my self-control. He was hardly the man to whom

complaints could be made. It is said that familiarity breeds
contempt, but I never lost my fear of Dutch Schultz. He was
not the gangster prototype the movies have shown the world.
He didn't carry a gun, and he never stood around and acted
sinister. He was businesslike, cold and incisive, colorless and
—deadly.

However, Dutch did have some sense of humor, and I
think he kept around the chap they called Abadaba because
he was funny, as much as for anything else. Abadaba—otherwise known as Otto Berman or Beiderman—was a mathematical wizard, who had some connection with the numbers
racket. I have since read that he advised about placing last-
minute bets on the pari-mutuel machines so that the odds
would change and a heavily played number would not pay
off. Anyway, Abadaba referred to himself as a "numerolo-
gist." He was short, fair, nearly bald and rather fat, and had
a droll way of talking. Since he amused "The King," like
the court jester of old, he got away with more than the
others—at least so long as he was in favor. He was another
who was killed with Dutch on that October night in 1935.

One morning when Dutch was at my place, there was a
sharp ringing of the doorbell, followed by a loud tapping at
the outer door. After a quick look, Lulu Rosenkrantz hurriedly opened up to admit a small, dapper fellow who was
escorted at once to the bedroom where the Dutchman was
sleeping.

The newcomer was with Dutch for several hours, during
which time there was much coming and going of various
members of the mob, and finally I was sent for. "Polly," said
Dutch, "this is Dixie Davis, my mouthpiece, and from now
on he's to be yours. He's on his way to the big time, and I
trust him."

I looked over my new lawyer without saying anything. At

least, I thought bitterly, he couldn't be any worse than Mr. Jayess, who was continuing to hound me even though I was paying off my debt as fast as I could.

"Dixie will be back this evening with six friends," Dutch went on, "and I'm letting you know in plenty of time to prepare a very special dinner with all the trimmings. Caviar and champagne and girls, all the best—get it?"

I felt exactly like the hired help, as if I should bow my head and curtsey, but I went out to give the necessary orders. A short time later, when Dixie Davis had gone, Dutch sent for me again. Now all his expansiveness had vanished. He was pacing up and down the room and appeared to be very nervous.

He told me that he had just learned of the kidnaping of Big Frenchy De Mange by Mad Dog Coll. Big Frenchy was Owney Madden's righthand man and Coll was holding him for thirty thousand dollars' ransom. "There'll be no safety for any of us while that crazy mick is around," said Dutch. He stopped his pacing back and forth and stood in front of me. His eyes narrowed and his voice became low and confidential.

"You know the Asterisk Club on Forty-fourth Street, Polly?"

I nodded.

"I'm told it's a closed-door club, but that you know the owner and can get in. Is that true?"

I nodded again.

"Good," he said. "That's where Coll's been hanging out. I want you to go there and take some of the boys with you. I'll let you know when."

It was as if he'd told me he would let me know what day I'd die. I knew that if I took any of Schultz's gang to the Asterisk, even if I survived the gunplay there, I would be rubbed out later the way witnesses always were. Fresh in my mind were the stories about the shooting at the Hotsy-Totsy Club the night Legs Diamond got drunk and knocked off a couple of guests. There were several witnesses including a chap named Hymie, Legs' own man, yet in a matter of days Hymie and the others were dead, and when Legs surrendered to the cops there was no one left to testify against him.

No matter how you looked at it, I was a candidate for a coffin and I decided then and there that I would refuse to have any part of this enterprise. If Dutch chose to pay off my mutiny with a bullet, I wouldn't have lost anything—I was sure of one anyway.

Dutch must have seen something of what I was feeling in my expression for his voice became hard. "Don't talk about this to anyone. Especially Bo."

I don't know why he specified Bo. Bo was his most trusted lieutenant and strategic adviser. He treated him better than the others and seemed to respect him. Could it be that he didn't trust Bo so much after all? Was he afraid he might tip off the Coll mob? Or did he think that Bo would sneer at him for hiding behind my skirts, for using a woman to protect him and do the work he dared not do himself? All the time I was getting the house ready for the evening's party, I mulled over this remark—maybe because I preferred to think about anything rather than my own position. I kept getting a picture of myself walking into the Asterisk Club with a gun-happy hoodlum behind me and an even crazier one in front of me. My only hope was that Dutch would abandon the plan. Meanwhile all I could do was let matters ride and pray there would be no necessity for me to defy him.

Promptly at seven, Davis returned with six others, including Ciro Terranova, called the "Artichoke King" because he levied tribute from the produce markets. Everyone drank a lot, including Dutch, which surprised me; it was the first time I had ever seen him really laying into the booze. Dixie and the others left about five A.M., but Dutch ordered some more champagne sent into his room and went in there with one of my girls, Ruth.

A little later Bo and Swede and I were having coffee in the kitchen when we heard terrifying screams coming from the bedroom. Bo and Swede tried to hold me back, saying that Dutch was in a nasty mood, but I tore myself away from them and broke into the room. Dutch was sitting on the side of the bed, trying to ward off a blow from a half-empty champagne bottle which Ruth was preparing to bring down on his skull. I grabbed her by the arm and pushed her out the door. Dutch looked like a madman, his eyes narrowed to pin points. Murder was on his face. I tried to calm him down with flattery, telling him he was too important a man to let himself get upset by a stupid little tart. But he just sat there repeating over and over, "That dirty bitch! That dirty bitch!"

Suddenly he leapt up and stormed out of the room, and ran through the apartment looking for Ruth. Bo told him she had gone home though he knew she was hiding in the maid's room. Frustrated, Dutch turned on me. "Polly, see to it that that dirty bastard doesn't make a quarter with you or anyone else in this town!"

I made the stupid mistake of saying I had no jurisdiction over anyone in New York, and he slugged me hard across the face, calling me a couple of names. I held back the tears and stood still, just looking at him, until finally with an oath he went slamming into the bedroom and locked the door.

I went to see how Ruth was, and what had happened. She

explained that Dutch had kicked her in the stomach for refusing to hand him a glass of champagne which was nearer him than her. She had thrown a glass at him, and would have conked him with the bottle if I had not stepped in. She was still furious. I gave Ruth some money and told her she must leave. She could not understand me; once I would have backed her up and thrown the customer out of the house. But Ruth did not know, nor did any of the other girls, that "Pop" was Dutch Schultz.

The following day I got an apology from my star boarder. It didn't cure my black eye.

II

Although Dutch never again brought up the subject of my fingering Coll for him, I lived in terror that he would do so, and my heart would nearly stop every time Coll's name came into the conversation. This was fairly often for, in that last summer of his short life, the baby-faced killer had instituted a reign of terror which appalled even hardened gangsters.

Shortly after the kidnaping of Big Frenchy, Coll was responsible for a murder which so horrified the city that gang leaders as well as the police were out to get him. At six thirty P.M. on July twenty-eighth a carload of Coll's men were touring the Upper East Side on the hunt, it was said, for Joey Rao, a member of the Harlem mob, allied to Dutch Schultz. As on all fine summer evenings the stoops were crowded with people getting the air, and the streets and sidewalks were filled with kids playing tag and hopscotch and stickball. But that didn't slow up the killers. When they spotted a man whom they thought was Rao, they blazed away with sawed-off shotguns and a machine gun. Their intended victim escaped, but five-year-old Michael Vengalli was killed, and four other young children were wounded.

Naturally, there was a great hue-and-cry, and some months later two members of the Coll gang, Dominic Odierno and Frank Giordano, were convicted of the murder and eventually went to the chair. However, Coll himself was acquitted when his attorney, Samuel Liebowitz, proved that George Brecht, on whose identification of Coll the state's case depended, was a jailbird, a "professional witness" and a perjurer.

But Coll was not taken into custody until toward the end of the year. Meanwhile, he was still on the loose, and warfare between him and Dutch continued with unabated vigor. In October, when a Schultz man named Mullins was killed, the newspapers said that the score in killings stood eight to four, with Coll in the lead.

I could almost sense when a murder was to take place. At such times the important mobsters in the outfit would hang around my apartment and wait until the job was completed by the underlings. I would have had to be deaf and blind not to know something was cooking. Lulu would be kept busy, running in and out buying different editions of the papers, which the mob would scan eagerly and then toss aside, until my apartment looked like one big wastepaper basket. Usually, if it was possible, I would sneak away on such occasions. I felt it was a good time to be someplace else. I was always afraid that if I hung around someone might let something slip in my hearing, and my only protection was ignorance.

On one such night, as I was on my way out, the elevator man handed me a note, saying he had been tipped a buck to deliver it personally. The note, which was unsigned, read: "It's urgent that you meet me at Papa Tony's at midnight."

Papa Tony's was the famous restaurant, run by Tony Soma, which was for so long the favorite hangout of writers and actors and other celebrities. The fact that this was the designated rendezvous reassured me, and I decided I would keep the date.

Outside the newsboys were calling, "Extra! Extra! Slaying in the Bronx!" I bought a paper, and diving into the nearest speak, ordered a Scotch and drank it off before I could nerve myself to read the headlines. It was even worse than I had expected—two killed and three wounded, and one of the dead and two of the wounded were innocent bystanders.

I knew this would call for retaliation, and somewhere in New York or New Jersey at that very moment men were gathering together laying plans to get even. Whether the Schultz gang had done the killing or not, the Coll men would be on the warpath, and it was quite in the cards that my apartment would become the scene of just such a slaughter as had occurred in the Bronx. What got me down more than anything was the thought that I was responsible for the girls and the maids being in jeopardy. I, at least, knew what risks I was running, but they were completely in the dark as to the identity of our customers. Yet there was no way I could warn them. I simply could not rely on them to keep their mouths shut, even though their own safety depended on it.

At a quarter of twelve I went over to Tony's where Mark Hellinger met me at the door. He said that he had sent the note, and took me to a table toward the back where we could have some privacy. I had not spoken with Mark since a night I had gone to the Follies to see his sketch about "Polly Adlervitch." He had asked then if I minded the use of my name, and I said to the contrary that was the kind of publicity I liked, and had kiddingly suggested that he ask Flo

Ziegfeld to put my phone number in the program too. But there was nothing humorous in the atmosphere tonight. As a well-known and respected newspaperman, Mark had many sources of information, and I knew I could bank on what he told me.

"Polly," he said, "I've been wanting to have a word with you for some time. You know I've always liked you as a person and admired you for your honesty and the way you've conducted your business. But I understand that lately you've surrounded yourself with some people who may get you in a lot of trouble."

"Believe me, Mark," I said, "I realize the danger I'm in— but I don't know how to keep these people out. I read the papers tonight—I know what's coming—but what can I do?" I tried to smile. "Who knows? Maybe tomorrow there'll be headlines about me pushing up daisies."

"Don't talk that way," said Mark sharply. "Don't you think that if this certain person knew it was pretty common knowledge he was hanging out at your place, he might consider it advisable to go elsewhere? Particularly now?"

What Mark said made a lot of sense. If it was no longer a secret that my apartment was the gang's hideout, then maybe I could persuade Dutch to move along. Even if he had no thought for the safety of the girls and the maids and me, he did attach considerable value to his own hide—and if newspapermen could learn where he was hanging out, then so could Mad Dog Coll.

I thanked Mark warmly for his interest and his advice, but it took guts to speak to His Lordship, the Dutchman—more, I am frank to admit, than I possessed. But I thought maybe I could acquire "Dutch courage" by a little judicious drinking, so I made the rounds of the bars until closing time. By then I was thoroughly plastered—so plastered that I had completely forgotten Dutch's order never to drink when he was around. He was afraid, of course, that I might get careless and talk too freely.

When finally I stood in front of my door I was weaving and had trouble finding the keyhole. I tapped lightly three times, the usual signal, and the door was whipped open with such unexpected speed that I almost fell forward on my face. There, lowering at me, stood Dutch with Bo right behind him. They grabbed me and yanked me into the kitchen.

Dutch said, "Where you been?"

I looked at him defiantly. "Out."

"Out where?"

"Just out."

"I notice you don't believe in taking orders. I thought I told you not to drink. . . . Well, answer me! Didn't I?"

Silence on my part. My new-found courage was all gone.

"Well, maybe this'll teach you a lesson, you so-and-so!" And his fist came down with a thump on top of my head.

I fell backward into the maid's room. Dutch followed to kick me, but Bo grabbed him and led him into the living room. The maid helped me to my feet and into a chair, and we huddled there together until we heard Dutch and his pals leave. Then she helped me into my room. By this time the liquor was wearing off, and the throbbing in my head became more severe. I felt so humiliated and ashamed I started to cry. "Did you see tonight's papers?" I sobbed, throwing caution to the winds.

"No, Miss Polly," said the maid. "They kept me on the jump." And then, trying to console me with how much money they'd spent, "They ran up a real big bill. They seemed in quite a gay spending mood."

I told her what they were celebrating. I couldn't hold in any longer, I was on the verge of hysteria. The liquor and the blow on the head had snapped my self-control and I had to release all the fear and misery that was locked up inside me. "You know why I drank tonight?" I told her. "To get up nerve to ask Dutch not to patronize me any more. But you saw how far I got with it!" Finally, she persuaded me to lie down. But when she turned out the light and left me, I rose up and looked out the window, wondering if Coll's mob already was staked out around the apartment building.

When a couple of weeks passed and Dutch did not come around again, I decided to move. Not, of course, that I could get away from him if he wanted to find me, but the apartment had become distasteful to me, and I could not get over the feeling that the Coll men were watching all the comings and goings. So I found a new place on West Fifty-fourth and began to receive a number of my old customers again.

Although I had discharged my five-thousand-dollar debt to Mr. Jayess, that didn't mean he was off my neck. He began hitting me up for small loans, and I didn't dare refuse him. I knew I wouldn't get a penny of my money back, even when he said he was making "investments" for me, but, so long as I was in business, I had to let him go on blackmailing me. Nevertheless, I was finally beginning to regain a little peace of mind, when one night in mid-December the elevator boy announced that a gentleman giving his name as "Pop Brown" was calling.

Dutch was accompanied by Abadaba and five other henchmen, two of whom I had never met before. One was a swarthy, rather shy chap whom I knew only by the name of Shorty. He seemed somewhat overcome by the elegance of the apartment, and was not exactly what you would call a trusting soul. Later, when he went to bed, I asked him why he didn't remove his shoes. "Listen, Polly," he said in a voice that was incongruously soft and silky, "I got twenty grand in them shoes and I ain't takin' no chances."

The other newcomer was "Pretty" Amburg, and why he was nicknamed Pretty I will never know. He was short and skinny and shifty-eyed, and had a deserved reputation for wanton cruelty and vandalism. (Pretty murdered the King's English, yet once, trying to impress me with his background, he told me that his mother was a schoolteacher. If it's true, I wonder what she taught. Pretty and two other of her sons were famous hoodlums and ultimately met violent deaths.) Now he came swaggering into the living room and inspected the pictures and furnishings as if he were a connoisseur of fine arts. Probably, I thought, trying to decide which are the more expensive things, so they can be smashed first. After the terrible tales I had heard of this destructive creature, I hated having him in my house.

Dutch made no mention of the fact that I had moved, nor did he apologize for the beating he had given me. Instead he took me aside and gave me five hundred dollars. "Next week is Christmas," he said, "buy yourself a gift. I may not see you until after New Year's."

Since he appeared to be in such a good mood, I took the opportunity to mention my fear of Pretty Amburg. "Pop," I began (it pleased him when I called him that), "I've been told how Pretty and some of his pals have acted at Sadie the Chink's and Jenny the Factory's. I've been told they abuse the girls and wreck the houses—slash furniture, set fire to beds, break windows—and carry away whatever they want for souvenirs."

"Relax," said Dutch. "Pretty won't visit you unless he's with me."

"Thanks, Pop," I said, "but I wish you could get him to behave when he's at Sadie's and Jenny's too."

"What the hell!" he said irritably. "I'm not pimping for their joints." He gave me a suspicious look. "How come you're so interested what goes on in other houses?"

"Because I know how tough it is," I said, "when you've been pushed around for years by the cops to have to put up with a lot of rough stuff from your customers too. And a word from you could make all the difference."

"What's your real reason?"

"Jenny did me a favor once. There were some cops in her place, and she heard them say they were on their way to raid me. So she kidded them along, fed them drinks and stalled them until she could get word to me to shut down. It was the cops themselves told me how Jenny'd put one over."

"Yeah. Well," said Dutch, "Jenny's a big girl. She can take care of herself. . . . You better get some more of your kids in tonight, Polly. I've got some friends coming down in a while."

The friends, I later learned, were members of the Harlem mob and were not anybody you would have cared to encounter in a dark alley—or even on Broadway at high noon. But strange to say, although several cases of booze were opened in their honor and the drinks were "tall, cold and consecutive," the mugs couldn't have behaved more decorously if they'd been members of the Union Club whiling away a Sunday afternoon at the Reading Room in Newport.

Although I entertained other customers when Dutch was not around, it was a terrible strain not knowing when he would turn up, and I thought ceaselessly of ways to get rid of him. But I never dared ask him point-blank to take his patronage elsewhere. I kept hoping that circumstances might change and it would not be necessary for me to insult him.

I knew he would regard such a request as a deadly insult.

Gangsters in general have a very low opinion of prostitutes, and while Dutch respected me for the way I ran my business and kept my personal life to myself, still he shunned any real tie-up with the house. (I think this is why he refused to intervene to protect Jenny the Factory from Pretty Amburg.) A big-time gangster regards a "prostitution man"—that is, a man who makes his money through procuring, even indirectly—as the lowest thing there is. He will not even be seen talking to such a man for fear the taint will spread to his name. So I could be certain that Dutch would hardly take any suggestion from me to move along, with a pleasant smile. I was a madam, and he did not take orders or suggestions from such a person.

Fortunately, it never came to that. One night toward the end of January a Mr. Abe and three gentlemen were announced. Not recognizing the names, I said I'd see them downstairs. But first I dug out twenty-two thousand dollars belonging to Dutch, which I'd hidden in the bottom of a double boiler, and gave it to Swede.

"They could be cops or stick-up men," I said.

"Or worse," said Swede. "Take it easy."

Two men were waiting by the elevator. One was rather attractive, with hair so sleek it looked as though it had been polished. The other was chiefly distinguished by an enormous nose. Two other men were standing by the outside door, their hats tilted low over their eyes. A child could have spotted them as mobsters.

The attractive man asked if they could come up.

"I'm sorry," I said. "I don't receive strangers."

The man with the big nose spoke up. "We are very good friends of Peggy Wild's."

"Good," I said. "Go there. I assure you my place is no different."

There was a lot more sparring around, and finally I agreed to admit them if they returned with someone whom I knew. I would have agreed to anything to get rid of them. I was convinced those boys had something on their minds, and it wasn't sex.

Swede was waiting anxiously upstairs, and he listened carefully while I described the visitors and related the conversation. He went at once to report to Dutch, and a few minutes later both men came out of the bedroom wearing their hats and overcoats. Without a word the other boys got their hats and coats and fell in behind Dutch and Swede. I was asked no questions and no one made any comment. They didn't even say good-bye. They just went.

I never knew who my visitors were that night, but whoever they were, I'm grateful to them. I didn't see Dutch again for over a year.

Because Dutch and his men spent so much time at my house, and it was unavoidable that I see a lot of them, it might be supposed that I knew much more than I am telling —that I had the "real inside dope" about what was cooking in gangland. But, as I have pointed out, quite literally my life depended on neither seeing, nor hearing, nor speaking of any of the evil around me. Consequently, I have no idea what connection, if any, existed between Dutch's departure and the murder of Vincent Coll which occurred not long after, on February eighth. Everyone who read the papers knew that Coll had beaten the Harlem baby-slaying rap and was running wild again, and everyone who read Winchell's column knew that "Five planes brought dozens of machine-gun and gat-bearing hoodlums from Chicago to combat the town's Capone. Local banditti have made one hotel a virtual arsenal because Master Coll is giving them a headache." Six hours after the edition carrying this item hit the streets, Vincent Coll went into a drugstore in the Chelsea district to make a phone call. While he was in the phone booth three men came in, and while two of them stood guard the other poured fire into the phone booth until Coll's body toppled out.

The murder has never been officially solved, but it was believed to have been done by out-of-town killers. It was also believed that they had been hired by either Owney Madden (in revenge for Big Frenchy De Mange's kidnaping) or by Dutch. However, the police finally absolved Owney, and some years later, long after his chief's death, George Weinberg, one of Dutch's aides, named Dutch as the man who signed the order for Coll's execution.

Maybe so. But I only know what I read in the papers.

III

However, I had little time in those days to sit down with the papers. Strangely enough, the notoriety I had received during the Seabury investigation, instead of alienating my uppercrust clientele, acted as a magnet. It had made the nation "Polly-conscious" on a scale I had never dreamed of, and socialites and money people—not just New Yorkers but from all over—came flocking to my apartment to be entertained. And I'm not ashamed to admit it gave me quite a lift to find that the entertainment many came for was an evening of conversation with me! To sophisticates, at least, I was somebody you had to know to be in the swim, and they were legion who dined out on anecdotes about me and happenings at my house. Inevitably much of what they had to report was embroidered and exaggerated or even a hundred per cent fabricated, but, although I naturally resented some of the stories which made me sound like an illiterate or a degenerate, or both, still these unpaid publicity agents did help to boost business.

Four years before, when I had begun to get the play from the theatrical crowd and what was now coming to be called "café society," I had begun to receive women as my guests. But at first it was only those who were so rich or so famous or so intellectual or so uninhibited that they could go anywhere. Now, however, dropping in at my place had become the thing, and from this time on I was running what amounted to a coeducational bordello.

It might seem that entertaining this respectable clientele would enable me to catch my breath between the visitations of the mobsters, but actually it was quite as much of a strain, though of a different sort. I had to be constantly on the alert to prevent husbands and wives from running into their respective mates, as in many cases a man did not know his wife was my customer, and vice versa. I became like a jailhouse matron guarding her charges, even though often all the parties concerned would just be innocently enjoying a drink, or a game of bridge or backgammon with friends.

Many women, of course, only came there out of curiosity, and they kept coming back partly, I think, because they got a vicarious kick out of knowing what was going on around them. I couldn't help but notice how these women would raise their eyebrows and stare when the maid would beckon to one of the girls and she would depart for the bedroom wing. And when a man would put his arm around a girl and say, "Let's take a walk" (the usual way for a customer to indicate he was ready for some sex), they couldn't take their eyes off the couple as they left the living room. For a moment conversation would flag, then they would ply me with

questions which I always turned aside with a kidding remark. Sometimes they would "third degree" the girls when
they came back. Did the men ever say they loved them?
Were the men very different? How long did they usually
spend? Some would even want a blow-by-blow account of
what had transpired.

Naturally enough, the girls resented these inquisitions and
often complained to me for allowing these legitimate women
in the house. "We don't want these dames gaping at us as
if we were freaks. Why don't they stay home and tend to
their own business and let us do likewise?" And I must say
I sympathized with them. But of course not all my female
customers were so ill mannered or so morbidly prurient.
Like many of my men, they regarded my place more as a
social club than anything, and their attitude toward the girls
was casual and unaffected.

Some of the girls were envious of my women guests, and
on one occasion this jealousy precipitated an incident which,
if it had ever become known, would literally have rocked the
nation. Since it still might very well do so if the identities of
those concerned were revealed, I cannot be too specific about
the date, but it was during the early days of the New Deal.

Bob, my writer friend, had asked me to arrange a dinner
party for six people so well-known that privacy was imperative. Would I, he asked, exclude everyone, girls as well as
customers? I explained that there was a big football game
on that day and many of my young college friends would be
disappointed to find my doors shut. Being an old Ivy League
man himself, Bob told me to go ahead and let the kids have
their fun, and settled for my reserving one wing of the apartment for his guests.

These turned out to be a truly notable assortment of celebrities, among them a U.S. Senator who was much in the

news just then, a famous woman writer, a movie idol, a prominent and lovely member of the fast fox-huntin' set, and a career girl, well-known both in Washington and New York, and very close to a member of the White House inner circle.

As Bob had requested, I had instructed the girls to keep away, but when they saw who all was there, they were extremely annoyed not to be allowed to join such a celebrity-studded group. In particular, Ellie—who was something of a sorehead anyway and had been boozing all afternoon—felt put upon at being excluded, and accused me of fostering class-consciousness. I told her I wasn't fostering anything but a private party, but she would be fostering a tremendous hangover if she didn't lay off the sauce.

Dinner went off well, but afterward the movie star excused himself to go into the bathroom and when he came out he had Ellie with him. This prompted Bob to observe, "Nice flushing, old man!" and everybody laughed, but I was furious and marched Ellie right back to the other part of the house. I told the maids to keep an eye on her, for Ellie was a bad drunk and often threatened suicide when she got loaded.

Meanwhile the entertainers engaged by Bob had arrived, and the party really was beginning to roll. The first to perform were three queer boys who were completely in drag, with wigs, false eyelashes, high-heeled pumps and beautiful evening gowns. Their act was hilarious and they were so convincing that for some time the Senator refused to believe they weren't women. However, the hit of the evening was their opposite number, Mabel, a big fat colored girl clad in white tie and tails, who flaunted a key ring on which was inscribed "With love" and the nickname of a well-known Park

Avenue matron. Mabel was famous for her risqué songs and tonight, as usual, she wowed her audience.

As I was busy all evening commuting between Bob's party and the football rooters, I did not know that Lola, the White House favorite, had asked one of the maids to show her around, and, just for a lark, introduce her as one of the girls. But about half an hour later, when I was back with Bob's party, Lola stumbled into the room, crying hysterically.

"Oh, my God! Ellie fell out of the window!" she sobbed. "I tried to hold her, but she fell."

In an instant everything was in an uproar. "Get to Ellie," I yelled at a maid. Then, like Paul Revere, I raced to every part of the house, knocking at doors and urging people to leave. "There's going to be trouble—get out! Hurry! There's going to be trouble!" I called over and over. The queers got so excited their wigs flew in every direction, their eyelashes fell off, and they began pushing and shoving to the nearest exit, stumbling along in their high-heeled shoes in the wake of Mabel who was cutting out with no time wasted. Her hoarse shouts made the pandemonium complete, and the football crowd couldn't have liked it more. In fact, they insisted on staying to see the rest of the fun, and I nearly lost my mind before I could get rid of them.

I found Bob alone, taking a cat nap in one of the rooms, and dragged him out of bed while he kept protesting that such a rude awakening was unfair to organized sleeping. But his sleepiness disappeared when Sam, the elevator boy, caught up with us. Sam was in a sweat of excitement. "She's alive," he reported breathlessly. "I carried her into the superintendent's apartment." Quickly we hurried down to Ellie. She lay brokenly on a bed, and kept repeating feebly, "I was pushed. . . . She pushed me out the window."

I knew Ellie was lying, for Lola was not the sort of woman who went around pushing people out of windows. But if Ellie were to persist in her story, and an investigation should result, I shuddered to think of the scandal. Turning to Bob I told him that he and his friends must leave at once.

"The hell we will, Poll," said Bob. "We're not going to leave you to take this all on your own shoulders. If we ran out and the girl died, you might be held for manslaughter. We're sticking right here until we find out how badly she's hurt."

I hurriedly got the neighborhood doctor on the phone, but when I tried to explain what had happened he cut in rudely, "What do you mean—a girl fell out of the window? You must be drunk. Call the police department." Finally, Bob had to take over and convince him there really had been an accident, and it was an emergency.

The doctor was unable to determine how seriously Ellie had been injured and called in a colleague, who advised us to take her to a private sanitarium. (The healers split two hundred and fifty not to talk about their visit.) I went along with Ellie and stayed till I learned that nothing ailed her except a few broken ribs. I also learned her "suicide leap" had been taken in two easy stages. Feeling slighted because she had been left out of the party, she had decided to get some attention and scare Lola, and had announced she was going to jump out the window. Lola tried to stop her and got a grip on her dress, but the cloth tore and out the window went Ellie. It was then that Lola had fled back to the party. What Lola didn't know was that Ellie was lying flat on her stomach on the fire escape, having jumped approximately two feet. As soon as she heard Lola run out of the room, she sneaked down five flights and dropped from the first floor to the ground.

When I got back to the house it was well after daybreak, but I found Bob and his friends still waiting. They were people who had everything to lose by becoming involved in a scandal, and it would have been perfectly easy for them to run out, yet they stood by. . . . Perhaps Ellie was right in accusing me of class-consciousness. For my dough, when people behave as these did, that's class.

IV

I suppose it has been pointed out before, but I always was very conscious of the similarity existing between happenings in Germany after Hitler took over in 1933 and the operations of American gangsterdom. The blood purges of the party leaders and the sadistic bullying and aimless destructiveness of the storm troopers seemed to me a large-scale version of the feuds between gangster chiefs and the "self-expression" of their followers.

A hotel not far from my apartment was a nest of these Nazi-type petty mobsters in training for big-time hoodlumism, and in many respects I feared them far more than the Hitlers and Görings of the underworld. In fact, since I could not appeal to the police for protection from their invasions, I would have been unable to operate my house in peace had it not been for Dutch Schultz. In the world outside the law, it takes the big boys to lay down the law to the lawbreakers, and while I didn't relish accepting protection from Dutch, there was no denying I needed it.

I had noticed a great change in the Dutchman when he reappeared upon the scene in the late summer of 1933. He was much calmer and more gentlemanly and seldom drank. Also, he was far sprucer in his appearance. A common friend with whom I had talked in Hot Springs said that Dutch had turned into a regular stage-door Johnny and had been seen hanging around all dolled up in top hat and tails, dancing attendance on a certain show girl. This surprised me. It was difficult to think of Dutch as a human being, yet there was a woman in his life all right, because whenever he stayed overnight at my place he had Bo or Larry telephone someone named Ida and tell her Dutch was okay.

Except for Bo and Larry, he no longer traveled with the old gang and now went around mostly with some important political figures. I would always be advised a day in advance of their visits, as I was not allowed to admit outsiders when Dutch and his friends were in the house. They usually arrived about ten in the evening and departed before daybreak, Dutch functioning as a trusted bodyguard to the politicians.

One night shortly after Dutch's return, six of the neighborhood hoodlums decided to pay me a visit. I was flabbergasted when I saw them at the door, and, though I tried to keep them out, they steam-rollered me out of the way and went stampeding through the apartment like a herd of stir-crazy buffaloes. Fortunately, there were only two guests present and one of them, an airlines executive who was sleeping off a hangover, never even woke up. The hoods stole two hundred and fifty dollars from his trouser pockets and then amused themselves by baiting the other guest, slapping him around and insulting him, until the fun palled.

"Let this be a lesson, you highfalutin bitch," said the leader as they departed. "We've heard your crack that you won't cater to racketeers, but you'll be seein' *us* around whenever we feel like it."

I replaced the money stolen from the airlines executive, and did my best to console the other customer, but even though I knew he would not report the incident (being married and prominent, he could not very well complain to the police), still if such invasions were to be repeated I knew I would have to close my house. I could not run the risk of exposing my clientele to such fright and embarrassment.

The very next night the hoodlums were back again. And when I heard them banging on the door, I didn't hang around to see the fun. I climbed down the fire escape to the floor below, found an open window, and made a three-point landing in the bathtub. Needless to say, the occupants of the apartment got quite a jolt when I popped in on them (it wasn't the time of year for Santa Claus, and anyway I was minus a white beard and red suit), but when I explained my plight, they were kind enough to let me stay. I could hear an awful rumpus going on overhead, but finally things quieted down and the maid called out the window for me, so I thanked the good samaritans and went back the way I'd come.

The hoodlums had really done a job. Lamps, dishes, glasses, ashtrays and knickknacks were smashed, tables, bureaus, desks and dressing tables were overturned, and nearly all the upholstered chairs had been slashed to threads. "At least," I said bitterly, "it looks lived in." Without a word, the maid straightened a chair and table and placed a bottle of brandy in front of me. She had the right idea. It was a time not for action but for anesthesia—and I drank myself into oblivion.

It was noon before I came to, and then I found that the marines had landed in the person of Bo Weinberg. "I've just sent for Dutch," he told me. "You explain everything to him." He looked around at the debris, shaking his head. "Too bad, kid. Those goddamned Indians sure made a mess of things."

When the Dutchman arrived, I told him in detail about the gang's two visitations and he was furious. "Why in hell didn't you mention my name?" he demanded. "All this could have been avoided."

"You've never before given me permission to do so," I said.

Since there was no answer to that one, Dutch turned to Bo. "Get Frankie on the phone," he snapped. "You tell those crazy fools I want an explanation, and I'll be staying here till I get it." However, word must have gone along the grapevine that Dutch was really sore, because the hoods could not be located. No doubt they were hiding out until he'd had a chance to cool off.

During the following week I was busy refurnishing the apartment, and I also was spending as much time as I could in Brooklyn, for my parents were soon to leave for Palestine. While I was sorry to see them go, yet, for selfish reasons, I could not help but be relieved. It was always a strain to be with them, and forever hanging over me was the fear that they would find out about my activities. So for once I was grateful for my father's restlessness. Although we had relatives in Palestine, I don't think my mother really wanted to make her home there, but she wasn't going to be left behind any more.

On my return from one of these visits I found Dutch in the kitchen, sitting with his feet propped on the window sill, reading *The Life of Al Capone*.

"Where the hell you been all day?"

"In Brooklyn," I said. "Did you hear from Bo?"

"Yeah," he said. "Frankie and the other boys'll be over tonight to apologize."

I looked at him. Suddenly I felt sick of the whole business. Perhaps it was because of the shame I felt at finding myself actually glad to say good-bye to my parents, but I amazed Dutch by bursting into tears.

"What good are apologies?" I said. "I appreciate what you've done for me, and I'm thankful for your protection, but when hoodlums like those get hopped up, you know yourself nobody can say what they'll do. I could lose an arm or leg, I could be blinded, I could be killed." He was staring at me so intently I began to be embarrassed. "I'm going to quit this damn business. I work like a slave twenty-four hours a day, and all I get out of it is a living and a headache. What money I do save goes in pay-offs when I'm pinched, or to fix up the place after it's been sabotaged by those strongarms. The hell with it! I'm quitting."

"Poll, you're not thinking straight," said Dutch. "You aren't gonna quit business because you can't. All this notoriety you've had—it's been great for bringing in customers, but it's gonna trip you up if you try to set up as a legitimate operator. Face up to it, kid; you're tagged as a madam and a madam is what you're gonna stay. . . . Breaking away from a racket, that's something that can't be done." He took the coffeepot and poured himself out a cup. "I tell you what I'll do. I will personally see to it that from now on you're not bothered by nobody in any of the mobs. Okay?"

I nodded, not very happily, and sat there, my chin in my hands, staring at the table. Bo came in, and Dutch finished the coffee and stood up.

"Brace up, kid," he said, giving me a little tap on the shoulder. "Everything's gonna be okay. See you soon."

Frankie and the others showed up that night, as Dutch had said they would. "Peace night, peace night," they chanted, marching around the apartment, and then asked me to give them several of the knickknacks which they had failed to destroy. In their moronic minds, this was a gesture of good fellowship. They were trying to convey that they appreciated my good taste. In their chastened mood, they even paid for their drinks.

Thanks to Dutch, that was the last I ever saw of such lice. And even though I had been put through hell during much of the time I had to entertain him, so far as I was concerned this kind deed evened things up and canceled out all the unpleasantness.

Although Dutch continued to patronize my establishment on and off during my remaining year on West Fifty-fourth, I myself saw very little of him, and our conversation in the kitchen was our last really personal contact. I have often thought that he lived a lonely life. In order to maintain his position and keep face with the mob, he had to hold himself aloof and conceal his emotions. He seemed to have no more warmth or need for human companionship than a machine, yet I think he knew that no one liked him and tried to con himself into believing it didn't matter, that money and power were what counted.

He was fatally wounded on the night of October 23, 1935, while drinking beer with Abadaba and Lulu in a Newark tavern. Taken to the hospital, he lived for several hours, and his deathbed wanderings were recorded by a police reporter. His last words were couched in a strange double-talk, the meaning of which, if there is one, nobody yet has fathomed. "A boy has never wept," Dutch said, "nor dashed a thousand kim."

I have heard that for several years before his death, Dutch had wanted to retire, but his fellow gangsters wouldn't let him. If this is true, then he must have been speaking from bitter personal experience when he told me that breaking away from a racket can't be done.

Chapter 8

Jump Collar

> Give us, in mercy, better homes when we're
> a-lying in our cradles; give us better food when
> we're a-working for our lives; give us kinder
> laws to bring us back when we're a-going
> wrong; and don't set Jail, Jail, Jail afore us,
> everywhere we turn.
>
> *Charles Dickens*   THE CHIMES

I

Heralded by a clinking of tin cups, the Aspirin Age followed
grimly in the wake of the Era of Wonderful Nonsense, and
the mid-years of the Thirties resolved into a period of desperate panacea-seeking, of bank holidays and boondoggling,
of technocracy and the Townsend Plan, of shots in the arm
compounded from the alphabet soup of C.W.A., F.S.A.,
F.E.R.A., F.H.A., N.R.A, N.Y.A., P.R.A., P.W.A. and
W.P.A.[1] In the 1932 presidential campaign, the Republicans had promised "a chicken in every pot," but it was the
Democrats who took over. And their bird was the blue
eagle, the National Recovery Administration symbol dis-
played by employers who had signed a code of fair competi-

---

[1] RESPECTIVELY: *Civil Works Administration, Farm Security Administra-
tion, Federal Emergency Relief Administration, Federal Housing Admin-
istration, National Recovery Administration, National Youth Adminis-
tration, Public Roads Administration, Public Works Administration,
Works Progress Administration.*

tion or the President's Re-Employment Agreement. Apparently, before there could be a chicken in every pot, there had to be a blue eagle on every product, and to General Hugh (Old Ironpants) Johnson fell the task of lining up the codes —no less than seven hundred and thirty-eight of them—for business and industry.

Down in Washington, the fall of 1934, with only fifty or sixty codes to go, the general was proceeding full steam ahead, blissfully unaware that his work partook of the nature of pounding sand down a rat-hole, for in less than a year, as a result of a Supreme Court decision invalidating the National Industrial Recovery Act, his beloved blue eagle would be a very dead duck indeed. At the same time up in New York, Madam Polly Adler, though not entitled to display the blue eagle (she had been given no opportunity to sign either a fair-practice code or a re-employment agreement), nevertheless was featuring a bird on her business cards—a scarlet poll parrot—under whose aegis she, too, was working night and day for economic recovery (her own), with no more premonition than the general that 1935 would be open season on symbolical poultry, regardless of species or color.

For some time many of my customers, in particular "Scottie," a multi-millionaire blueblood, owner of a noted racing stable, had been objecting to my West Side location. Scottie often remarked on the hard-boiled characters hanging around outside a near-by hotel, and was afraid they might recognize him and stage a kidnaping. (Scottie was no prissy worrier. This was the heyday of the kidnap racket and every wealthy, well-known man had to face the possibility he might be snatched.) Unless I moved to a better neighborhood, he said, I was going to lose some business, including

his, and he even offered to make up the difference in rent if
I would locate on the East Side.

After my long sojourn at the West Fifty-fourth Street
apartment, I had come to look upon it as practically the old
homestead, and the rental agents offered to lower the rent
if I would stay on and (something unique in my experience)
praised me as a model tenant. But I did not feel that I could
disregard the wishes of my clients, and so, armed with impressive social references supplied by Scottie and others, I
went house-hunting and finally settled for a twelve-room
apartment at Fifty-fifth and Madison, in the heart of the
café society country. In addition to being a "good address,"
it was a perfect setup since it occupied the whole second
floor, with nothing but shops underneath.

As always, before I signed a lease I made the nature of
my business known to the building superintendent, who was
extremely cold about the whole deal until I mentioned the
handsome stipend he would receive monthly. Then he became all charm and warned me to be wary of the elevator
man, an elderly Negro who had been there, I guess, ever
since they brought in the first load of bricks. But I had a
little talk with this white-haired old codger, and, after the
usual palm-oiling assumed all was well in that quarter.

The apartment was one of the most beautiful I have ever
had. The living room was Louis Seize, but not arbitrarily so
—you didn't feel as if you'd wandered into one of the period rooms at the Metropolitan Museum—and the decorator
keyed the color scheme to my collection of rose quartz and
jade lamps. The walls were warm gray and the draperies
pale green satin. In the cosy paneled library the walls were
lined with shelves displaying my fine collection of books,
most of them, I regret to say, as yet unread—at least by me.
My friend Bob and a famous woman playwright had advised

me on "must" books, classics and contemporary works, and I had supplemented these with sets which, frankly, I got less for their contents than for their decorative bindings. There was a shelf devoted to autographed copies of books written by or about my customers, and it was in the library that I kept my collection of old phonograph records.

The taproom, as the decorator called it, had a military motif. There was a drum-shaped blue glass bar, and the color scheme was red, white and blue, the chairs were blue piped with white, and the bar stools were red leather. In the dining room, the idea, according to the decorator, was to suggest the interior of a sea shell. All I can say is he must have had in mind a damn big sea shell—I could accommodate fifty for dinner. The chairs were upholstered in oyster-white antique leather, the table, buffet and serving tables were of some sandy-colored, highly polished wood, and the walls and draperies were coral and gold.

Since peach is a color that brings a glow to wan faces, I did my four bedrooms in peach and apple green, and the baths also were peach and green. In the service wing, there was a large and well-equipped kitchen, a butler's pantry, maids' bath and three maids' rooms—one of which I fitted up for myself as a refuge for days when I wanted to "get away from it all" (but not too far).

Along with two maids and two cooks (one for the day shift, one for nights), my household consisted of four hand-picked young ladies, the cream of my list: Nora, Rosalie, Kit and Angelica. Nora, a stunning blonde, as a child had acted in pictures and was attending dramatic school in her spare time. She was bright and vivacious, and a good foil for Rosalie, who was the slumbrous, siren type—ebony hair, camellia-petal skin and the figure of a streamlined Venus de Milo. Rosalie was a Cuban, and had a repertoire of Spanish dances, which she performed occasionally at night clubs. Kit, though not as beautiful as the others, had a wonderful personality. She was twenty-nine, which was considered old by my clients, but being a veteran night-club hostess, she knew how to handle men intelligently and many would tell her their troubles, which took a load off my shoulders. Kit was my lieutenant; if I was not present I knew I could count on her to see that things went smoothly and, in an emergency, to keep her head. (As a matter of fact, she held her liquor much better than I did.) The fourth girl, Angelica, was the cutest and my favorite. She was little and piquant and her pert grin and saucy ways made her a favorite with the customers too.

Angelica's two older sisters, Betsy and Nana, had worked for me back in the Twenties. They were Kentuckians, with a better education and background than most of the girls, and I often pleaded with them to get out of the business, particularly when I learned that their kid sister was soon coming north to join them. They left my establishment around 1928, and I next saw Betsy in the summer of 1934. She called me at a beauty salon which she knew I patronized, told me she was married, and asked me to come and see her. Her apartment, in a brownstone walk-up, was plainly furnished but clean, and while Betsy had gotten fat and sloppy, she still had the same soft voice and charming smile. Her husband, she told me, was a swell guy and I could see for myself that her baby was a husky, happy-looking little tyke. Nana, I learned, also had married happily and was living in Baltimore. It was the kid sister, Angelica, who had turned into a problem.

"I should have listened to you, Polly," said Betsy, "when you warned me not to bring her to New York. Now she's hustling in cheap hotels, running around with bums and addicts, and though she denies it, I think she's on drugs herself. If she must be a prostitute, I would like her to be with you. You take a personal interest in your girls, and I know that if Angie is taking drugs, you'll help her kick the habit."

When I talked with Angelica, she was quite frank about her drug habit and agreed to take the cure if she could come and work for me. I arranged for her to be treated at a sanitarium and, in due time, she became a member of my household. But, although she succeeded in pulling the wool over my eyes, Angelica was continuing to use heroin, and, as a result of her deception, I was to spend some very harrowing hours.

While my new apartment won me many compliments, my overhead had increased enormously, and I was forced to keep open twenty-four hours a day. This suited the idle rich set to a T. Since Repeal, bars closed at four A.M., and it was convenient for them to have a place where they could drop in after hours for a nightcap and hot cakes and sausages. (Cocktail snacks and late suppers were served with the compliments of the management; the cost was more than recouped by the additional business this brought to the bar.)

Convenient though this nonstop hospitality may have been for my guests, it was hell on the hostess. I was tired to the point of slap-happiness. Often I couldn't have told you the day of the week—or even the time of day. Since the windows facing on the front were heavily draped and the curtains always drawn, I wouldn't know whether it was noon or midnight. The air I breathed was dead and heavy with the aroma of alcohol and perfume. My eyes burned and smarted from fatigue and cigarette smoke. My ears were constantly assailed by the ringing of bells, the blaring of phonograph and radio, the ceaseless chattering of the guests. If it hadn't been for an occasional weekend in the country, I would never have seen the sun, never have breathed fresh air or known a night's sleep. . . . Why, I thought to myself, I might as well be a mole working in a factory again; this life is the same as being buried alive.

By New Year's, 1935, after three months in the new house, I realized I'd wind up a basket case if I didn't take a vacation, so I booked passage on a West Indies cruise. Then one night, a week or so before I was scheduled to sail, I received a visit from four policemen. It was sheer good luck—and, I may add, the last I was to have for many a moon—that the girls had been engaged to entertain a visiting royalty and his entourage, and were spending the evening at the Waldorf.

When the cops walked in, a couple of them whistled appreciatively and the sergeant remarked, "Boy, what a layout! Where do you keep your gambling paraphernalia?"

"Huh?" I said. "My what?"

"Your roulette wheel."

"Don't kid me, gentlemen, you know my name, and it's not a roulette wheel you're after."

But strangely enough, it was. Later I learned that the elevator man, despite taking handouts from me, had passed on the names of all my guests to the building agent. (The double-crossing so-and-so had no trouble finding them out, since it was a rule that everybody had to be announced, and my customers, being sure I would protect them, always gave their right names.) Anyway, the building agent, never dreaming that so many socially prominent men and women would be going night after night to a whorehouse, had deduced that I was running a gambling joint and had phoned in a complaint.

The cops and I had a few drinks together, and I thought my best move was to lay my cards on the table. Doing my best to impersonate a broken blossom—which was not hard, the way I felt—I showed them my reservations for the cruise and said it was to be my first real vacation in five years, but I supposed now I'd have to cancel it.

"Oh, I don't know," said the sergeant. "This complaint may not be too serious. For the time being, close your place, and I'll get in touch with you in a few days."

Actually, it was only two days until he called to tell me everything was under control, and in gratitude I asked the four cops up to dinner. They were so gentlemanly I almost forgot my pet peeve against bluecoats and invited them to the cocktail party which I gave the afternoon I sailed. I was both surprised and touched when I got to my cabin and found a huge basket of flowers inscribed, "Bon Voyage from your four friends." It seemed to me a good omen, and I thought hopefully that maybe my cop-fighting days were over . . . I must have been soft in the head.

II

On my return, six weeks later, I found a new clean-up campaign was on. A Reverend J. D. Egbert was preaching sermons about vice conditions and the evils of the policy racket, and a "Committee of One Hundred" had been formed to stamp out sin—or at least give it a couple of kicks in the pants. With the Seabury investigation still fresh in their minds, I doubt if the cops were too keen about participating in a "crusade," but there was a new administration in City Hall—LaGuardia had come in on the Fusion ticket—and if the new broom was hell-bent on sweeping clean, the police department had no choice but to co-operate.

Nevertheless, in view of the ease with which the previous

complaint had been disposed of, I wasn't particularly
alarmed and saw no reason to take extra precautions. It
would have done no good if I had. Naturally I didn't know
it, but I already was surrounded, and the cops were only
waiting for the psychological moment to swoop in and make
the kill. Although the maids had mentioned there was a new
man on the service elevator (which opened directly into
my kitchen), and had said he was ever so accommodating,
helping them count the laundry and open the cases of
champagne, I had no more idea he was a police spy than I
had that my wires were tapped and two cops were planted in
the janitor's apartment, listening in on all my calls. Maybe I
should have checked personally on the "accommodating elevator man." Maybe, in the old days when I was constantly
on the alert for police interference, I would have smelled a
rat. But the fact remains I didn't, and having not the slightest
premonition that a sneak attack was in the making, I carried
right on with business as usual.

Like most women in my profession, I had a number of pet
superstitions, one of them being that Tuesday was my lucky
day. It is a notion I no longer cling to. In fact, if anything, I
am less partial to Tuesday than the other days in the week.
Tuesday, March 5, 1935, was the date of my personal Pearl
Harbor—Tuesday you can have.

The evening of this "lucky day" found me very low in my
mind. Ever since my return I had noticed that Angelica was
behaving oddly, and finally that afternoon I had asked her
point-blank if she was back on drugs. She denied it vehemently, but when I asked if I might examine the contents of
her locked suitcase, she refused permission. "You must take
my word for it, I'm no longer an addict, Polly," she said, and
flounced from the room. But a little later on, she came back

and without a word handed me a hypodermic syringe and two packages of heroin.

I didn't reproach her; she knew without my having to say it that I was heartsick about the whole thing. I merely asked if she would let me help her again, and she said brokenly that all she wanted was another chance. She'd gladly take the cure, and this time she wouldn't fail me. I immediately telephoned Dr. Gould, and he said to send Angie to him in the morning. Then, as soon as she had left the room, I hid the heroin and the syringe in—of all intelligent places!—the pocket of one of my suits, which was hanging in the closet.

I went out to dinner and when I returned found a message to call a certain number, which I did, and was connected with the precinct police station. Figuring it was somebody's idea of a gag, I hung up. Also, I found a telegram from a policeman friend who was vacationing in Florida. He had guessed wrong at the races and asked me to wire him train fare back to New York. I did so, and then placed the telegram, which was signed with his own name, under the jewel box on my bureau.

Many times since I have wondered where my wandering mind was that night—one place it wasn't was in my head. In the space of two short hours I had been guilty of three inexcusable lapses. I had failed to destroy a message linking an officer of the law with a law-breaker, I had totally ignored the possibility that a blind call from a precinct station might be an attempt to tip me off to a raid, and, worst of all, I had made myself a candidate for a federal charge by planting drugs on myself.

At five minutes to midnight on "lucky Tuesday," my telephone rang. "This is Uncle Lester, Auntie Polly. How'd you like to come over to the Waldorf for a little drink?"

I recognized the customer and knew what he was asking, so I replied gaily (*toujours gai*, that's me), "I have everything the Waldorf has. Why not drop over here?"

"Fine," he said. "We'll be right over."

I asked him what he meant by "we"—did he have a rat in his pocket? (which would have been a wonderful cue for the two cops who were listening in to say, *No, lady, but you've got a bug on your line*), and Lester laughed and said he had an old classmate with him. About ten minutes later they arrived, both of them in extremely good humor, and his friend was introduced to me as Mr. Paul Pepper. I liked him better than Lester, who was a bit too stuffy to suit me and had made a poor impression the first time he had visited my place. He had come with some business friends and had given me a check for his share of the bill, and I heard from one of his companions that he was worried for fear the check might be raised. Naturally I resented this slur on my honesty.

Over our drinks, I told the men about my recent West Indies cruise and mentioned that I had taken some movies. The three girls present—Angie and Nora and Rosalie—coaxed me to run them off, and Nora went to fetch the films while Lester set up the projector. All the films were kept together in one carton, and, as bad luck would have it, mixed in with mine were some of the blue variety, the property of a patron who had parked them with me a few days before. The cans containing the lewd films were unlabeled, as were mine.

The first reel I put on was my boat trip. Not being much of a mechanic, I had quite a bit of difficulty with the machine, and my audience kept heckling me, shouting wisecracks and instructions. "A little slower, Polly! . . . You're going too fast now . . . Slower! . . . Now that's the way I like it." These shouted exhortations were, of course, quite audible to the cops who, as soon as the two customers had arrived, had come out from under their respective rocks, and were coiling up to strike.

When I put on the next reel, suddenly there flashed on the screen a scene which had no place in home movies of a vacation trip. The room rocked with laughter. The episode being depicted was not only very pornographic, but it was upside down.

At this point I resigned as a projectionist. I removed the machine and reels from the bar, and settled down to do a little drinking with Pepper and Nora. About four o'clock the house telephone rang, and a Mr. Fitzgerald was announced. The only Fitzgerald I knew who might be turning up at that hour was a cop, and if it was "Fitz," it meant he was coming to warn me of a raid. I said I would go down to the lobby to meet Mr. Fitzgerald, but I never got that far.

As I opened the door, five husky plain-clothes men practically fell in on top of me and went plunging on into the apartment. For the next few moments all I could hear was doors opening and closing and the thunderous trampling of flatfeet as they chased from room to room like a posse of Keystone cops. Then my mind leapt quickly to the things this raid might uncover, and I nearly collapsed when I recalled the two decks of heroin and the telegram. Somehow or other I must get to my room and destroy them before the cops had a chance to search thoroughly.

I got into conversation with the policeman who had remained behind to guard the exit. He was a poker-faced chap with a holier-than-thou air which I didn't care for, but he was a human being (at least I thought he was) and maybe I could get to him.

"Why so many cops?" I asked. "You can't be after Dillinger—he's dead."

"When we raid you," said Poker Face, "it ain't no ordinary deal. The Inspector and the Lieutenant come along, the both of them."

This gave me an opening to bring up the telegram. I figured he had the normal flatfoot's resentment of brass, and wouldn't want them to find evidence which would hurt a fellow cop—my friend also belonged to the Fourth Division—and if I could get to the bedroom I would have at least a sporting chance of getting rid of the heroin.

His poker face never changed when I told him about the wire. "Let's go get it," he said. We hurried into the bedroom and I extracted the telegram from under the jewel case. But as I started to tear it up, Poker Face twisted my arm and yanked the wire away from me just as another cop appeared in the doorway.

When he saw me, he grinned broadly, exposing what appeared to be a double handful of gold teeth. "Say, Polly, this is one swell joint!"

"Joint!" I said indignantly. "You've got a nerve calling this a joint. This is an A-number-1 house of assignation!" He made a note of my remark in his book, and too late I realized I had made a very damaging admission. Of course I knew better than to exchange backchat with cops, but this just wasn't my night.

Gold Teeth said I was to come to the living room at once. As we passed by the bar, I saw my three girls—Kit was not in that night—huddled together, pale-faced and frightened. I tried to stop to reassure them, but was shoved into the living room to face Inspector Neidig and Lieutenant Smith. Lester and Pepper were seated side by side on the couch, looking very unhappy and sheepish.

"Don't worry," I said to them. "This is only a jump collar."

"Jump collar!" said the Inspector. "Huh! We've got you cold and you know it."

"Look, Inspector," I said, "I've been a good sport all these years. I've never harmed anyone. I'm not running a brothel —this is a decent house. Why pick on me?"

It was a waste of breath. "We know you have some lewd films here," said the Inspector. "Hand 'em over or we'll tear this place apart."

I glanced toward Lester, and he quickly looked away, so I knew the coward had talked. (I soon learned he had also admitted the purpose of his and Pepper's visit.) Nevertheless, I denied having any such films in my possession, and the Inspector turned his bloodhounds loose. Every nook and corner of the apartment was searched, but having a specific object to hunt for—a round tin of film—they didn't bother to look in places too small to conceal it (such as the pocket of my suit). Of course I couldn't know they would overlook the heroin and when I saw the contents of my closet strewn around the floor, I thought it was all over but the sentencing.

In the meantime, Poker Face had turned the telegram over to Lieutenant Smith, and I was being questioned about this, but—even distracted as I was—I would admit nothing. (Later my friend who had sent the wire was broken and put to pounding a beat. It was a while before he found who had stooled on him, but he told me that he'd known all along it couldn't have been me.) Finally, the films were discovered in a locked closet, by which time the apartment was a shambles and so, needless to state, was my nervous system. Then Lester and Pepper were ordered to leave, and the three girls and I were taken to the Thirtieth Street Police Station in the patrol wagon.

III

It was a busy night at the station house. Drug addicts, drunks and streetwalkers were being hauled in, and cell doors clanked open and shut continuously. The drunks were vomiting all over the place, and no one was permitted to flush the toilet. This was the job of the matron on duty and she only got around to it about once an hour. The sleeping accommodations consisted of loose boards suspended from the wall by chains, and the mattresses were old newspapers, but finally I passed out from sheer exhaustion and slept till court time.

At the courthouse, I met with a press reception which would have flattered a Hollywood celebrity. Photographers lined up for pictures (I cannot say I was looking my best), and reporters clamored for a statement. I merely told them what they already knew—that I was a good target whenever there was a clean-up campaign and that for years the cops had been trying to hang me in a jump collar. "I've been the fall guy so many times I feel like a rubber ball," I was quoted as saying.

Although Magistrate Anna M. Kross is truly one of our most fair-minded judges, it seemed to me that morning that conviction followed after conviction, and I began to feel increasingly as a goose must in the moment before it is whisked into the oven. At long last the name Polly Adler was called, but I didn't stir. I had been booked as "Joan Martin," and it was the only name I would recognize. This didn't soothe the judge any, and when finally I answered to the name of Joan Martin, her voice fairly dripped acid as she set my bail at two thousand five hundred dollars instead of the customary five hundred.

The bond was paid and then my old pal, Poker Face,

stepped forward and tapped me on the shoulder, and my attorney (*not* Mr. Jayess) informed me that I had another charge pending: possession of lewd films. I blew up and reminded him that the films were not mine, but he carefully explained the law of possession, and I realized the charge was justified. However, the lewd picture charge was the *only other one,* which meant that the cops had not, after all, found Angelica's package of dope. My relief was so great that I practically skipped all the way to the patrol wagon.

At the Fifty-seventh Street Courthouse I had my hearing, the bail was upped another grand, the bail bond was paid, and I was off for home, newsmen and photographers in full pursuit. At the apartment a charming surprise awaited me in the form of a uniformed cop—assigned by the city to "protect" me while the case was pending. He told me he thought my home was in exquisite taste (he was that kind of a cop— a Ferdinand the Bull—probably put there because he wouldn't be susceptible to women), but I was in no mood for compliments.

"This isn't a home," I told him. "This is a house. Or anyway," I added quickly, "that's what it's alleged to be."

But it wasn't even a house much longer. Having no desire to be chaperoned by Ferdinand, I made arrangements to put my furniture in storage and moved to a hotel. The one I went to was a flea-bag, but I had no choice in the matter. A notorious person like me would have been about as welcome as the bubonic plague at a first-class hotel.

The reporters, on the other hand, greeted my return to the spotlight with whoops of joy. I was pleasantly surprised at the tone of much of the publicity. It was more jocular than condemnatory, I was treated more as a "character" than a public enemy, and even the comparatively staid *Herald-Tribune* reported with some amusement the ambiguous re-

marks overheard by the cops while the film was being run
off. Even more cheering to me was the editorial run by the
Daily News on March twelfth under the heading POLLY
ADLER'S "LITTLE BLACK BOOK." It said in part:

The police vice and policy crusade, apparently started by Tammany
District Attorney Dodge, and at least not discouraged by Fusion Mayor
LaGuardia, makes us a little sicker each day. Take the Polly Adler phase
of it. Here is a woman who keeps an expensive house of ill fame, conducting it on the quiet, without complaints from the neighbors, and with
every regard for outward decency. This is in accordance with Mayor
Gaynor's stipulation as to what is the wisest way to handle this terrible
problem.

The police tap this woman's wires, set spies on her, and in other ways
keep her under surveillance as if they suspected her being the Lind-
bergh kidnapper. They seize, without a vestige of right to do so, her
"little black book" containing the names and addresses of various well-
to-do patrons of her establishment. Thus they obtain opportunities for
blackmail for anybody who can get a peek at this book. Already whispers
are going the rounds that the book contains the names of a motion picture star and a Broadway stage favorite.

It is this crusading against personal and private habits and instincts—
the sex instinct, the deep-rooted human fondness for gambling as shown
by the prevalence of policy gamesters—which is futile and sickening,
just as the prohibition of drinking liquor was.

That kind of stuff has eventually tripped city administrations which
have tried it. It is the same story as the liquor prohibition story. Much
as we all deplored bootlegging and the graft and crime that sprang from
it, the best thing to do during prohibition was to patronize the bootleggers and defy the law in order at last to smash the prohibition law.
The Mayor would do well to remember, we think, that it was the vice cop
frameup revelations which started the Walker Administration toward its
ruin.

At my next court appearance "a packed courtroom of
eager thrill seekers sighed in audible dismay when the first
public hearing was postponed. But there was general re-
joicing and a renewed rush for passes when it was learned
that the Adler case would be transferred from the cramped
quarters of woman's court to more spacious quarters in the
Crime Courts Building." I was held to be tried at Special
Sessions and the girls were slated for the Lower Courts.

Meanwhile Lester and Pepper were getting panicky. One paper ran a front-page caricature of two headless figures captioned: WHO ARE THE UNKNOWN MEN IN THE POLLY ADLER CASE? The day after it appeared the two "unknowns" summoned me to a conference in a private suite at the Waldorf. They had strong political connections, and I was in hopes they could help me. Present at the meeting were Lester, Pepper and a retired police officer whom I had known for years.

"What will it be, Polly, Scotch or champagne?" asked Lester.

"The way I feel," I said, "a little of both."

But Lester did not smile. Removing his pince-nez, he looked me in the eye and said, "Why don't you plead guilty and get it over with?"

"When I need advice," I said, "I'll ask a lawyer."

"You got us into this mess," said Lester. "The least you can do is plead guilty and save our reputations."

"Has it never occurred to you that if you hadn't shot off your mouth, admitting everything under the sun but rape, none of us would be worrying tonight?"

Pepper interrupted at this point to ask me to think of their families. I smiled at the old fool. "Were *you* thinking of them when you were with the girls?" And then, turning to Lester, "As an old newspaperman you should be smart enough to know that the buyer is as guilty as the seller in any kind of rap."

This infuriated him and he shouted, "Goddamit, if you don't plead guilty I'll have every newspaper and press association in the country blast you! You'll never be able to make a living again—in New York or anywhere else."

I raised my voice to match his. "Keep your cheap threats to yourself! The worst part of my business is dealing with crumbs like you. Think of your reputation? Why should I? Did you think of what it was doing to me when you blabbed to the cops behind my back?"

I was so angry I burst into tears. The ex-police officer, who had been silent till now, put his arm around my shoulder and offered to drive me home. He seemed sympathetic, but it was all a build-up to a bribe. He said that Lester would pay me ten thousand dollars to plead guilty. I told him I would play the game the way I always had. I would take my chances and Lester and Pepper could take theirs.

On the day of the girls' trial I accompanied them to court, but when the testimony began I was too nervous to sit still, and sweated it out in the bail-bond office across the street. As I was sitting there, I noticed some queer-looking characters hanging around, some of them busy on the phone, others roaming in and out. They didn't strike me as pimps, and I wondered what connection they had with the place. I had planted an emissary in the courtroom who reported to me at intervals, and when at last he said it looked like a conviction, I became very upset. One of the characters approached me and said, "I think it's swell the way you stick to your girls. It ain't usual among madams. But a lot of your troubles could be avoided if you became a member of our combination." He went on to explain that his "combination" operated on a weekly payment of ten dollars per girl, which insured her of bail in case of arrest. He boasted of his strong connections and claimed that none of the girls registered with his outfit had ever been convicted. But when he offered me his telephone number, I declined with thanks. I had no wish to get mixed up with a vice combine.

Although Lester and Pepper were called as witnesses, they were spared the humiliation of testifying. Magistrate Jonah J. Goldstein declared the prosecution had made a prima facie case without them, but he added, "I don't think it's fair to spotlight the women and whisper about the men. It takes two to commit the offense, although under the law only one is brought in. Even though the men are in places of that sort by choice, the procedure in these cases, as in prohibition, makes only the seller and not the buyer liable to prosecution. There is no logic in this distinction, but I am compelled to administer the law as it is written."

And the law found my girls guilty. Rosalie was deported to Cuba, Nora received a suspended sentence, and Angie was sent to Kingston Avenue hospital for a drug cure.

My case did not come to trial until April twenty-seventh, but many postponements kept the story fresh in the newspapers. Ironically—or, perhaps, appropriately—on the evening of my thirty-fifth birthday the *Daily Mirror* was on the streets with what purported to be my biography. "Everyone knows her. No one knows anything about her—" except, presumably, the gentleman who wrote that I was born and reared on the Lower East Side and "as her social ambition increased with her rising fortunes, she passed up Broadway for Fifth Avenue and Park Avenue. From the Ghetto to the heart of the Four Hundred, this is Polly Adler's success story."

My attorney, Samuel J. Siegel, had informed me that District Attorney Dodge was just as anxious to dispose of the case as I was. The D.A. had said that if I would plead guilty to the lewd-picture charge, he would dismiss the disorderly house charge. Since this was the major charge, I agreed to do so. However, when the day came, I had no sooner pleaded guilty than Assistant District Attorney Wahl asked the judge to set a later date for my trial on the charge of running a disorderly house.

As it dawned on me I was getting a royal double cross,

I turned to my attorney and insisted that he withdraw the guilty plea at once. On his immediate request, the case was recessed until afternoon. My attorney and the D.A. went into a huddle, and at the afternoon session Mr. Dodge went before the court and explained that there had been a "misunderstanding." I never did find out who misunderstood whom, but I wound up with a date for a new trial.

On thinking it over, it seemed to me to be in my best interest to plead guilty to the disorderly-house charge. I knew that even if I beat the rap on the house-running charge, I would get the limit for having the lewd pictures in my possession. Also, it would give my customers more confidence in me if they saw that I would go to jail rather than stand trial and be cross-examined about the people named in my "little black book." This is the true reason why I pleaded guilty, and not, as some papers said, because there was underworld pressure on me to do so.

As a matter of fact, if it had not been for my underworld acquaintances, I could easily have received a three-year sentence. It was a good and powerful friend from the illegal side of the tracks who came through for me after my friends on the legitimate side dummied out. A few days before I was due to be sentenced, I had talked with this man, and he had promised to see what he could do. From our conversation later, I gathered that there was a possibility of leniency, and on the way to the courthouse I told my attorney that I thought my sentence would be thirty days and a five-hundred-dollar fine or ninety days and no fine. He asked where I had gathered this information, but when I could only tell him it was from a reliable source, he snorted and said, "Poppycock!"

Nevertheless, the sentence was thirty days and five hundred dollars' fine, and the lewd-picture charge was dropped. Considering that I was "the center of a city-wide drive against vice" and "elected to be the goat after the Committee of One Hundred was formed," I felt that I had come out of it rather well.

IV

At the Jefferson Market Jail, I was ushered into the front office where a matron demanded all my personal property. This was handed over and checked and recorded for safe keeping. Then I was passed along to another matron who told me to undress. She stood by as I showered in the uncurtained shower room, commanding me to put my head under water. When I complained because I'd just had my hair done, she snapped, "This is a jailhouse. Here you do as you are told."

Next came the physical examination. While I was awaiting my turn, there were blood-curdling screams from the inner office and another prisoner explained that "Doc" was a little rough at times, especially when it came to the blood test. . . . I had seen newsreels of South Sea Islanders spearing fish, and I think that's where "Doc" learned his technique.

I was assigned to a cell on the sixth floor, and, when we got up there, asked my warder if there had been a jailbreak —the place was deserted. My joke went over like a lead balloon. She explained coldly that it was recreation period. Wondering what would be considered recreation here, I sat down gingerly on my cot and surveyed my new quarters. In one corner was a washbasin, in another a toilet bowl, which also served as a chair for the small writing table, and that was the works.

Still restless and keyed up after the trial, I walked to the tier gate and stood there, more than a little uncertain what to do with myself. A Negro woman was the first inmate to return from recreation. She rushed up to me and said excitedly, "I just heard that the big shot, Polly Adler, is going to be put on this tier. Have you seen her?" As I had been sentenced under the name Joan Martin and intended to use that name while serving my time, I denied knowing anything about the "big shot," and abruptly returned to my cell. I was sorry at once. These were my fellow prisoners, and it was up to me to get along with them. I wanted to make up for my coolness to the colored girl, but now all the other inmates had returned, and I felt shy about going out among them.

A face appeared in my cell door. It was framed with jet-black hair, cut in uneven bangs. The body it belonged to was short and buxom, and both body and face looked as if they'd seen hard wear for all of fifty years. When the face broke into a smile, I saw two front teeth were missing, but the smile was merry. A warm, friendly voice said, "My name's Rosie. What's yours?"

"Joan Martin."

"Have it your own way," she said, "but I know who you are." She winked. "Say, do you know Owney Madden?"

I acknowledged that I knew Owney, and she beamed. "I knew you was okay! I was born and raised in Owney's neighborhood. Yes, sir, I knew all them boys from Hell's Kitchen." She looked my cell over. "Why didn't they put you on my side where you can get some sun? I'll speak to the head screw tomorrow and get you changed over."

"Thanks, Rosie, but I won't be here long enough to get a suntan. I've only got twenty-five days to serve, providing I don't lose my five days off for good behavior." I was trying to tell her that I didn't expect any favors and, more than that, I didn't want to endanger those precious five days.

"Your first visit, huh?" said Rosie. "Me, I'm an old-timer in this clink. I know how to get things done."

I asked her where to get the toilet articles I needed, especially soap and a toothbrush, and she said the commissary was closed for the rest of the week, but "I'll round you up a piece of soap, and don't worry about the toothbrush, kid, you can use mine." Before I could refuse this handsome offer, Rosie darted away and in a flash was back carrying a piece of knitted string.

"Here," she said. "This is for you. I knitted it myself." When I looked bewildered, she shoved it into my hand. "It's to tie your hair up." And it turned out to be darn useful, too.

We cut up a few more touches about Owney Madden, who seemed to be her particular hero, and I felt I had made a friend. At eight thirty a bell rang, and Rosie explained that it meant all prisoners must return to their own cells for the night count. She said a cheery good night and "See you in the morning." I replied that it would be funny if she didn't, and this killed her. At nine o'clock the lights were put out, and I settled back for my first peaceful night's sleep in three months.

At six thirty the next morning, a harsh voice called out an "everybody up" and soon the air was filled with the screech of cell doors. A few minutes later the inmates were hurrying back and forth with their mops and scrub-buckets. Not wanting to shirk any duties, I asked the lady in the next cell to lend me her scrubbing utensils. If I was to live in this cell for the next month, it would have to be clean. I washed the walls as well as the floor and barely made the breakfast line. But when I tasted the slop that was served, I decided I had made the trip for nothing. The oatmeal was scarcely cooked, and served without milk or cream.

I got up to leave but a thunderous voice stopped me dead in my tracks. "Say, you, where d'you think you're going? Remain seated until class is dismissed." The voice came from a police matron with a thin-lipped, sadistic mouth and metallic blue eyes. Pointing toward me, she deliberately winked at one of the prisoners who was collecting dishes from the table and placing them in a portable wagon tray. Her voice took on a sneering tone. "We'll show Miss Rich-Bitch some manners, eh?" I sat down. The woman next to me said, "Pay her no mind. She's the meanest one in the place. Some of the others are kinda decent."

A thin-faced woman opposite interrupted us. "Say," she said, "aintcha gonna eat your chow?" I shook my head. "Okay, then, can I eat it for you?" I pushed the plate over and she devoured the mess, stuffing the leftover bread into the bosom of her dress. "This is for Johnny and Bill," she explained. "My pet mice. It gets kinda lonesome nights, so I keep 'em in my cell for company." I was very happy that she and Johnny and Bill were not in my tier. I wasn't that lonesome.

Since I had to wait for the report on my physical examination before I would be assigned my work, I had nothing to do until lunch hour. I sat on my cot staring at the blank walls, taking stock of my past and thinking of my future. I didn't feel too good about either. My arrest and the various trials had used up my savings. I'd even been forced to borrow. There would be other debts to pay when I'd paid my "debt to society," and I wondered if society would have any suggestions about how I should go about doing it. . . . It seemed a century before I heard the footsteps of the other prisoners returning from the workroom.

Rosie was coming down the corridor, waving a pack of cigarettes. "For you, kid," she announced triumphantly. "I bummed 'em from one of the 'Poppas'—told her you'd pay 'em back when you got your commissary."

I was grateful for the cigarettes and curious about the giver. What was a "Poppa?" Rosie laughed at my question and winked broadly. When she saw that I really didn't understand, she explained that "Poppa" was the jail-house term for Lesbian, and I made a mental note to return the cigarettes as soon as possible, without dividends!

Rosie asked why I had been so late at breakfast and was furious that I had stopped to clean my cell. "Didn't I tell you I was getting you moved to the good side? It's all fixed. I'll help you move over right after lunch." I looked around the tiny cell. "Maybe we better call a moving company," I said. "With all this stuff to move, it'll take a couple of vans."

Laughing together, we started to lunch, and on the way Rosie took time to introduce me to her special friends. The inmate of one cell was a sweet-faced, soft-spoken elderly woman in her late sixties. Except for her prison uniform, she looked like the kind of grandmother any kid would love to have.

Rosie's friendly voice boomed out, "For God's sake, Mary Shane, are you in again?" The old lady chuckled contentedly. "Yes, Rosie, and for a sixer this time." *Six months,* and she seemed grateful for it!

When I marveled at her attitude, Rosie told me her story. Although now she was a hopeless alcoholic and jail habituée, Mary had once been the happy wife of a police lieutenant and the mother of a large family. She had grown children now and was a grandmother, but none of these things kept this old lady away from liquor. Her family had long ago deserted her, and jail was her only home. Whenever she finished a sentence, she would wave gaily and promise to be back by nightfall. She rarely stayed away from "home" more than two days before she was picked up.

My thoughts were interrupted by a hoarse whisper from Rosie, "The next cell is Dago Jean's." The girl in the cell was packing. "She must be checking out. She's been in for an indefinite sentence for running a nautch house." Rosie's tone was apologetic as she remembered the reason I was there. "Say—wait a minute! I just thought of something." She bustled into the girl's cell and emerged with a pair of low-heeled shoes. "Think these would fit your dogs?" They were near enough for comfort, and I was glad to have them instead of the "scuffies" provided by the city. Nobody remembered who had been the original owner. They had been handed down from inmate to inmate, and to wear them was considered a mark of honor.

We joined our "sorority sisters" in the chow line, and this time I sat next to Rosie. Although I was hungry, I could not eat the dreadful food. Rosie whispered, "You better eat. It don't get any better at dinner." So I drank some tea and finally managed to swallow a little cold potato, and Rosie ate the rest.

In the afternoon I moved to the cell with the "southern exposure," but it takes more than sunlight to warm up a prison cell. While the matron made a routine search for sharp instruments from the workroom and food smuggled from the kitchen, I wandered into the corridor and looked out the barred window, facing the Sixth Avenue side. When I saw the free people going about their business, I suddenly realized that being in jail didn't mean only being locked up—it meant being locked out. Now I truly understood the expression: *outside the pale.* . . . A sharp voice interrupted my thoughts. "Hey, you, get away from that window. What are you doin', sendin' a message to your pimp?" It was the hard-faced matron of the breakfast episode. My better judgment stopped me from answering. I did not want my privileges taken away.

During the four-o'clock count, after the working hours were over, a new matron came on duty. In the brief glimpse I had of her as she passed my cell, I knew I was going to like her. She was a plump, neat, little brown-haired woman, with a quiet voice and kind eyes. The inmates all spoke to her respectfully, and she returned their greetings in a friendly manner, calling each by her first name. There was never any show of belligerence during her time on duty because Mrs. McCarthy treated the prisoners like human beings. And when I saw how they responded, it seemed to me there was the key to many social problems.

I thought of the aged prostitutes in the jail. Without their youth and looks, they were no longer "marketable." Maybe some of them could eke out a living working the docks and saloons of the poorer neighborhoods, but I knew that to stay alive most of them would have to become (if they were not already) shoplifters and pickpockets and dope peddlers. The only "reform" offered these women is a term in jail with bad food and harsh treatment. The moment they have served their sentences they are shoved back into the world, with their bitterness against society more deeply rooted than before. Where could they go? What could they do?

I felt an impulse to go among my friends after my release, and enlist their aid in some rehabilitation project. Perhaps a farm—not only for the old outcast prostitute or drunkard but for the young girls who feel the lure of the bright lights—a farm staffed by sympathetic, socially conscious volunteers, not the sort of stuffed shirts who tell you, on a full belly, that YOU are not hungry.

Why couldn't I go out and campaign for such a farm,
I thought to myself—and then I smiled, a little sourly. Polly
Adler in the role of a social reformer was a lousy piece of casting, even in a daydream. I remembered the time I had written to the head of a Jewish orphanage for boys, offering to
pay for a vacation for twelve of their youngsters at a beautiful
resort at Amawalk, New York. The offer included providing
the clothing the children would need for a summer vacation
and a salary for a tutor. But apparently the orphanage people
concluded it was holier to snub one sinful woman than to
give twelve little boys a summer of sun and happiness. My
letter was never acknowledged.

Dinner consisted of a lone and withered frankfurter, a
smattering of beans, two slices of bread, and prunes—always
a melancholy spectacle. When Rosie warned me of the dan-
gers of fasting, I told her I was running a scientific test; I was
going to determine how long it took for a person to get so
hungry he'd eat anything.

After dinner, we went up to the roof, to the "grand ballroom," as the prisoners called the recreation hall, a large,
bare, shedlike place furnished with benches and a piano and
radio. A young girl with a pale, serious face was at the piano,
playing a Chopin Polonaise in quite a professional manner.
Struck by the incongruity of this obviously cultivated girl in
such surroundings, I asked Rosie how she came to be there.
Before she could reply, a shrill voice called out, "Hit it, Paderewski! Jazz it up!" Lost in her music, the girl at the piano
seemed not to have heard the voice. Rosie, in answer to my
question, tapped her forehead significantly.

"She's so screwy," said Rosie, "she even thinks she showed
that guy Paderoo how to play."

"But why is she here?" I persisted.

Rosie shrugged. "She don't talk to us, and there's no other way to find out. Besides, who cares?"

Rosie's next information, conveyed in a whisper, was about two girls who entered arm in arm. "Joan, here come a 'Poppa' and a 'Momma.'" The two women looked the same as the others in the room; neither one appeared more masculine than the other. I asked, "Which is which? How do you tell them apart?" Rosie's eyes grew wise. "See their belts? Well, the one with the buckle in the front of the dress is the 'Poppa.' The 'Momma' puts her buckle in the back."

As we moved toward the door to the roof, a cheerful voice greeted us, "Hiya, Rosie, who's your new friend?"

"Sally, this is Joan, a Righto, our kind of a gal."

I looked Sally over. She stood about six feet tall, towering over me, and when she reached out and squeezed my arm, it was as if she were prodding a loin of beef in a slaughter house.

Rosie said, "I heard you were promoted from potato peelin' to head chef, Sally. If you can't improve on the stuff we get, you better swipe somethin' decent for Joan to eat. She ain't had enough to keep a bird alive since she got here." Sally didn't answer, but Rosie wasn't letting the opportunity slip by. "Sal, I guarantee that Joan will not stool on you. You gotta get her somethin' fit to eat."

Sally agreed to take the chance, but she stated emphatically, "I ain't doin' it for Shorty here; I'm doin' it for you, Rosie."

Rosie promised to return the favor. She would knit a sweater for Sally, if Sally would get the yarn. I thought it was time for me to express my gratitude, so I offered to have the yarn sent in, and our three-way friendship was cemented by Sally's laughing answer, "Don't forget to knit it two sizes larger than I am now. I won't get my diploma for another year, and since I'm in the kitchen now, I'm aiming to get fatter."

Sally went off to substitute for a girl on the basket-ball team and I surveyed the rest of the roof garden—a wide graveled terrace surrounding the "ballroom." The entire roof was enclosed in a finely meshed wire, which formed an enormous cage. As I looked up I had an almost uncontrollable impulse to throw something against the wire mesh, and then I remembered I had seen caged animals do just that. I sat down quickly, lit a cigarette and puffed furiously. Rosie watched me for a minute and then said quietly, "The cage gets everybody the first time they see it. You'll get used to it."

We watched the game for a while and after Sally had made a good shot, Rosie began to brag. "Sally's a big heist woman," she said, "and that takes plenty of guts. She's got enough guts to steal a railroad train."

I laughed and said that was quite a trick; she must be good.

"She sure is," said Rosie. "If she hadn't been on the hop, she would never get caught, she's so fast. Why, she got so loaded one night the damn fool went into a police station and stole a cop's uniform. Then she went to the Pennsy station and changed into the uniform in the woman's can, and then walked right into a liquor store and stuck it up. And by God, she nearly got away with it! But she was so fractured with drugs she just strolled away instead of hopping a cab. So they picked her up, and she got the limit for impersonating an officer."

I wiped away the tears of laughter. "Rosie, did you make up that mad story just to cheer me up?"

"Honest to God, Joan. It's the gospel truth!"

"Then all I can say is that gal's gall outclasses her guts. She should get smart after this stretch and keep away from drugs."

Rosie wagged her head and looked at me with a somber expression. "I feel real bad about what she did because I sold her the stuff that same afternoon. I got bagged myself a few days later, so she was here to say hello when I blew in."

Up until now, I had no idea why Rosie was behind bars, and for a moment, my old hatred for drug peddlers flared up. Then I thought, "Who's judging who?" and controlled myself.

Rosie was in the mood to talk. "I've been a damn fool. I'm past fifty, and here I am serving an indefinite term. I've been here so often I know every nook and corner; I know what the girls are thinkin' and what they're gonna do before they do it. I've got a boy, too." Her voice broke a little. "He's in a military school, supported by relatives who want to give him a chance in life." Her voice was proud. "Joan, my kid is the brightest and the best-lookin' kid in that whole school."

I ask her if her husband was still living.

"Yes. He's servin' time at Riker's Island. We both got pinched at the same time." Her tone was apologetic. "We didn't always do that, Joan. One time my old man was in good with Bill Dwyer and Owney. Durin' prohibition, when they were the bootleg kings, he made a lot of money workin' for them. But he wasn't satisfied with peddlin' hooch. He got to drinkin' it. Then he got so bad, he'd drink alky; then he got on drugs. He lost his job, and I went to see Owney and begged him to give him another chance. He did it, for me, but the same thing happened again, and so"—she shrugged— "we both wound up peddlin' the stuff."

"Is he taking the cure now?"

Rosie's laugh was short and bitter. "Sure, he's got to take it; he's doing a stretch. But you know the old sayin'—'once a junky, always a junky.' " Her expression changed. "If he don't make a man of himself this time, I'm gonna get my kid and go where he'll never find us. My boy ain't gonna suffer all his life like I did." She cried, unashamed. "Joan, I don't know why I'm blabbin' all this to you. But I guess you ain't had no bed of roses either, and maybe you understand how I get to feelin' low."

I understood so well that if the matron's call of "Time's up" hadn't intervened just then, I might have wound up telling Rosie the story of *my* life, matching my mistakes with hers.

I was awakened out of a deep sleep by frightened cries from the floor above. A woman was screaming, "Please, God, let me die." Then she called for help again and again. Then, suddenly, the screams were shut off. In the silence I wondered what time it was. I tossed from side to side. I counted sheep. The last hour of rest was interrupted by screams from the floor below. A woman kept shouting hysterically, "You dirty sons of bitches, let me out of here. I'll kill you for this, you sons of bitches." Other voices bawled at her, "Shut up! . . . . Quiet! . . . . Go back to sleep! . . . . Nutsy, keep yourself gagged."

Suddenly it was six thirty. The main switch that opened the cell doors creaked into action. I rushed off to the shower room. "Jeez, I didn't get a wink last night," said one inmate. "Me neither," chimed in another. "I felt sorry for the poor dame. I think it was Big Cliff; she musta wanted to die; it's her fourth day in the tank and that's the worst time."

(The tank is a section on the eighth floor: a series of small cells with iron doors, solid except for a tiny heavy glass window at eye level, through which the matrons and doctors can observe the drug addicts taking their cure.)

That day one of the inmates asked me how long it would be before I was well. I didn't know what she was talking about. It turned out that she assumed I had a venereal disease because I was wearing a brown uniform. All healthy girls wore blue, she told me. Extremely upset, I marched at once into the laundry room and demanded of the matron why I was wearing a badge of sickness when I was perfectly well.

She looked me over and replied in a cool voice, "*Madam,* this *house* is three-quarters full of negative women. We ain't got enough blue uniforms to go around." When I said nothing, and she saw I was not going to be baited into losing my temper, she spoke more pleasantly. "You start work in the sewing room tomorrow," she said. "You'll get a blue uniform in the morning."

I felt better next day, in blue, and while my work in the sewing room was a bore, I preferred it to idleness. I learned to make rag rugs. I even made a beaded bag. Perhaps I inherited some of my father's talent for tailoring.

My sanity test was at least a break in the monotony of sewing. The psychiatrist was a young, attractive blonde, resembling many of the girls who had passed through my life. (In fact she wore more make-up than I permitted my girls to use.) Motioning me to a seat, she placed a box of colored blocks in front of me and told me to arrange them according to a sketch placed beside them. While I performed this feat, the doctor studied me through tortoise-shell-rimmed glasses as if measuring me for a size-fourteen strait jacket. When I had finished, she inquired about my schooling.

"Two years of high school—evening high school," I said.

"Why did you stop there?"

"Because I was on my feet all day working in a corset factory, and it was two miles to school and back, and I couldn't spare the extra dime for carfare, and the two-mile walk got me down."

There were no more questions on that score. But when she tried to delve into my family background, I refused to give.

I resented being treated like a child—and a backward child at that. If I was sane enough to conduct the most famous house in the biggest city in the world, smart enough to cope with cops and drunks, to amuse and be on friendly terms with people on the top intellectual and social levels, I didn't need advice from a girl who probably hadn't one tenth the human experience—clinical experience—I'd had.

She kept questioning me, but, as I may have mentioned a time or two, when I don't feel like answering, a stone wall is just as responsive. Finally, giving up that pitch, the doctor said, "I want you to identify the pictures on the wall over my head."

Facing me were three pictures in dilapidated frames and—God knows what the gimmick was!—all depicted the same identical scene, a shack surrounded by a few trees. When I had made sure they were exactly alike down to the last detail, I said, keeping my face absolutely dead-pan, "The first is Whistler's Mother, the second Grant Wood's 'Midnight Ride of Paul Revere' and the third"—I squinted a little—"the third seems to be either a dog or a rabbit drawn by James Thurber."

The doctor burst out laughing, and this broke the ice. Soon I felt on a friendly enough footing to ask, "Doctor, do you usually keep mentally ill women here?"

"Not after we find they are ill. Then we send them to a place where they can receive the indicated therapy."

"Then what about that poor girl they call Paderewski? Why is she here?"

The psychiatrist's eyes narrowed a little. "She is refined and well-educated, but she is a hopeless kleptomaniac. Her family life is a complete mystery. She will not disclose even the smallest clue. She has been here twice in my time. I've had several talks with her about books, art and music, but when she is with the other inmates she just shuts off her mind. She couldn't bear the life here if she didn't."

"But what about her fantastic story about teaching Paderewski?"

The doctor laughed. "That's the cleverest thing she does. She pretends she is crazy so the other women will leave her out of their conversations and their activities. This allows her to escape into her own world."

The door of the office burst open, and in came the Assistant Warden. Her voice was harsh, filled with anger. "What's the meaning of this laughter, Doctor? Am I interrupting a social call?"

That concluded my psychiatric examination, in which, incidentally, the press took a great interest. On May twelfth, the New York *Journal* observed rather cattily: "Polly Adler, who posed as a wit in New York's most famous bordello over which she reigned as mistress, yesterday was subjected to a scientific test to ascertain just how smart she really is," and promised to let its readers know how I made out. I expect it was quite a letdown when they had to print on May thirteenth that I was "healthy and sound mentally."

Dorothy Kilgallen interviewed me at this time, and quoted me as saying in regard to my cell, "It's not bad. Of course it ain't big, but it's home." And of the jail routine, "I don't mind the work, but the hours aren't so good." It was a funny interview, and I admire Miss Kilgallen, but I kind of resent that "ain't."

Outside prison walls Sunday is considered a day of rest. Inside it's just the opposite, although not a working day. On Saturday the girls blossom out with toilet-paper curlers in their hair and take great pains laundering their uniforms, bribing the laundry girls, if they have extra cigarettes, to iron them with extra care. Then, on Sunday, the girls attend in order the Catholic, Protestant, Christian Science and Salvation Army services. This makes it possible for them to "keep up socially" with their friends, particularly those on other tiers. Rosie took me in tow and I made the pilgrimage with her each Sunday, making all four services.

On my last Sunday in prison, as I entered the chapel for the Salvation Army service, I was stopped by Major (now Brigadier) Agnes McKernan. She handed me some leaflets and said, "I understand you are leaving us, Polly, and I want to talk to you."

"I know," I broke in. "You followed me around all during my trial, pelting me with pamphlets. I have them at home, and I can't wait to get out and read them."

"Polly, you may not know that I used to be a member of the Committee of Fourteen. I've watched your disgusting career for years. Is there no way to stop you from forcing young girls into a life of shame?"

I burned. "Major, if you have investigated me as thoroughly as you say you have, then you must know that such an accusation has never been leveled against me. I never permit a girl to work for me unless she is already committed to the life."

When the Major sniffed and stated that was not the way she'd heard it, I lost my temper completely. "Well, then you heard wrong, and in any case you should have checked up, if only for your own peace of mind. Or is believing evil of others a new addition to the Salvation Army credo?" I was really lacing into her until suddenly, remembering my five days off for good behavior, I shut up like a clam.

There was a regular welcoming committee awaiting me when I got back to the tier. Major McKernan had given some of the girls a pain in various places for some time, so I was a heroine. "You're an okay broad," said Sally, pumping my hand. "You sure got that preacher dame told."

The night before my release I hardly closed an eye. I knew friends outside were throwing a "gates ajar" party for me, and I planned to spend most of next day at the beauty parlor. But in the midst of mentally enjoying a hot tub, hair-wash, manicure, pedicure and facial, I thought of Rosie and a sense of guilt swept over me. What could I do to repay her countless kindnesses? As a small return, I decided to send ten dollars a month for her personal commissary needs. Then my thoughts drifted to the other girls, and I thought of ways of playing Santa Claus—gosh, just a pair of silk stockings for Sundays can make a world of difference in jail. . . . Just being remembered.

In the morning when the cell doors ground back, I was up like a flash, laughing and kidding in my best "pre-prison" style. But when the girls gathered around to say good-bye, Rosie wasn't among them. I found her in her cell crying. Putting my arm around as much of her ample figure as I could reach, I told her how much her friendship had meant to me, and asked if there was anything I could send besides the remittance for the commissary. She begged me to "write a letter now and then," and gave me a fictitious name to use on the letters, as former prisoners are not allowed to correspond with inmates.

Leaving Rosie was the only bad moment. Almost before I knew it I was wriggling into my musty, wrinkled street clothes, saying one more sentimental good-bye to all my "classmates," shaking hands with the nice matrons and ignoring the others. I was all set to go swinging out the door, a free woman, when I saw the gentlemen of the press gathered like a besieging army, armed with their cameras and their pads and pencils. I rushed to the matron and begged to be let out a side entrance, but she said they were all covered too, and I'd be spotted no matter what exit I left by.

We were talking near the Receiving Gate, and I saw a patrol wagon arrive with a load of prisoners. This gave me an idea, and I pressured the matron into giving me a break. All she did was turn her back a moment and then—presto!—right under the noses of the reporters I rolled away from jail in a style to which I had become only too accustomed, namely, in the caboose of a pie-wagon.

V

For a few days, just the great fact of being free made everything look good to me, but the jail experience had cracked the armor of my self-confidence. Doubts and fears began to seep in, breeding inferiority feelings, and I became more and more reluctant to face the world. Were my friends really glad to see me, or was it just that they regarded me as a curiosity, as anecdote fodder—an ex-jailbird and town character whose sayings and doings might provide tales for them to dine out on? As this state of mind gradually took possession of me, I accepted no more invitations and began to dread going out of my apartment for any reason at all. It seemed, if I may take a whirl at a classical allusion, as if society had at last found my Achilles' heel, and like Achilles I was sulking in my tent.

After a couple of weeks of this self-imposed "solitary" some old friends dropped in and insisted I go out with them on the town. "You've got to snap out of it, Polly," said Tom H. "If you keep on like this, next thing you know you'll be counting your fingers at the University of Paper Hats. All right—so you've been in pokey—so you're out—let's live a little."

We went to Lou Richman's Club on Fifty-second Street. Perhaps because I was unsure of myself I made a point of walking in with my head high, so high that I promptly tripped over a man's outstretched legs and landed in the best possible position to observe that his shoes were from French, Shriner & Urner. The man helped me up apologizing profusely. He was a handsome six-footer topped off with a beautiful head of iron-gray hair—my particular weakness.

"I guess my legs are too long for these small tables," he said. "I hope you weren't hurt."

"Nope, just knocked the wind out of my sails," I told him, and he laughed and asked if he might make amends by buying my party a drink. Tom H., who was standing by, invited him to join us. His name was Harold M., and Tom performed the introductions.

When my name was mentioned, there was an awkward moment. "I suppose you're no relation to the notorious Polly, are you, Miss Adler?" Harold said kiddingly. And when I said we were one and the same person, "But it can't be! You're not—well, you're—you're so different." Apparently, like so many others, he had expected something more on the order of Diamond Lil. I explained that my diamond stomacher and my aigrettes were at the cleaners, everyone burst out laughing, and Harold soon recovered from the embarrassment he felt at showing his surprise. We stayed until closing time, and I was pleased when he asked me to round off the night at Reuben's.

At four in the morning Reuben's is always jammed, and, as our taxi drew up at the curb, the Scotch courage I'd found in a highball glass suddenly deserted me. How could I face

the sly glances and snide cracks of the Broadway back-
stabbers and hatchet men? Harold must have sensed my
panic for he gave me a reassuring wink and offered me his
arm with a flourish. As we entered there was a hush, heads
turned and the buzzing began, but Pop Reuben came hurrying over to shake hands and himself took us to a table reserved for favored customers. It was very heartening to be
treated with such graciousness. It did a lot for my morale.

Harold and I talked until daylight. It was like the old days
with Casey, except that this was not romance, this was friendship. He was separated from his wife. She was a good egg,
he said, but in recent years he had taken to serious drinking
and had worn out her patience. Why did he drink? Well,
like so many men when they reach a certain age, Harold no
longer found life particularly interesting. Everything had
lost its savor, he was bored all the time, nothing was worth
doing and life didn't seem worth living unless he had some
drinks under his belt. He asked me about my plans, and I
tried to explain what jail had done to me, how I had nothing to show for years of hard work, and how I would like to
get into a legitimate business—maybe something in the manufacturing line. He was most sympathetic, trying to show me
that my fears of "society" were groundless, and to lend me
courage to make the break from my old life.

The basis of our friendship was our desire to help each
other. My part was to give him some of the zest for life
which I still had in abundance. His was to show me how to
make my way into a legitimate field. Soon we were seeing
each other constantly, and Harold was tops as a cavalier; every
day he sent me more gardenias than most people go to the
grave with. For weeks we followed a routine of meeting for
cocktails at six, then dinner at some fine restaurant, then a
tour of the town's most amusing joints, which seldom ended

before daybreak. Finally I had to call a halt. I just couldn't stand the pace.

When I moved into a new apartment on East Fifty-fourth, I thought maybe it would help him to ease up on the boozing if we had dinner at my place and spent our evenings there. But I'd hardly had a chance to get the furniture in place before I was tripping over the cases of Scotch that Harold had supplied for our "quiet evenings at home."

When I had been out of prison six weeks, I received a visit from the police, and was stunned to learn that they had been tapping my wires ever since I'd moved into the new apartment. "We hate to do this to you, Polly," the lieutenant said, "and we know you're not conducting a business in this place, but—well, take a friendly tip and move."

"Where to? Do you think Park Commissioner Moses would mind if I pitched a tent in Central Park?" I was so angry my fingers shook when I tried to light a cigarette. "I refuse to be hounded because my name is Polly Adler. Here, take my house key, visit here any hour of the day or night, and convince yourself I'm not breaking any law."

Lieutenant Smith said that wasn't the point. There was pressure on the police department to make me move. The owner of a club near by had complained about me. "He thinks you're living too close to his club, and you might hurt his business," said Smith. "He's pestering us daily for results, and I know he'll resort to anything to get you moved." He hinted that the club owner—whom, by the way, I had met at a party given for Mayor Walker—might even resort to planting a gun or drugs on me. The lieutenant's parting words were, "Get smart and get out."

When Harold called for me that evening, he was too excited at the news he brought to notice I was upset. He said he had lunched with a friend who was planning to open a small factory in New Jersey and was offering a twenty-five per cent interest to a competent person willing to take full charge and invest a small amount of capital. It sounded ideal; the only fly in the ointment was that Harold had neglected to inform his friend I was Madam Polly. As I had feared, when he learned my identity, the deal collapsed with a dull thud. "It took many years of hard work on my part," the friend said, "to build up my rating with Dun & Bradstreet. And I can't help but wonder if a partnership with Miss Adler would hurt my credit. . . . No offense to Miss Adler's character, you understand."

When we were alone, Harold apologized for his "conservative" friend. "I'll offer to finance the business. That ought to bring him around."

"Don't bribe my way into a legitimate business," I snapped. "I've been bribing people all my life, and I'm sick of it. Let's just skip the whole thing. And you stop filling my head with pipe dreams! I'm stuck with myself, and I know it. I'm going back to the whorehouse business where I belong."

But Harold told me I was a weakling, and finally I promised to keep trying. I remembered a night-club owner who had urged me to come into partnership with him. He had been so impressed with my ability in handling people that he wanted no other investment on my part. However, now when I called him, he said, "Sure I'd like to go in with you, Polly, if the police would ever let you alone. But I doubt if that day will ever come. You've had too much notoriety. The cops are bound to hound you out of anything legitimate."

I made two other calls and got the same word. Next I tried to get into a business where I could stay in the background. I thought maybe I could be the silent operator of a hat-check and cigarette concession. So I called a restaurant owner, an old friend, and told him my plan.

"I'm sorry, Polly, no dice," he said. "There's a new city ruling that all concessionaires as well as the girls who work for them must be fingerprinted."

For many days I tried every possible angle; I exhausted all my contacts, but every door was closed to me, sometimes with a tactful lie, sometimes with the blunt announcement that people couldn't afford to be associated with me. Then I got a wild idea—so wild I thought maybe it was good. I'd go and appeal to the police commissioner in person!

What happened was succinctly reported in the *Daily Mirror*:

The lady is not unused to having men call on her, not only policemen but gentlemen. No one remembers though when she last came a-calling on a man, and that man both a gentleman and a policeman. She was demurely clad, her approach was sedate and her expression naïve.

"May I speak to the Police Commissioner, please?" she half-whispered.

"Sorry, ma'am, but the Commissioner is very busy. Can I have your name?" asked the secretary in a routine manner.

"Hm? Don't trouble. I'll write him," she said, and tripped out. A reporter, entering as she was exiting, addressed her, but she hurried out and ducked into a waiting limousine.

"What did she want?" he called to the secretary.

"I don't know. We have hundreds of cranks——"

"Cranks!" bellowed the reporter. "She was no crank!"

"Well, who was the lady?"

"That was no lady, that was Polly Adler!"

This was one joke on myself I couldn't laugh at—or off. Dutch had been right; once you're tagged as a madam it's for keeps. I could never be a legitimate operator, my reputation would always be an insurmountable stumbling block. I had wanted to impress on the Commissioner the seriousness of my intention to go straight and to ask his co-operation. I thought if he was convinced of my good faith, he might tell the cops to lay off and give me a chance to get started. But I didn't try to see him again. What was the use? I was no lady. I was

Polly Adler. I was a madam—or would be as soon as I'd plunked down a month's rent and opened my little black book. I couldn't live my reputation down—all right then, I'd live up to it.

Chapter 9

A House

Is Not a Home

> It is a mere absurdity to assert that prostitution
> ever can be eradicated. Strenuous and well-
> directed efforts have been made. . . . The
> whole power of the Church where it possessed
> not merely a spiritual, but an actual secular arm,
> has been in vain directed against it. . . .
> Absolute monarchs have bent all their energies
> of will, and brought all the aids of power to
> crush it out. . . . The guilty women have been
> banished, scourged, branded, executed; their
> partners have been subjected to the same
> punishment; held up to public opinion as im-
> moral; denuded of their civil rights; have seen
> their offenses visited upon their families; have
> been led to the stake, the gibbet and the block,
> and still prostitution exists. . . . Prostitution
> is coeval with society.
>
> *W. W. Sanger, M.D.*   THE HISTORY OF
> PROSTITUTION

I

As Miss Pearl Adler, the reformed procuress and honest citizen, I was a social outcast. As Madam Polly, the proprietress
of "New York's most opulent bordello," society came to me. I
took a six-room apartment in the East Fifties and before
many days had passed was back in the old familiar routine.
My clients said how they had missed me and how glad they

were I was once again "at home" to them, but to be honest, I could not return the compliment.

It is one thing to embark on an enterprise under your own power, but when you are pushed into it—when it seems, as it did to me, that you have no other choice—then you start out bogged down by the chips on your shoulders, in the mood to make the worst of things instead of the best, prepared to magnify every difficulty and exaggerate every hurt. Not only did I find it harder to put up with the drawbacks of the profession, but my state of mind was such that I could no longer enjoy its great recompense—the company of those gifted and amusing and celebrated people whose patronage and friendship I had set such store by.

In reality nobody had changed toward me. There always would be patrons who would despise me for being a madam, who would go wash their hands after shaking mine, who would make use of me, and then—because I was associated with the side of their own nature of which they were most ashamed—would get rid of their feelings of guilt and self-disgust by making me the target of their ridicule and contempt. And there would always be the others who, in spite of my calling, saw me as a human being with qualities which appealed to them, whose liking for me personally would outweigh their prejudices against my profession, who, being neither cowards nor hypocrites, would not make me the whipping boy for their own consciences. But at this time I was not, as Dutch would say, thinking straight. My mental set was rebellious and sullen and self-pitying. The world had given me the brush-off, and I retaliated in kind. I retreated into a shell of indifference; I gave my customers what they paid for, but nothing of myself. I neither looked for nor gave sympathy or interest or friendship. And, as a result, the next two years were to be the unhappiest I spent as a madam.

Now when I was called on to listen to the troubles of tired businessmen and discontented wives and unhappy mistresses, I would pretend to sympathize, but it was only from the lip out. I would have no patience with their complaints about being bored and misunderstood, and, in particular, with their lamentations about "that man Roosevelt," who it seemed was personally responsible for their domestic hardships ("we had to cut the indoor staff down to eight") and the cancellation of their plans to winter in Bermuda or abroad ("we'll be criticized if we don't open the Palm Beach place and spend our money in this country").

I don't mean to say that only poor people have problems, or that because a person is rich, he may not be just as much in need of sympathy as the guy on the corner selling apples. But at a time of nationwide distress, I found their whining about "economics" almost more than I could take. (On the other hand, some of my best friends are millionaires, men like Scottie who did—and do—far more to help out the "submerged tenth" than all those parlor pinks and leftist windbags whose altruistic schemes always simmer down to saving the country with somebody else's hard-earned money.) In any case, whether I found my clients' point of view congenial or not was very much beside the point. The only things that concerned me during their monologues was the amount they spent on drinks. When possible, I'd encourage backgammon instead of conversation. It meant far less talking and, since it left a hand free to hold a glass, just as much drinking. I was considered a whizz at the game, and, as play was usually for high stakes, this became a good source of income.

Now that I was at the beck and call of my customers twenty-four hours a day, I saw less and less of Harold. He was bitterly disappointed in me for returning to my former life. Moreover now that I had the "madam" in front of my name again, I felt our association would have to end. I was grateful to him for his loyal friendship during a difficult period and for his efforts, even though they were fruitless, to "rehabilitate" me. But I hope I had helped him too. At any rate, Harold and his wife became reconciled and, so far as I know, are still together.

I had been back in business only a couple of months when Inspector Neidig came to call. The last time I had seen him was at my trial, and I remembered his embarrassment on being called to the stand. It was unusual for a cop with the rank of inspector to appear as a witness against a mere madam.

When the maid woke me to say he was waiting in the living room, I was out of bed in a flash, and, only half-awake, started throwing on my clothes. It was one in the afternoon, but some Washington men had left just three hours before.

Inspector Neidig greeted me with a scowl. "Polly," he said gruffly, "why don't you get wise? Why don't you quit before the Feds take you in tow? Look what happened to Diane B. (One of my competitors who had been arrested by the FBI.) This is off the record, but they're on your tail too."

Since I was not an interstate operator, the reference to the federal men didn't faze me. I told the Inspector in detail about my attempts to get out of the business and concluded with the defiant assertion that, as no other vocation was open to me, I expected to be running a house until the day I cashed in my chips.

"Do what you like," he said curtly, "but do it someplace else." He added that he'd be back in a few days to make sure I'd vacated. He didn't care where I moved to—just so it was out of Fourth Division territory, out of the "silk stocking district."

So back went the furniture into storage (at least I was

popular with the storage company—I gave them more business than any other customer), and I moved to temporary
headquarters at a flea-bag on Sixty-fifth Street. The colored
elevator boy there was a "king pimp" with a system all his
own. For ferrying men up to the prostitutes living there, he
received a fee of a dollar a head, and the prostitutes paid
him half what they received from the men he procured for
them. In addition, he collected five dollars a week for keeping
their telephone calls straight, and was paid extra when he
introduced new girls to madams in the city. He was a regular
jack-of-all-trades. There wasn't anything he couldn't get,
from a shoelace to a hop layout. No wonder he drove to work
in a Cadillac.

Inspector Neidig's visit was the opening passage of the
second of the dominant themes, or motifs, of these years—the
"move along" motif. I was to be constantly on the run not
only from myself, but from the cops. As in my early days, I
was kept hopping from one address to the next.

New Year's, 1936, found me in an apartment on Central
Park West, and, since I had been there almost long enough to
catch my breath, I was prepared to believe that maybe the
coming year would be better. It was a feeling I shared with
people in general, for it was beginning to look as if the depression had been licked—the federal dole had ended the
month before—and, except for the Italo-Ethiopian war, the
international scene was reasonably calm.

But in New York another vice investigation was under
way, and the papers were full of stories about the impending
assault on the various vice rackets by racket-buster Thomas
E. Dewey, who had been appointed Special Prosecutor by
Governor Herbert Lehman. As I had no affiliation of any
nature with the "combination" (I have told of my one encounter with the combination men that time in the bail-bond

office), I felt I had nothing to fear. But on Friday, January thirty-first, I got an anonymous tip-off which made me think that the Seabury history was going to repeat itself. My caller informed me there was to be a wholesale raid on houses of prostitution that night. The cops, he said, would not be told till the last minute which houses would be raided, and I didn't hang around to find out. I checked with the maid every hour all through the night, but the word was "all serene" and, until I saw the papers, I thought perhaps it had been a false alarm.

Far from it. The headlines blazed with the news that Dewey's men had raided nearly fifty houses, and had rounded up and hauled in a great drove of girls and madams with such picturesque names as Cokey Flo, Gas-house Lil, Frisco Jean and Silver-tongued Elsie. There was a statement from Mr. Dewey that he was not interested in wiping out prostitution, but in nabbing those who organized vice on a wholesale scale. "If this were merely an attempt to suppress prostitution, gambling and lottery games," he said in reference to the investigation, "I feel sure the governor would never have ordered it. . . . [Our intention is to] deal only with vice where it exists in organized form." He added a few words to the effect that he did not intend "to make Polly Adler the hub of this investigation."

But in spite of Mr. Dewey's statement, I was sceptical, and when I couldn't get any information as to who would be next on the list for scrutiny, I decided to close my place and get lost. I had friends on the Coast who had given me a standing invitation to visit them, and what better time to take them up on it? So inside of a week I was basking in the sunlight on the beach at Santa Monica, trying to pretend that the only Dewey I had ever heard of was the one who took Manila.

Now that I was on the Coast I made a point of looking up a former madam, whose house in Hollywood had enjoyed the same high repute as mine in New York. Although we had not met before, she was most cordial and invited me to lunch. I found her attractive and refined, almost prim in manner. It was hard to believe that this lady, who looked so like a schoolteacher, could ever have been a madam. We had lunch at the Beverly Derby, and while we were chinning over our coffee I noticed a group of people in an adjacent booth whom I had known in New York some years before. My mind went clicking back, and I recalled that a man in the group had once been the sweetheart of Louise M., who ran a call house in New York. I was trying to think of his name when the waitress handed me a note, asking me to phone him that evening.

The first five minutes of our telephone conversation was taken up with a blow-by-blow description of his personal success story and what a big shot he had become. I wasn't impressed, and I implied that if he wanted to beat the drum for himself, okay—but not on my nickel. So he got down to business.

"You know, Polly, there were many of your friends at the Derby this noon who would have come over to say hello to you, but they didn't dare on account of the person you were with. She's the most notorious woman in Hollywood."

"So am I a rabbi's daughter?" I exploded. "Was Louise M.? You have a very short memory, bub!"

And I banged down the phone. In his lean days, when this inflated jerk was romancing a madam, he wasn't too proud to let her put the clothes on his back—the Sulka ties and the Charvet dressing gowns and the monogrammed shirts. He wasn't too proud to eat three squares a day at her expense, to guzzle her whisky and drive her car, and finally to accept the plane ticket to Hollywood and the cash which had carried him until he had begun to click. But now a madam was dirt beneath his feet. . . . Success does something to jerks like that —it protects them from their memories.

When my hosts went away on a business trip, they urged me to be sure and have friends in, and I invited the former madam for the weekend. My first impressions were confirmed. She proved a woman of heart, of discrimination, of sound good sense. It was a relief to be able to open up about my own problems with someone who could really understand. But after she left, I was twice as lonely in my friends' big house and moved to a hotel in Beverly Hills. This was a mistake. The other guests cold-shouldered me industriously; they really worked at leaving me out of things. I had hoped for anonymity in Hollywood, but what I got was isolation. When my masseuse suggested a trip to Honolulu, I bounced right up off the table and called the Matson Line. I found that if I took a plane I could catch the *Lurline* which was sailing from San Francisco the next afternoon.

Killing time, I stopped in at Dave Chasen's only to find no drinks were being served as it was Election Day. However, when I caught sight of a certain well-known and beloved face, I felt as a wayfarer lost in the Alps must feel when he sees the lights of the hospice shining through the snow— Robert Benchley was there, and waving at me to join him. With characteristic foresight, Bench had prepared for the Election Day emergency, and offered me a Pink Lady from a flask that would have broken the neck of a St. Bernard. Soon we were deep in reminiscences about old times, about Papa Tony and Dorothy Parker and the members of the Algonquin Round Table.

We were well on the way to getting lost in a pale pink fog, when I heard brays of greeting, and there were some of the hotel guests bearing down on us, their cold shoulders magically defrosted at the sight of my companion. I whispered that up to now these characters had done nothing but snub me, and Bench responded by giving them the full treatment —a brush-off that sent them scattering in all directions like a busted strand of dime-store pearls.

Robert Benchley was the kindest, warmest-hearted man in the world, and ordinarily he would have cut off his right arm rather than do or say anything to make another person uncomfortable. But such petty gratuitous meanness always infuriated him, and he despised snobs and hypocrites. To cheer me up, he told me of the time a great friend of his, an international stage star, opened in a play. As always, she was snowed under with telegrams wishing her luck, most of which were signed with internationally famous names. But in the place of honor at the top of the dressing-table mirror was the telegram from me. Speaking of this actress, I remember that Bench used to kid me about my husky voice, saying that I sounded just like her with a cold.

Between Mr. Benchley and the Pink Ladies, I nearly missed the plane. I'm glad I didn't though, or I would have missed a most happy and refreshing holiday. No one knew who I was, and I reveled in the novelty of being treated like everybody else. If it had not been for the bills piling up, I could never have pried myself away from those friendly islands.

On my return journey I stopped off at San Francisco and spent a few days seeing friends (including Mr. and Mrs. Climber, who remembered "Baroness von Weiner" very well indeed) and the sights. One tour took me to Alcatraz, where Al Capone was then in residence. I left a note and some cigarette money for him with one of the guards. I don't know if he ever got them, but I felt I should at least leave a card on "Baron Al" when I called at his walled castle.

Mr. Dewey was a man of his word. I was never called for questioning. However, I was astonished to learn that he was seeking to link Charlie (Lucky) Luciano with the prostitution racket. It was inconceivable to me that any such connection could exist. For one thing, I used to supply the girls when Charlie Lucky entertained in his plushy hotel suites, and it hardly seems logical that if he had the alleged tie-ups, he would patronize a madam outside the combine. Of course it was no secret that Charlie Lucky was mixed up in all sorts of rackets, and his activities were openly discussed by the men who were "too light for heavy work and too heavy for light work." But not once was it ever even implied that he derived any part of his income from prostitution.

I think Mr. Dewey never called me as a witness because the only testimony I could possibly give was in favor of the defense. As Dewey said, "We can't get bishops to testify in a case involving prostitution," but his case against Charlie Lucky was based on the word of frightened, ignorant prostitutes, many of them alcoholics and drug addicts.

I knew one of the star witnesses, Mildred Harris, who testified that Charlie Lucky spat in her face when she appealed to him to allow Pete, her husband, to quit his racket of booking girls into houses. I could not accept a word of this story. What may have happened is that some new bookies muscled in on Pete Harris, and Mildred, realizing that a word from Luciano would have scared these men off, went to Charlie Lucky for help. As I have explained elsewhere, a "prostitution man" is considered an untouchable by big racket men, and if Mildred did use such an approach, Charlie would have been so insulted he would have refused even to discuss the matter, let alone intervene. But if she had said Pete was on someone's rub-out list, it is my feeling he would have done all he could to help her.

I say this because in the years of my acquaintance with Charlie Lucky, I never found him to be other than gentlemanly. I knew him before he became the kingpin of the rackets, but success didn't change him. He was always quiet, clean-talking and considerate of the girls and maids. I remember on one of his visits, the building superintendent was fixing the kitchen sink, and Charlie, noticing the man looked terribly gloomy, cracked, "What's this guy doing in a house of joy? He looks ready to croak!" But when we were in the other room, and I explained that the man was ill with leukemia, Charlie was deeply embarrassed by his unintentional unkindness. He gave me three hundred dollars for the poor fellow and said to let him know if more was needed.

Another time Charlie was entertaining a group of friends at my place, among whom were Terry McGurn and Bugsy Siegel, the West Coast racketeer who was killed in the home of Virginia Hill. Terry and Bugsy decided to give me a lesson in interior decoration and began by hauling the sofa into the kitchen and moving the stove into the living room. They got the stove about halfway through the door when they noticed Charlie Lucky looking at them—not saying anything, just looking. In two seconds flat the furniture was back in place, and there was no more horseplay for the balance of the evening.

One day shortly after Lucky's trial opened, I received a phone call from a big racket man telling me to meet him outside my apartment house in ten minutes. This man had never called me before nor had he ever been in my house. I knew him by name and reputation only.

As I stood in front of my apartment, a battleship-size sedan pulled up, and the man who had called jumped out. Without a word he helped me into the back seat. Another man was sitting there, but we weren't introduced. The driver waited until another large black car pulled up ahead of us, then we followed after it. I looked out of the rear window and saw a third big sedan following. The man who had telephoned smiled reassuringly. I knew that he was a friend of Lucky's and surmised this trip had something to do with Lucky, so I wasn't too worried. But if I hadn't known this, I would have sworn I was being taken for a ride.

It was dark, and as we cut swiftly around corners and sped down dimly lit streets, I soon lost all sense of direction. I had no idea where we were going, and I didn't ask. At last we turned into a tunnel and emerged in a garagelike underground area where a number of cars were parked. My caller took me by the arm and, with the rest of the men following, led me through a series of offices into a large conference room. I caught my breath! Gathered there were men from all the biggest rackets in New York. It was the first time I had ever seen all these men under the same roof. It may well be the only time they all were assembled.

I was led to a chair by a desk and asked to be seated. I recognized the man behind the desk as one of New York's most prominent lawyers, a man whose name had never even been breathed in connection with the Lucky Luciano case. He thanked me for coming and then explained the reason for my being brought there. All the men present, he said, were doing everything possible to prove that the testimony being given by certain women were false. They were trying to uncover facts which would discredit that testimony. Handing me a list of names, he asked me if any of the girls on the list were known to me. After I had studied the list carefully, I shook my head. Although I would have liked to aid these men in their efforts to exonerate Charlie Lucky from a charge all those there felt was false, none of the girls had ever worked for me. There was nothing I could have done or said to help.

Charlie Lucky was convicted of compulsory prostitution on sixty-one counts, and on June sixth was sentenced to thirty to fifty years at Dannemora, which is a long stretch even if it's served on both ears. However, after serving only nine of them, his sentence was commuted by the same man who had sent him up, Governor Dewey, and he was deported to Italy.

Quantities have been written pro and con on the question of Lucky Luciano's guilt, not of his being a racket man, for Charlie himself never denied that, but of his being guilty of the charge on which he was convicted. Certainly I believe that in the many years I was associated with prostitution if there had been even a hint of a rumor of a tie-up between Charlie and the combination, I would have heard of it. And if he was indeed "ninety times guilty," then why was he sprung?

II

Maybe it was the weather—July 10, 1936, was the hottest day of the year—but after the raid which occurred on that date I decided New York was too hot to hold me, and I'd go elsewhere to conduct my business. I had been spending the evening quietly enough writing letters when a friend of mine, Gracie M., a dancer, not one of my call girls, dropped in to repay some money she'd borrowed. While she was there, a customer telephoned asking me to line up dates for him and a friend, and I asked the two men up for a drink. They arrived about ten minutes later, and, as they walked in the front door, four cops came in through the back. They instantly pounced on Gracie, who was sitting in the kitchen drinking a cup of coffee.

I pleaded with them to let her go, pointing out that if she

were in my house to make money she would hardly have her dog with her, and she wouldn't be wearing a housedress, nor would she be living in a cheap rooming house around the corner. Any girl who worked for me certainly fared better than that. But I had not as yet telephoned to make dates for my two customers, so Gracie was the only "evidence" the police could find, and they insisted on hauling her in.

"She's a blonde, ain't she?" said one of the coppers. "And you promised your johns to get 'em blondes." So I knew my wires were tapped.

On the day of the trial, Gracie was dismissed, but I was held on what seemed to me a mental charge. I was *thinking* of furnishing some blondes, but I hadn't produced them. As I said to the cops, "I am innocent of any law-breaking this evening. Yesterday, perhaps, but not tonight." Realizing the tough spot I was in, I was compelled to ask the men who were in the apartment to testify in my behalf that they were not at my apartment for immoral purposes, and it was their testimony which got me off the hook.

The papers headlined: POLICE STATION IS OBSEQUI-OUS TO POLLY ADLER, and said that "the most publicized madam in New York whose arrest in 1935 created much of the furor leading up to the Dewey Vice investigation . . . was so courteously treated at the W. 68th St. Station that Commissioner Valentine ordered an investigation." This was typical of the way newspapers exaggerated every little thing connected with me. When I went to be booked, the desk sergeant leaned over to shake hands and said, "How are you, Polly?" I put my finger to my lips and said, "Psst! The name is now Kay Bell." He said, "Ooops! Sorry," and asked me if I wanted to see the reporters, then took me to a back room when I said I didn't. I wouldn't call that obsequi-ous. (The same newspaper story, describing my apartment, said I had a bust of Beethoven on the radio cabinet and a red silk canopy over my bed. Well, it happened to be a bust of Mozart and there was no canopy of any description, but I guess in hot weather it's easier to exercise your imagination than your eyesight.)

In any case, I was fed up with the wire-tapping and police double-crossing (the leader of the arresting flatfeet had fallen out of one of my beds the very morning of the pinch), and I decided they could find another target. I was getting out. The burning question, of course, was what town to settle in. There were not many which could support a de luxe establishment such as mine, all the year around. Outside New York, as I knew, so many madams depended on the convention trade—or, at resorts, on seasonal business—to keep operating.

I had got to know quite a lot about houses in other towns, from hearing the girls talk about where they had worked. For example, on their "vacations" in Florida, my girls usually would work either for Gertie Walsh or Colette. At Colette's a girl was required to drop her own name and assume that of the movie star whom she most resembled. A blonde might call herself Lana Turner, a brunette, Hedy LaMarr, and a redhead, Lucille Ball. Perhaps because of this gimmick Colette did a thriving business. Men flocked to her place to meet the namesake of their favorite movie queen and to be able to say next day, "I spent the night with Lana Turner" —or whoever. But the girls preferred to work at Gertie's house because it was the busiest and best-paying. There was no time wasted in conversation and "sociability" as at my house. Men came there for one reason, and one reason only. The girls worked in shifts. In the dining room there would be two spreads: the girls going off duty would have breakfast before retiring, the girls going on duty would have dinner before starting work; and a buffet setup would follow later for a midnight snack.

One of my girls told me she had once worked for the famous Madam Swift. The girl was new in town (one of the Madam's requirements, by the way—she would not hire local girls whom her clients might recognize), but a friend told her about the Madam's place, and she went to see about work. Madam Anna Swift ran a massage parlor advertised in the newspapers as a legitimate business and conducted as a legitimate business, but with variations. A client who came to her building and asked for a massage or a high colonic got what he asked for. A trained nurse took care of his needs. Then a "finisher" came in, a pretty girl who proceeded to give him a rubdown. This young lady was part of the establishment. No price was discussed. Madam Swift charged ten dollars for his massage. His gift to the girl was her pay for the "finishing," which could involve pretty much whatever he wanted, and the amount was up to him.

The girls lived upstairs, but even they saw little of the Madam. A white-haired grande dame, said to be in the Social Register, she dined alone, formally, her table gleaming with fine linen and silver and graced by candles and flowers. My girl told me she found it hard to believe that Anna Swift really was a madam and knew what was taking place in her house. For years the cops had tried without success to get the goods on her, but eventually Madam Swift got careless. Some girls whom she had sent out on call got tagged, and the cops, when they finally had the evidence to raid her, found all the equipment for the off-beat pleasures sought by a sophisticated and twisted clientele. Whips, cat-o'-nine-tails and a whole torture chamber convinced them and the world that the Madam had known what she was about all right. Having raided her once, the cops kept at it until at last she was driven out of town. She went to the District of Columbia and foolishly opened up there, where every crime is a federal offense. As a result the old lady has done a lot of time.

But of the million-odd prostitutes in America, only a very small percentage are fortunate enough to be employed in the first-class parlor houses and call houses. While I seldom came in contact with the madams who ran cheap whorehouses, I had learned something about them from Rose Blake, a well-known out-of-town madam, whom a patron had brought to my house one night after a big fight at the Garden. With her was one of her girls, Trixie, and from them I got a fairly comprehensive picture of the operation of the lower-priced establishment which goes in for quantity rather than quality, and depends on volume of business and a quick turnover for profits.

Rose's house was in Pennsylvania in a wide-open town. "I have ten girls working for me regularly," she said, "and when the mines are in full operation, I increase my staff to fifteen or twenty. My girls work in shifts, as we are open from eight in the morning till midnight. The girls alternate. Those who start at eight and quit at four will take the four to midnight shift the following week. Of course the night shift is the busiest."

"How many men a day visit your house?" I asked.

"From two hundred to two hundred and fifty," she said, smiling at my look of amazement. "My girls must have contact with twenty-five men a day to net thirty dollars a day. I run a strictly three-dollar house." (Of the seventy-five taken in, half would go to Rose, and the odd seven-fifty would go for tips, personal expenses and so on.)

"Well, Rose," I said, "I guess you're better off than I am. With all the raids and shakedowns and my high overhead,

I'm always winding up on the wrong side of the ledger. But you must make quite a profit."

"My average gross is eight thousand dollars a month," Rose said, "and I know that sounds like a real bundle. But let me tell you where it goes. I pay five hundred dollars a week to the Chief of Police for protection. The collector doesn't tell me how this money is passed around, so I don't know. All I know is that it costs me fifty dollars a week per girl to stay in operation, and when I have fifteen girls with me, the five hundred jumps to seven hundred and fifty. The two uniformed cops who patrol my beat get one hundred and forty dollars weekly, or twenty dollars a night. Then there's rent. I pay five hundred dollars a month for a house in the slums on the outskirts of town, a house nobody in his right mind would pay fifty a month for. But I'm told that the landlord is a friend or relative of the police officials, and this is the only place they'll let me keep open. Actually I operate with two partners, the landlord and the police.

"I, as the madam, am an outcast," she went on, "but my partners rake in the profit and still stay respectable. What's more, I have to help them stay that way. I'm expected to take at least one pinch a month, more at election times. They warn me in advance of a coming raid, and I see to it there's only one girl and the housekeeper around to take the rap. The girl's bail is set at three hundred dollars and the house-keeper's at five hundred. We forfeit the bail so they won't have to appear for trial. Thus the city becomes my third partner, because these pinches cost me from eight hundred to one thousand dollars a month." She hesitated a minute. "What gripes me most is the parade of compulsory charities. Every month they hit me for tickets to the Policemen's Ball, or the Firemen's Outing, for contributions to the church bazaars and baskets of food for the poor. . . . There are lots more, all of them compulsory. So just to meet this monthly pay-off, my house has to bring in eight thousand a month."

I had been running over the figures she had given me and now I said, "Supposing the graft you have to pay off adds up to five thousand dollars. If your house makes eight thousand, is the other three thousand yours?"

She laughed. "Aren't you forgetting running expenses? Besides the graft, I have to have two maids and a housekeeper. The maids get fifty each a week, the housekeeper a hundred. I have fifteen mouths to feed, including my girls and the cops who drop in around midnight for a snack. My table costs me around two hundred dollars a week. This is partly because the grocer jacks up the prices for me—everybody gets his cut, you know—and besides, he's like the others on the outside, figures all we do is coin the money."

I said, "Yes, and there's laundry."

She smiled again. "You keep thinking of my house in terms of yours. You see, we use trick beds. These look like regular beds, but instead of a box spring, there's a mattress over the slats—it's easier on the girls' backs. Then, we don't use sheets but just throw a cotton spread over the bed and the pillow, and put a small rug on the foot of the bed for a man to rest his dirty shoes on. I hand out paper towels and Lifebuoy soap."

I broke in, "What's a man doing in bed with his shoes on?"

"Listen, all he's got is fifteen minutes. You don't think he's going to waste time taking his shoes off, do you? Why, even with the girls' trick dresses—zippers all the way down front so they can peel them right off and nothing underneath to take off—still the men complain they don't get ready fast enough."

When I asked about paying the girls, she told me that each girl was paid off at the close of her shift when she turned in her "lace curtain"—the card that bore a punch mark for every customer entertained. "If her lace curtain matches the card on which the housekeeper keeps her tally, everything's fine. I have a special puncher that makes a different mark that can't be copied. Each punch-hole means a dollar fifty, and if I left it up to the girls and didn't have my special punch, their cards would be like old lace at the end of the first hour." As it was, she said, a girl was timed from the moment when a customer entered the bedroom, and after fifteen minutes the housekeeper tapped to indicate that time was up. "Of course a man is privileged to remain longer, but the girl must collect at fifteen minute intervals."

At this point the maid beckoned to me, and I excused myself to Rose and went to see what was the matter.

"You better straighten yourself out with the girls," whispered the maid. "They're on my neck, complaining about that Trixie who came here with Miss Rose. She hasn't left the bedroom since she got here." She pointed to the bill of the guests present. "You can see for yourself, no other girl's name is on it, only Trixie's. She sure works like lightning."

Later, when I called Trixie aside to give her her share of the money she had earned that night, she declined it saying, "Split it among your girls. They work here. I'm just vacationing." I insisted, but she was firm. Remembering what Rose had told me about her girls having contact with twenty-five men a day, I realized this must have seemed just a light workout to Trixie.

The kid puzzled me. Here she was, a cute little blonde with all the qualifications to work in a high-class call-house, and yet she chose a three-dollar house in a coal-mine territory. When I asked her about her home town she said, "My home is in whatever town I'm booked. I make the same circuit every year and, like a good actress, I have no trouble getting return bookings. My 'landladies' tell me I increase their business when I'm performing in their houses. They start billing me with their customers weeks in advance as 'Bedroom Trixie.'

"But I guess you'd call Detroit my home. Six months out of the year I work there in the two busiest houses. I never leave the bedroom, except for my meals, from the time I start to work. That's why they nicknamed me 'Bedroom Trixie.' Right now I'm staying in New York because my man had a stroke. He's under a doctor's care here, and I'm going to stay with him until he gets well. But the doctor's bills are terrific, and I have to get to work. Can you refer me to a house with lots of action?"

"You scored a hit with my patrons, Trixie. You can keep dates for me."

"Jack may object if I work in a call-house. There's not enough money in it. And, besides, I never worked in a high-class house. I probably wouldn't know how to get along with a better class of men."

"A man's breeding, education, social or financial position," I said, "have nothing whatsoever to do with the way he behaves when he enters the bedroom of a whorehouse. So be at ease."

Early next evening Trixie phoned me. "My sweetheart gave me permission to give your house a tryout," she announced. She remained in New York until Jack had his second stroke—this one fatal. After that she drifted back to the "circuit" again, and the last I heard of Trixie she was working in a crib in Panama. It made my blood run cold to think of it. Panama was one of the lowest spots on the face of the earth for a prostitute—the bottom of the barrel, the last port of call.

On my West Indies cruise in 1935 there had been a stopover at Colon and in the course of seeing the sights I had visited the red-light district. Here the street was lined on both sides with cribs—small rooms, about twelve feet wide and eight feet deep, whose front walls were great wide doors which pulled back so that the entire room could be exposed to the street. Each room had a large double bed, splashed over with a bright satin spread, a table, a washbowl and mirror. One large chair stood near the open door, and it was here that the room's occupant sat during her leisure hours, chatting with the girl next door or mending a piece of clothing, but always with her eyes swiveling toward the street to watch for a customer. When a man strolled down the street, the girls shrieked out their prices, dickering at the top of their lungs until he had made his selection and settled upon the price, and the big doors had closed on the incipient romance.

Most of the "girls" were anything but that. Some were fat and greasy, others thin and peaked, and all wore heavy make-up slathered on like paste. They were of every age and nationality—Cubans, Germans, Italians, Chinese, Americans and a mixture of races, Latin-Indian-Negro. I talked to one of the girls. She showed me her treasures, proudly displaying for my approval a kewpie doll, some pictures of her family and, the joy of her life, a phonograph. I congratulated her on her wealth and was somewhat startled when she informed me that she was getting married the next day.

"Tomorrow!" I exclaimed. "But then what are you doing here? Why not leave right now?"

She regarded me with amazement. "Leave now? I wouldn't think of it! My rent is paid up until tonight."

On another occasion I had learned more details about operating a cheap house from the housekeeper in a bordello in a small California town. As in the locality where Rose Blake had her house, this also was a wide-open town, and, as in any open town, the rule was that the powers-that-be allow just so many places. It's all the same to them who runs them, they get paid so much per girl in any case.

This place was run by a man who owned four other houses in the state. The housekeeper had worked in them all and reported they all were run the same way. The rental on the Mission House, as her current place was called, was fifty dollars a month and three girls were employed there, working one shift only, from noon until midnight. The girls lived on the premises, and each paid fifteen dollars a week for room and board. They had their own rooms, which were not used for hustling.

Once a week the pimp would drive over with a car full of girls, and the housekeeper would pick those she wanted for the coming week. Then he would drive on to distribute the rest of his girls. Before the work week began, the girls were examined by a doctor, the fee for the examination being five dollars. Each girl was guaranteed one hundred and fifty dollars a week, and the house never had to make up a deficit because the girls always earned at least that much (at the rate of two dollars per customer). The girl was given a card, and the housekeeper had a duplicate. The two were checked at the end of the night and that was when the girl learned how much she had made. Here the customers were allowed only five minutes in the room with the girl.

House money was kept separately. The housekeeper held the money for the girls, turning it over to the pimp when he came around at the end of the week. The girls never so much as touched their earnings. Once or twice the housekeeper would try to hand money to the girls, but they would always say, "Give it to Bill" or Joe, or whatever his name was. They were not allowed to leave the house, except to go to the hairdresser once a week, and many times they would refuse even that in order to save money for the pimp.

In all the housekeeper's experience, there were only two girls who had no pimps. One of these was a married woman with a child, which she had placed in a boarding school. Her husband was a truck driver, and she was hustling in order to help him buy a house. This woman seemed, in comparison to the other girls, extremely refined and well-educated. She spent her spare time knitting sweaters for her child and looking forward to the weekends when her husband would come to see her. She did not appreciate that to all intents and purposes, her husband was as much of a pimp as the others. The second pimpless girl was often kidded by the other prostitutes and accused of being a Lesbian. She took the razzing quietly, as she did everything, and sent all her money to her parents every week. She stayed by herself, and having no recreation and no apparent outside interests, soon cracked up mentally and was taken away.

So far as the housekeeper knew, these houses did not pay protection. The Mission House operated across the street from a police station and, in the event of trouble, a cop could be summoned simply by raising a certain window shade which caused a red light to flash on over the sergeant's desk. The one drawback in operating so openly was that the police refused to allow them to sell or serve liquor, since this would cut in on the revenue of the town saloons. (The only time there had been any trouble, according to the housekeeper, was when a woman called Russian Ruth opened an opposition bordello. Ruth operated at cut-rate prices in order to build up a clientele, and at last the other madams hired a picket to march up and down in front of her house wearing a sandwich board which read: "Don't patronize this place!") The housekeeper told me that even houses such as these, with such comparatively small operating costs, ran very close to the red and only made a very little profit each month. So I asked myself, If the madam and the girls don't make the money, who does?

Well, Rose Blake had provided a partial answer when she named her "three partners"—the landlord, the police, and the city officials. And in a way, every outsider who has business dealings with a house of prostitution makes a profit. Not only the merchants who purvey food and goods to the madams, but also the storekeepers who sell clothing and knicknacks to the prostitutes, have no qualms about marking up their goods two or three hundred per cent. Prostitutes are free with their money (when the pimps let them have any). They are prone to squander it on silly trifles, often things they neither need nor want, and they do this in spite of all advice to the contrary, almost, you might say, compulsively. It is a trait which the shopkeepers cash in on, as do the traveling salesmen (often doubling as pimps) who come into the house with their cases of junk jewelry or sleazy underwear, and who can get from the girls any price they ask.

What it comes down to is this: the grocer, the butcher, the baker, the merchant, the landlord, the druggist, the liquor dealer, the policeman, the doctor, the city father and the politician—these are the people who make money out of prostitution, these are the real reapers of the wages of sin.

III

Having mentally cased the nation for a likely site, I packed up my belongings lock, stock and barrel, and headed for Chicago. Maybe it was because the words "Gold Coast" evoked associations reminiscent of "Golden Land," but I decided that it was here I would stake out a claim and try my fortunes. However, first it seemed politic to sound out the "early settlers," and see if they had any objections to my opening a house there. I knew from past experience that madams sometimes resent newcomers, and cutthroat tactics on their part could be just as big a nuisance as framing cops. But far from discouraging me, the old established firms were all in favor of my opening up there. "We need someone like you to pep up these old skinflints out here," they said. "Maybe you can pry loose some money from them. They're such cheapskates they've never even been inside a really good expensive house."

Well, it causes me much chagrin to record it, but my career as a Windy City madam was strictly a one-night stand. I leased an apartment and called up a few friends, but my opening laid a terrific egg. The very same men who spent generously when they patronized me in New York were tighter than the bark on a tree in their own backyard. I guess in Chicago even sex has to have a New York label. Or, as an actor friend told me in an attempt at consolation, "The thing is, Poll, the provinces just aren't ready for you yet."

Anyway, so far as I was concerned, the famous Variety headline should have been rewritten to read HIX NIX SEX —P. A. CHI SERAGLIO IN 5 G FOLDEROO. But I wasn't ready to go back to New York yet. I guess I was still mad at the town and everybody in it and thought I'd "punish" them by staying away. So for the next few months I was a lady of leisure, catching up on my sleep days and spending nights chinning with the bartenders.

One night I decided to pay a call on Vicki Shaw, a notorious old-time madam who had been in the business since the days of the Everleigh Sisters. I wanted to talk to someone who knew all the ins and outs of the business, who could tell me what future there was for a person like me, what I could expect from life if, as seemed inevitable, I must go on being a madam to the bitter end.

The cabdriver almost fell out of his seat when I gave him Vicki's address. "Lady, are you aware that place ain't no night club?" he asked. I explained that I had lived most of my life in Europe, where it was not at all unusual for women to visit houses. He bought this, and drove me to Vicki's without further ado.

The door of the little two-story red-brick house was opened by a pale-faced, gaunt woman, whom I assumed to be the housekeeper. I couldn't help but wonder, as I was ushered into a small sitting room, if she had been one of the girls in her younger days. I could almost feel her resentment at my being there. Evidently she thought I was one of those thrill women, seeking some excitement. But when the colored maid served me a drink I gave her a five-dollar bill and told her to keep the change, and that brought a smile of welcome.

"Is it possible for any of the unoccupied girls to join me in a drink?" I asked.

"Sorry, ma'am," she answered, "we're very busy tonight."

And indeed they were! The house was playing to standing room only. Men were coming and going as if it were Bargain Day.

I scribbled a note to Vicki, introducing myself, and gave it to the maid. Almost at once I was ushered into the madam's bedroom where a fire crackled cheerily in a big fireplace. Beside the hearth in a rocking chair sat Vicki, and when she reared herself up to greet me it was an enterprise. There was a good three hundred pounds of her. While I was trying to dope out if Miss Shaw's hair was white or an over-bleached blonde, my hand was crushed in a Strangler Lewis grip.

"So you're the famous Polly Adler!" she boomed in a voice that shook the house. "Your reputation certainly don't match your body. How do you manage to stay so little? Sit down and pour yourself a drink." And with a wide sweep of her hand, she motioned to both a bottle and a chair.

I helped myself to a drink. Though I'm a Scotch drinker, she insisted I try her Melwood bourbon. It had been put in bond before prohibition, she said, and none of the distilleries operating today could touch it. Then we talked for a while of conditions in the business, and I quoted the other madams on the parsimoniousness of the Chicago clientele. " 'Twasn't always that way," said Vicki with a sigh. "Back in 1900 we had the goddamndest bunch of spenders here. 'Course they wasn't all local. Why, goddamnit, Polly, men came from all over the whole goddamn world just to spend a night at the Everleigh Club!"

Since I had always been curious about the Everleigh Sisters, the most famous madams in American history, I asked Vicki to tell me something about them, and she didn't have to be asked twice. From midnight till six in the morning, while we got steadily mellower on the Melwood, she told me the story of the Everleighs.

They were Kentuckians, the daughters of a successful lawyer, and were born not long after the Civil War—Minna in 1868 and Aida in 1871. When their respective marriages went on the rocks (they had married brothers), the sisters went on the stage, that and schoolteaching being about the only careers open to women in those days—except, of course, the one they finally got into. In 1898 they inherited thirty-five thousand from their father and went to Omaha, which was the scene of the Trans-Mississippi Exposition. Learning that the biggest money was being made by high-class brothels, they invested in one, and by the time the exposition was over had parlayed their stake into seventy-five thousand dollars.

On the advice of a Washington, D.C., madam, Cleo Maitland, they decided to locate permanently in Chicago, and spent more than two thirds of their capital furnishing the Club on South Dearborn Street, which opened February 1, 1900. The fame of the establishment spread so rapidly and widely that in 1902, when Kaiser Wilhelm's brother, Prince Henry of Prussia, visited America and was asked what sight he would most like to see, he instantly replied, "The Everleigh Club." In fact, from that time until the Club was closed in 1911, the two "musts" on the list of every foreign potentate visiting Chicago were the stockyards and the big three-story house on Dearborn Street.

Among its wonders were an art gallery, a thousand-book library (both Minna and Aida were bluestockings in their leisure moments), and a Turkish ballroom, complete with fountain. Among the fourteen special reception rooms were the Rose Parlor, the Moorish Room and the Gold Room, which featured eighteen-karat gold cuspidors, gold-rimmed fishbowls, a fifteen-thousand-dollar gold piano and golden chairs and hangings. The boudoirs upstairs boasted mirrored ceilings and marble-inlaid brass beds, and each had some special attraction. One was equipped with a Turkish mattress on the floor and another had an automatic perfume spray over the bed. In every corner of the house there were always fresh roses, and on special nights Minna would have live butterflies fluttering about.

A well-known Chicago lawyer, Colonel MacDuff, used to spend his annual two-week vacation there, and among the Everleigh Club fans were such great figures of the sporting world as Gentleman Jim Corbett, Stanley Ketchel ("The Michigan Assassin"), and Bet-a-Million Gates. Almost every celebrated actor who came through the town spent at least a night there, and John Barrymore reported on the felicities of the establishment in the most glowing terms. A Congressional committee, in Chicago to conduct an investigation, shacked up at the Everleighs' and did most of their investigating in the boudoirs upstairs.

In 1911, the Sisters issued an illustrated brochure which described the thirty beautiful hostesses, such extra added attractions as the three four-piece orchestras, and such mundane comforts as "steam heat in winter, fans in summer" and valet service at all times. But the brochure proved their undoing. The city authorities felt that in openly advertising their wares the sisters were going one step too far, and regretfully required them to close down. The Club was opened again briefly in 1912, but closed down again for good and all the same year.

But by that time their nests were well feathered—and why wouldn't they be? The price for an evening there was fifty dollars—which in those days was the same as a couple of hundred or more now; and food, wine and tips often brought a man's bill up to five hundred or one thousand dollars. I don't know what their operating expenses were, but they were said to have netted one hundred and twenty thousand dollars a year and to have retired with a half-million in cash and two hundred thousand dollars in jewels. After their retirement they were hounded for years by police and reporters and the curious public, but finally succeeded in disappearing from sight.[1]

All Vicki could tell me about their present status was that they were living in some Eastern city—"probably writing po-

[1] *Until Minna's death, in 1948, only a half-dozen trusted friends knew that the sisters were living the life of respectable clubwomen at a home they owned near Central Park in New York. I am indebted to Irving Wallace, one of the few who knew their secret, for this information.*

etry and going to lectures. They was more like a pair of female professors than madams."

When I asked what their particular intellectual interests
were, Vicki replied vaguely, "Oh, they was interested in all
them long-hair things." Rising with a grunt, she went over to
her desk and after opening several drawers and sorting their
contents, extracted a slim leatherbound book. "This was
Minna's," she said. "I got it when some of the Club furnishings was auctioned off. Can you read French?" And when I
said I couldn't, "Well, me either, but it's all odes or some
kind of poems about this famous historical prostitute Rhadopis. She was a Greek girl, see, and they shipped her over to
Egypt, and she done so well hustling that she saved up her
dough and bought herself a pyramid."

This really caught me off balance. "A pyramid?" I repeated
numbly. "You mean a pyramid like the—like *the* pyramids?"

Vicki was delighted at my amazement. "Yeah, a regular
pyramid," she said. "Same as King Tut's, same as on the
Camel package." She chuckled. "Ain't it the goddamndest
thing? Tickles me every time I think about it."

"But a pyramid's to be buried in," I said.

Vicki shrugged. "Pyramids was stylish then. Lots of stylish
things ain't much use. Hell, Polly, the way I heard it, in them
days they was all working for pyramids—or *on* 'em. And so
this girl Rhadopis, she was going to be right in the swim. If
it hadn't been pyramids, it would have been something else."

A maid came in to report that the last guest had gone, and
I accompanied Vicki while she saw to it the house was locked
up for the night. When we returned to her bedroom she insisted I have "one for the road." The fire on the hearth was
long since dead ashes, and without its warm light Vicki looked
all her seventy-odd years.

"Miss Vicki," I said hesitantly, "I'm curious to know why

you've never retired. Here it is six A.M., and you've spent the night playing watchdog to a lot of revelers. You must have enough money to quit. Why is it you haven't?"

"Maybe I should," she said. "I've enough money—why wouldn't I have? I been running a house fifty years. But goddamnit, I'll never quit. I was born in a whorehouse, and raised in a whorehouse, and I'll die in a whorehouse."

As she spoke, it seemed to me I heard Nettie Gordon saying: *Who'd come to visit a whorehouse madam? Who wants to sit alone and die of loneliness?* I heard Dutch Schultz saying: *You'll never quit because you can't. You're tagged a madam, and a madam you're going to stay.* . . . And suddenly tears —probably pure bourbon tears—began to roll down my cheeks.

"I wasn't born in a whorehouse," I sobbed, "and I'm not going to die in one!"

Somewhat startled, Vicki drew me to her massive bosom and patted my shoulder consolingly. "What the hell you talking about dying for—a kid like you? Why, I'm more'n twice as old as you are, and dying don't worry me. It's something we all got to go through."

I launched into a rather incoherent explanation to the effect that it wasn't dying that worried me, but living. "I can't ever be anything but a madam," I wailed in conclusion. "Society won't let me."

"Seems to me," said Vicki slowly, "it's a waste o' breath bellyachin' about the cards being stacked. You still got to play the hand that's dealt you. And the way I look at it, *somebody's* got to be a madam. Maybe madams ain't considered respectable, but by God, Polly, the world ain't ever been able to get along without 'em. . . . Leastwise not since civilization set in. I guess back when we was all living in caves and a guy got to feeling randy, he just picked up a rock and went huntin'——"

As no doubt she had intended, Vicki's anthropological lecture started me laughing and snapped me out of my self-pitying mood. I had always told my girls: If you have to be a prostitute, be a good one. Well, the same applied to me. If I had to be a madam, I'd be a good madam. Instead of sulking in Chicago, I'd go back to the town I loved and where I stood for something, even though that "something" was what most of the world regarded with disapproval. Nobody knew better than I that a house is not a home, but in the words of Edgar Guest's famous poem: ". . . ye sometimes have t' roam afore ye really 'preciate the things ye lef' behind."

IV

If I was to make my living as a madam, I could not be concerned either with the rightness or wrongness of prostitution, considered either from a moral or criminological standpoint. I had to look at it simply as a part of life which exists today as it existed yesterday, and which, unless there occur changes more profound than can at present be visualized, will exist tomorrow. The operation of any business is contingent on the law of supply and demand, and if there were no customers, there certainly would be no whorehouses. Prostitution exists because men will pay for sexual gratification, and whatever men are willing to pay for, someone will provide.

I had found that being cynical and half-hearted about my profession had worked out to the disadvantage both of my customers and myself. But if I could think of myself as fulfilling a need, as one in a long line which stretched back to the beginning of civilization, then, no matter what stigma attached to my calling, at least I was not "antisocial." I had a very definite place in the social structure. I belonged, I had a job to do, and I could find satisfaction in doing it the very best way I knew how.

To the uninitiated it might seem that there can hardly be much difference in houses, and of course in the bedroom the procedure is fairly well standardized, varying only with the customer's whim. (This last item would make a book—or, rather, a whole library—all by itself, and is a subject I will leave to Kinsey and to Freud.) Actually, however, the atmosphere, surroundings and quality of entertainment depend on such factors as geography, economics and contemporary tastes. In America today you would find no counterpart of an Algerian peg-house or the Yoshiwara in Japan or the Fish Market in Cairo. In fact, for the most part, the red-light district is a thing of the past. And, in fact, the old-time sporting house has vanished like the old-time saloon. There are no more establishments like the Everleigh Club or like the famous house in St. Louis run by Babe Connors (she of the diamond-inlaid teeth), where Paderewski once accompanied bawdy songs on the piano and in which, so it is said, a Republican platform once was written.

Yet all whorehouses, past and present and wherever located, exist to cater to an instinctive appetite, just as all eating places exist primarily to supply food. But aside from their common reason for being, you will find little resemblance between a "greasy spoon," an automat, and the Colony or Chambord. Similarly there is a world of difference between a two-dollar house and a ten-dollar house, between a twenty-dollar house and what a punning friend of mine once called a *maison carte blanche*. Moreover, just as in top restaurants it is the personality of the maître d' which gives a place its particular cachet, so does the personality of the madam count for a great deal, and in the long run the difference between my place and other houses in the same price bracket was me.

Leaving modesty aside, I still cannot say what, in particular, it was about me which put Polly Adler's house in a class by itself. (I guess maybe I'm too close to the subject to write of it objectively.) But I can say that I did have a somewhat different attitude toward my customers than did the other madams. To me (once I'd dislodged those chips on my shoulders) my patrons were not just ambulatory bankrolls, but individual human beings—social acquaintances and often friends—entitled to the cordiality and consideration one extends to an honored guest. There is a Polish saying: "When a guest enters the house, God enters the house," and this was the golden rule of my hospitality.

The way I looked at it was this: When a woman marries a man she knocks herself out (or should) to gratify his every wish. She will cook to please his stomach, dress to please his eye, behave to suit his mood. After all, why not? Isn't he supporting her? Isn't he giving her his love and respect? Well, I didn't get the love, and I didn't always get the respect, but there were certainly a lot of husbands supporting me, and I figured it was my duty to find out what they wanted and give it to them.

I recall meeting an old-time madam in, of all places, a Turkish bath, and while we were sitting there in the steam room, as was to be expected we got to talking business. "Tell me, Polly," said Evelyn, "what is the secret of your success? I'm a much older hand in the make-believe love game than you, but I've never seen anything like the way you've come to the top. What's the angle?"

"If I have an angle," I said, "it's quality and consideration—the quality of my establishment and consideration for my customers. Bergdorf's and Bonwit's dress their windows attractively to pull in trade. I give my customers an attractive house. People in stores prefer to patronize good-looking, capable sales girls. I give my customers good-looking, capable hostesses. In the finest and most exclusive shops, the customers are treated as privileged friends of the management, their special likes and dislikes are tabulated, and they are given personalized service. Well, that's the way I try to run my business."

Though I didn't go on to say so to Evelyn, there were two other precepts which I applied to running my house: *Cleanliness is next to godliness,* and *Honesty is the best policy.* I was a fanatic on the subject of cleanliness. It was a must that both the house and the girls be immaculate. As for honesty, I considered it a keystone in my relationship with the customers. The men knew they would never be rolled at my house, nor be given a padded check. As my reputation for square-shooting became established, I had a number of customers who would simply hand me a signed blank check when they arrived, and tell me to fill it out in the morning—and they were men whose bank accounts did not contain peanuts. Also, often when a patron had an out-of-town guest whom he wished to be entertained, he would telephone me and name the amount which he was prepared to spend on the evening, and he could be sure his guest would not be shortchanged. Sometimes, my patrons made me handsome presents when they were particularly pleased with my brand of hospitality. And if I liked the man I would accept his gift. After all, if Washington officials can accept deep freezes, why shouldn't I grab off a little ice?

A man's visit to Polly's meant more than just sleeping with a woman. He expected to be amused and even informed. He knew he could count on conversation about the latest plays and the newest books; he would hear fresh and funny stories and anecdotes about the town characters. Good talk and good liquor, good-looking girls in good-looking surroundings, these were the ingredients which went into the making of a good night, and when my men said, "Good night" (though usually it was five or six in the morning), they really meant it had been.

I had to protect my customers more ways than one. I'll never forget the time a big advertising man was in the house on a truly epic binge. He was very much taken with a girl called Dorothy, and when his secretary called to remind him of a conference next day in Philadelphia, Mr. Huckster decided he had more important business with Dorothy. The secretary then called me and begged me to see what I could do. It was an extremely important meeting, she said, and it was vital that Mr. Huckster be there looking brighteyed and alert.

So I coaxed and pleaded with Mr. Huckster and at last he consented to pull himself together and make the trip—but only on condition Dorothy went with him. I reminded Mr. Huckster that if he took Dorothy along he'd be guilty of violating the Mann Act, but he paid not the slightest heed. "Either Dorothy goes with me or I stay here," he said. "An' I don't care which." Finally, I pretended to give in, and told Dorothy to get ready. I said I'd drive to the train with them, and, as soon as we got Mr. Huckster sobered up, we set out for the station. Once there, I stuck close to the two of them and insisted on getting aboard to see them settled. Then, just as the train was about to pull out, I latched on to Dorothy and whisked her from the Pullman to the platform.

She was furious. "What's the big idea?" she demanded.

"Here I've gone and broken my date with Johnny. I told him I was going to be in Philadelphia the next few days."

"When did you tell him that?"

"Oh, I telephoned him when I went to pack."

Mr. Huckster never knew what a narrow escape he had. Johnny, Dorothy's boyfriend, was a notorious shakedown artist, and he'd have taken Mr. H. for plenty on the threat of reporting his violating the Mann Act.

Because of episodes like this, I had a reputation for dependability among the secretaries, agents and managers of my clients. One man whom I had to keep a special eye on was a famous musician. Blue, as I'll call him, began spending a lot of time at my house after a much publicized marital bustup. He was bitter and hurt and sought consolation among my girls. He drank a great deal too, and when he reached a certain stage of intoxication always got an urge to go driving. Anything on wheels would do—trucks, motorcycles, ambulances, garbage wagons—anything he could get his hands on, and it was my job to keep him away from the rolling stock. It was also my job to keep him from giving away everything he possessed. I remember one night he smiled at me lovingly and said, "Polly, baby, I have a surprise for you."

"What kind of a surprise?"

"I'm gonna buy you a big fat Cadillac all for yourself."

I said, "Sure, sure," and thought no more about it. But the next day his manager phoned and began a long oration on the subject of Blue, how he was throwing all his money away buying people presents, passing out Cadillacs as if they were cough drops. I laughed and assured him I had no intention of accepting the car Blue had promised me. The manager, a hair-tearing type, was much relieved and became one of my biggest boosters.

Then there was the time B. J. was taking a "rest cure" at

my place. He came for cocktails on Monday, and the following Sunday was still there. His whereabouts were known only to his confidential secretary, Miss Compton, who phoned to say he must attend a directors' meeting on Thursday. Would I please get him in shape for it? I said I would try and, God knows, I did. I argued, kidded, pleaded and conned, but the more I cajoled, the less he listened. He would stop when he was good and ready, and that was that.

My house was always in an uproar during his periodic binges. It became a regular sanitarium with a doctor calling daily to check his blood pressure, shoot vitamins into him and oversee his health in general. I myself watched him constantly because Miss Compton warned me that when he was on a spree, he often tried to commit suicide. I had to make sure all the cutlery and sharp things were locked up where he couldn't get at them. His personal barber called every day to shave him. Two operators from a leading beauty salon appeared at regular intervals to manicure him and massage his face and feet. A male nurse checked in to administer a body massage and a high colonic. His Sulka pajamas were changed twice daily, and the bed linens morning and night. For all the punishment his body was taking, he was in tiptop shape, not a hair out of place. Roaring drunk, he was still a fashion plate. In between these attentions, he popped vitamin pills into himself. I used to think it was like entertaining a drugstore, and my private name for him was "Mr. Walgreen."

After a week, I usually had other names for him. He demanded meticulous service. He never seemed to relax, and night and day I was hopping up and down—like the Hop Toy of old—waiting on him. After a week of this, I was a wreck. So, one day, when his doctor was there, I asked him to check me over too. The doctor examined me and began to shove pills at me. "Stop worrying about B. J.," he said. "He's fine;

you should be the patient. Your nerves are in a state. Get some rest and take these pills."

"It's all my fault," B. J. said, turning on the charm. "I know I'm a difficult person to handle. Now, Lulu Belle (this was his pet name for me), I'll promise to stop drinking and you can relax."

I smiled weakly, thinking now there was a chance he'd be up and in shape for Thursday's meeting. He told the maid to bring him a glass of milk and ordered a highball for me and for each of the girls. I drank mine slowly, watching him pour milk down his throat practically by the pint. The girls' drinks I knew would be tea. Fancying the situation was under control, I sneaked off to my room for a nap. I was really beat.

"Lulu Belle, do you feel better?" It was a sweet voice whispering in my ear. I opened one eye and peered at B. J. He was drunker than sixteen million dollars. "What time is it?" I asked. "And where are the girls?"

"They left me, Lulu Belle." His glazed eyes filled with tears, then he brightened. "We went riding up and down the elevator until the elevator man caught up with us in the cellar. They went away. They said they were going for a walk in Central Park with two Scotch bottles. They wanted me to come along, but I came back," he ended virtuously.

The girls appeared after they had killed the bottles and had a nice nap in the middle of the park.

"The grass looked so inviting," they explained.

I got out of bed and went investigating. I had been taken. The milk B. J. had been gulping so fast was three-quarters brandy. The girls' tea had been spiked to the hilt. Everybody got drunk while I sipped on my highball. It was a great joke to everyone but me. I knew I was in for four more days of playing nursemaid to B. J.

Yes, he got to the meeting.

But perhaps my biggest responsibility was to my younger clients. Often boys were brought to my place by their fathers—and these men were not evil-minded old rakes, bent on debauching their sons. It was simply that they believed this was the wisest and best way of handling one of the most difficult problems a father has to face. They knew the physical and emotional damage that can result if a youth begins his sex life with some furtive, sordid episode which may forever make ugly and shameful this aspect of human nature. They realized the importance of a satisfying and psychologically right initial sex experience, with nothing undignified nor cheap about it, and they relied on my tact and good judgment in selecting a congenial partner and putting the boy at his ease. I took a special interest in such boys, and was proud of their friendship and their trust in me. As they grew older, they often would discuss with me their future brides, and it was then I thought of them, rather sadly, as my own sons.

I remember one customer of mine who had two sons in Yale. As part of his farewell advice before sending them off to college he had adjured them, "Now don't get yourself mixed up with any floozies! Not that I want to keep you from having fun, but play it safe—go to Polly's." When the boys objected that their allowance was too anemic for the healthy prices I charged, he said expansively: "Don't worry about the expense. Just charge it to me."

The boys took his advice to heart—so much so, in fact, that they turned up bringing six classmates. "Just charge the whole thing to Dad," they said.

Next day when I called Dad and broke the news, he took it good-naturedly. "Chips off the old block," he chuckled. "Even have their old man's habit of picking up the tab. But," he added, "I waited till I was earning my own money before treating the town. It's okay this time, Polly, but tell the boys next time they call on you that I don't intend to pay for the sex life of the whole damn Yale University!"

Chapter 10

Season in
the Sun

> What about sexual intercourse: was that an
> opium of the people? Of some of the people.
> Of some of the best of the people.
>
> *Ernest Hemingway*   THE GAMBLER, THE NUN
> AND THE RADIO

The four years preceding America's entrance into the war
saw the beginning of the metamorphosis of New York from a
big town to a world city. Almost overnight it seemed the Manhattan scene was repopulated with a new cast of characters.
On the streets, in shops and restaurants, you heard French
and German and Polish and Spanish; you saw the flags of
many nations arrayed outside the Waldorf and the Plaza; you
heard the stories of refugees and the speeches of delegations;
you watched preparedness parades; you attended benefits and
joined committees and replied to appeals—for no matter
how isolationist might be the feeling in other parts of the
country, you in New York could never forget that Europe was
just a day away.

In the light of Mussolini's aggressions in Africa and Al-
bania, Hitler's gobbling up of Austria and the Sudetenland,
the dissolution of the Czechoslovakian Republic, and the Japanese invasion of China, it seems incomprehensible that such
a phrase as "Peace in our time" could evoke anything but

hollow laughter from the citizens of the Western democracies. Yet we bought it, and while in Europe the munitions factories worked overtime, in America we had a fair.

During these last peacetime years, I, as New York's premier madam, ran a close second to Grover Whalen as an official greeter. Whenever it was a question of providing a visiting V.I.P. with the more informal type of female companionship, I was usually appointed chairman of the subrosa entertainment committee, and, as a result, could boast a clientele culled not only from Who's Who and the Social Register, but from Burke's Peerage and the Almanach de Gotha.

Looking back, I suppose I had now arrived at the climax of my career as a madam. A homely (or maybe I should say "housely") incident will illustrate the distance I had traveled since the days I had "loaned" my apartment to Tony and his lady friend. I was laid up in bed with a severe cold, red-eyed and runny-nosed and about as unglamorous as a woman can be. However, I wasn't too ill to receive, and in one evening the visitors who dropped in to cheer the patient up included a famous composer, two well-known authors, a magazine editor, a top-flight interior decorator, two members of the Russian nobility who were now U.S. citizens, and a prince of a reigning royal house, his equerry and his American host.

At one point one of the Russians asked me the old familiar question, "Polly, why are you in the business you are in?"

"Look at me," I said, "and then look around you—see the people who are here. I'm not beautiful, I'm not educated, I'm the daughter of a poor Jewish tailor from a little town in Russia. Ask yourself what I have in common with people like you—except being alive, except being human. It isn't my brains or my birth that entitle me to your company—and God knows it isn't my looks—so what ground is there left to meet on? If I weren't a madam would you and he"—I nodded at his royal highness—"be sitting on my bed?"

The editor said, "But, Polly, we don't come to see you because you're a madam. If it was only that—well, then, why would we be in here with you? Why, as you say, would we be sitting on your bed, instead of a bed containing one of your girls?"

"Don't get me wrong," I said. "Your being here—how can I tell you what it means to me? If I could cut up my heart and hand you each a piece, would that tell you? You could go anywhere, you could be with anybody——" And, as always seems to be happening to me, I started to cry. "Why, when I look around this room I don't know whether to pinch myself or jump for joy. It's like a dream. Who am I, Mrs. Vanderbilt, that I've got princes and famous celebrities sitting around watching me blow my nose on a piece of Kleenex?"

How could I help but be proud and happy that such people thought enough of me to come and see me when I was sick? There was nothing I could give them or do for them; they came out of friendship, because I was a person who meant something to them. It was true. We wouldn't have met if I hadn't been a madam, but, as the editor said, that wasn't the reason they were there. . . . Maybe the royal gentleman thought I was hinting, but I finished up the evening blowing my nose, not on Kleenex, but on his royal handkerchief. I still have it. I sent him another with the message that I would like to keep his as proof that sometimes kind hearts and coronets come wrapped in the same package.

There are many things about those years it gives me pleasure to remember. For one thing, I realized an ambition which I guess every woman must have—I had a movie star for a beau.

Our first encounter could scarcely have occurred under more unromantic circumstances. I was down in Hot Springs, Arkansas, and there one morning in the elevator of the bathhouse, I came face to face with Wally Beery. He smiled at me. He should have laughed out loud. My hair was in curlers, and I was wearing a heavy flannel robe and flat straw slippers. Beside the tall Wally I looked like a prune—and that was the name he was to call me throughout our friendship.

Wally's arrival had caused quite a stir among the hotel guests, and that evening in the lobby a lady sitting next to me pointed him out, remarking that she had known him quite well twenty years before, when he was married to Gloria Swanson. She wrote a note reminding him of their acquaintance and had it taken to him by a bellboy. In a flash, Wally came loping over and, completely ignoring the note-writer, greeted me like a long-lost friend. By the time I'd explained, she had stomped off in a huff, no doubt to expostulate thereafter on how he had become a snob since reaching stardom.

I told Wally that the closest I had ever come to meeting him was in the bathhouse that morning, and then, with some trepidation, added that my name was Polly Adler.

Wally pursed his lips. "Polly—Wally. Sounds good, don't you think?"

We stood and chatted for a few minutes, but our conversation was constantly being interrupted by people asking for his autograph. "Come on," he said. "Let's get out of here. Will you join me for a bit of supper?"

In the restaurant I ordered a beer while Wally asked for a sandwich. I had always been under the impression that he was a heavy drinker, but now I learned otherwise. In fact, he couldn't stand being around drunks. (After that, when I

went out with Wally I drank water till it ran out of my ears.)
We sat and talked for a long time. He spoke mostly about his
daughter, Carol Ann, whom he adored, about his recent divorce, and about his early struggles before he became a movie
star. He told me how lonesome he was, and apologized for
being in such low spirits, but even in a blue mood he came
across as a warm, vital, big-hearted man.

"I expect to be in New York before long," he said. "How
about us making some dates right now? I want to see some
shows and go to some of my favorite restaurants, and I sure
would like the pleasure of your company."

It occurred to me then that he did not understand the situation with regard to me, and naturally I could not accept his
invitation if our being seen together would hurt him professionally. "Wally," I began hesitantly, "I think there's something you ought to know about me. It might be a mistake for
us to go out together in New York. I'm—well, everybody
there knows what business I'm in. I run a whorehouse."

Wally didn't even blink. "So what?" he came back instantly. "You can run fifty of them. To me you are a very
nice person."

Well, hearing him say that would alone have been enough
to make it a very big day for me. But—the cherry on the par-
fait—that was the night of the March of Dimes ball in honor
of the President's birthday, and thanks to my famous escort,
that was one ball I was the belle of.

Wally was going on to New Orleans the following morning, but before he left he took me for a spin in his plane. He
had his own Howard, and later, on one of my trips to California, taught me to fly. He telephoned every night while I
was in Hot Springs, and always sounded very paternal and
comforting, warning me not to catch cold leaving the bathhouse and reminding me to take care of myself in general.

Gee, I thought to myself, what a grand guy! His concern and interest did more for my health than all the spring water in Arkansas.

When I returned to New York, I did not know exactly what day he would arrive, and I remember what a lift I got, hearing that cheerful voice over the phone. "Hello, Prune. This is your cowboy. Open up the corral gate. I'm coming right over to see you."

I tried my level best to dissuade him from coming to the house, but when he insisted I told the maid to take care of the calls and not allow any visitors. I didn't want Wally to see me in my role of madam. Hearing about it is one thing, seeing it is another.

(Although I didn't know it, when Wally talked with me on the phone, there was a reporter with him, H. Allen Smith. Mr. Smith's account of the conversation was subsequently included in his book, *Low Man On A Totem Pole,* a best-seller of 1941.)

When Wally arrived, we talked for a while, then suddenly he jumped up, pulled me out of my chair and put his arm around me. "Come on, darling," he said. "Let's take a walk."

Now for years I had been watching men put an arm around a girl and say, "Let's take a walk." To me it meant only one thing—a walk to the bedroom. So there I stood staring at him, dismayed and bewildered. I had thought in spite of my profession he had some respect for me, and anyway there had certainly been nothing amorous in our previous conversation. "Why—why, Wally," I stammered. "Do you—do you really think that's such a good idea?"

He looked at me, lines of puzzlement wrinkling his forehead. "But it's so beautiful out," he said. "I bet you haven't even been out today. Wouldn't you like to take a walk and see the sunset?"

In my embarrassment, I blushed so hard that I produced a pretty good replica of a sunset all on my own. "Oh, a *walk!*" I gushed. "A walk! Why, I'd love nothing more."

So we went for a stroll along Fifth Avenue, a fact which was duly reported by none other than Walter Winchell, who wrote that he had seen "Polly Adler arm-and-arming it with Wally Beery, bowing to their respective fans." . . . Wally and I remained devoted friends until his untimely death in 1949.

It was in July of 1939 that I received the ultimate, untoppable tribute to my business career. I entered the Valhalla of the American executive. I could feel that my name would go down in history inscribed on the rolls with Morgans and Mellons and DuPonts, with Henry Ford and John D. Rockefeller. I, Polly Adler, was written about in *Fortune* Magazine! At the time, however, I had no time to savor the glory and wonder of it. The anonymous writer of the article mentioned that my apartment was "not far from Central Park West in the Sixties," and I had to move at once to avoid a raid.

This particular issue of *Fortune* was devoted to New York City, which was playing host to the world at the great fair which had opened on April thirtieth. Agreeing with Mayor LaGuardia that the fair's greatest exhibit was the city itself, the editors assembled a sort of super Baedeker, containing the straight-from-the-horse's-mouth dope about everything from Manhattan's intellectual life (as exemplified by what was called "the fauna of the publishing world") to its illicit pleasures which, needless to state, is where I came in.

The article, which seemed to me remarkably accurate, commented on "the cop's loathing for Vice Squad work—a nine-year heritage of the Seabury investigation," after which arrests for prostitution declined by fifty per cent. Speaking of the Dewey investigation, it said that "the law's heat did bring about one outward change: it finished off the 'parlor house'—or 'sporting house,' as some still call it—in New York City." My place and Peggy Wild's and Diane B.'s were mentioned as "some of the fanciest parlor houses in the U.S. until the law closed them all up." Then, after noting that Peggy and I had "opened again on a less extravagant scale," the article continued: "The would-be visitor has small chance of getting into an establishment like Polly Adler's unless he is on her card index—a priceless and heavily guarded file that gives not only the patron's name, business address, and telephone number, but also such information as his preferences in women and liquor and his degree of liberality. Peggy Wild is not quite so cautious as Polly Adler, but one must still come well recommended to get in."

Well, I would still like to know who recommended the writer of the article; somebody certainly held the door open and let the flies in! It is quite true that I did have a card index as described, with symbols in a code which was known only to the maids and myself. In my absence, this enabled them to ascertain whose credit was good and which men paid what. (Incidentally, call girls too had a code in their address books listing the Good Time Charlies. For example, an exclamation mark after a man's name meant he was a liberal spender; a question mark meant it was up to the girl and the man's mood whether she struck it rich or not; and a comma denoted a poor sport. As one girl once told me, "It took me six months to go through my exclamation and question marks. Then, when they began to ask me to bring girlfriends along, I knew they were getting tired of me, and I'd better try another town.") The article was also correct in saying that my place could scarcely be called a parlor house, it was a "glorified call flat, *i.e.*, a place run by a madam who calls girls in for the evening." After my arrest in 1935, I never had girls living in, and it would be technically correct to describe me from that time on as a call-house madam.

Speaking of prostitution in general, the writer said it was impossible to guess the number of prostitutes in New York City. "True it is that prostitution *seems* to have leveled off in prevalence since the start of the depression—a statement that apparently runs counter to the notion that prostitution *flourishes* in depression. . . . A great many women take to the streets in hard times, but the general effect is a lowering of price standards, and a fall off of business in the upper brackets of harlotry." (This is untrue. I was certainly operating in the upper brackets and my business *never* fell off, regardless of depressions or anything else.) "Moreover, there is the important fact of shifted moral standards—particularly in a city like New York—by which men have freer associations with women of their own social strata, and less reason to seek out prostitutes."

Well, that raised a point about which I often wondered myself: why men came to my house for something which they could so easily secure—for free—elsewhere. And so, after reading this article, whenever a client asked me how I got into the business I countered with the query, "Why do you keep me in business?" Most of the men replied that sex was their most important form of relaxation and since they couldn't find it at home they sought it elsewhere. Some said their wives were good mothers, but indifferent bed-partners; others that their mates were naggers and after that "hard day at the office," they wanted companionship, not needling. "I don't want to hurt my family," said one man, "but I have no outlet for my emotions at home. If I took a mistress, that might lead to complications. Coming here is simpler and safer." The feelings of my bachelor clientele could be summed up this way: "Why waste the effort wining and dining and sweet-talking a girl just on the chance that you may score? It's going the long way around when we know you're here to arrange things. And besides, an experienced girl is never a disappointment."

For a bachelor, perhaps a house is the best solution for his sex life, but I truly do believe that nine times out of ten a wife could keep her husband on the reservation if she used half the effort to hold him that she did to hook him. When a woman sets her cap for a guy, she goes all out to be attractive to him. She keeps herself groomed to perfection, she always has that dab of perfume in the right place, she laughs at his jokes, she goes along with his whims, she flirts with other men just enough to keep him up on the bit, and whatever she does, she convinces him she does it all for great big wonderful Him. But after girl gets boy, why should a two-buck marriage license entitle her to turn off all that charm she turned on during the courtship? Why doesn't she continue to dress up for him? Why doesn't she use her eyes to see how he's feeling, and her ears to listen to him, and her tongue for compliments and interesting conversation instead of digs and gossip about her neighbors? And why, after waving her sex like a flag to get him, doesn't she at least pretend to enjoy his caresses? And yet I suppose I should thank such wives instead of criticizing them—they helped keep me in business.

Why wouldn't a man turn from such a wife to my girls, who were always beautifully groomed and lovely to look at and gay and responsive, who were always flattering him, sympathizing with him, telling him what a terrific lover he was? Of course they were getting paid for it, but doesn't a wife get paid too? It is not a new point of view, but so far as I'm concerned a prostitute is anyone who sells herself for gain. The women who take husbands not out of love but out of greed, to get their bills paid, to get a fine house and clothes and jewels; the women who marry to get out of a tiresome job, or to get away from disagreeable relatives, or to avoid being called an old maid—these are whores in everything but name. The only difference between them and my girls is that my girls gave a man his money's worth.

I will admit there are some men who couldn't be kept home by a whole harem of wives. And there are some wives who do their darndest, but just don't have enough of the old Eve. It's my hunch that some of the legitimate women who visited my establishment came there expressly to find why men, including their own husbands, frequented places like mine and sought the company of prostitutes. And if, as sometimes happened, they asked my advice about how to keep a husband faithful, I would quote to them a line from Clare Boothe's play, *The Women*. Speaking of losing her man to another woman, one character says bitterly, "I should have licked that girl where she licked me—in the hay!"

I have said that nine times out of ten a wife can keep a husband on the reservation. As an example of the tenth time, there was the customer who told me that his wife had done everything possible to make herself attractive to him. "She wears a different colored nightie each night, she tries like hell to be alluring, and I know she loves me dearly. But what do I do? I stay in my bed and read *The New Yorker*. I feel sorry for her, but I just can't do anything about it. She's repulsive to me." This wife was truly to be pitied, for her husband was all mixed up in his sex behavior. A house of ill-repute was the only answer to his problem, and, as a matter of fact, it was a psychiatrist who had given him my address.

While I do not intend to go into it, I think I should put it on the record that toward the end of the Thirties, an increasing number of my clientele seemed sexually maladjusted. As the tension in Europe grew, and war became ever more imminent, people's peculiarities were intensified. They seemed to get more and more off the beam. Whorehouses always draw twisted people who are unable to satisfy their desires normally, but now it got so that I began to think of a patron who wanted the simple, old-fashioned methods as a "truck driver."

In this connection, I remember one time a patron of mine called and said he was sending over a friend of his who had a very peculiar request. Half an hour later I admitted a man of about forty-five, quite the toff in appearance. He spoke with an Oxford accent, and told me that he had been born in America but had lived most of his life on the Continent. I had arranged for one of my prettiest girls to join us for cocktails and when she appeared the gentleman blushed, grew confused, and asked with some embarrassment if he might speak to me alone. I thought: So—another one with funny ideas. Now what can his perversion be?

"Miss Adler," he said when the girl had gone, "no doubt this will seem odd to you, but I am not here for the reason you so obviously suppose. I am here to select a wife."

My mouth fell open. Then I started to laugh. I just couldn't help it. Of all the twists I might have imagined, that one was the topper. "Please forgive me," I said when I was able. "But surely this is some kind of a gag. I'm not running a marriage bureau, you know."

"It's no joke," he assured me. "You see, many of my friends think it strange that I've remained single for so long. But I've seen so much infidelity, so many shrewish demanding wives, so many messy divorces, that I simply don't want to let myself in for that sort of thing. Nevertheless, it does seem expedient for me to get married, and I believe the answer to my problem lies in marrying a prostitute. Being unused to any real affection, her gratitude to me might be the factor that would

keep her faithful, and as a prostitute is trained to please
men, I'm sure I shouldn't find her disappointing sexually. In
return I could give her a home and advantages which perhaps
she has never had, as well as the protection of my name. Do
I make myself clear, Miss Adler?"

He made himself clear all right. I thought, This guy is a
complete crackpot, but I better humor him or he'll start
frothing at the mouth and busting up the bric-a-brac. So while
Little Rollo described the exact type of girl he was looking
for, I sat there serious as an undertaker, and even pretended
to jot down the specifications for his bride. He gave me
a handsome present for the girl whose attentions he had
spurned, and I promised to get in touch with him as soon as
I had lined up a selection of "fiancées."

The door had hardly closed after him before I dismissed
my eccentric visitor from my mind. If I thought about him at
all, I figured he'd gone back to playing bridge at his club, or
else had been taken away to some retreat for those with
more money than sense.

But I was so wrong. When he didn't hear from me, Rollo
went elsewhere with his weird request and actually married
one of my former girls who was then working in another
house. After their marriage, they went to live in Paris, and my
last report on this zany mating came from a socialite friend of
mine on his return from a trip abroad. According to him,
Mrs. Rollo had become the toast of Paris, one of the most
sought-after and smartest hostesses in the international set.
"You see her everywhere," he buzzed. "My dear, I ran into
her at the races, and she was absolutely *embedded* in gran-
dees. And you know what? She had the nerve to snub me, the
snob!"

As unusual in its way as the story of Little Rollo is the story
of Maureen, a story with a twist that might have come

straight from the pages of O. Henry. One afternoon the maid ushered in a girl who said she had come to me at the suggestion of an actor named Edgar L. I liked Maureen's looks very much. She was trimly turned out, carried herself well, had a pleasant speaking voice and excellent manners. During our interview I was interrupted several times by phone calls, and I was hurrying to get dressed, so perhaps my cross-examination was not as searching as usual. I don't recall all that was said, but I do remember that she impressed me as rather naïve. (When I asked if she was French, she looked somewhat surprised and said, "No, I'm Irish.")

I had a man due up in a quarter of an hour, an old customer, and I asked Maureen if she would like to keep the date. She said she would be delighted. When the customer arrived I introduced them, and, after the usual small talk to break the ice, excused myself. A few minutes later Maureen burst in on me almost hysterical. "That man! . . . That man!" she sobbed. "He's crazy!"

I jumped up. "What did he do to you?"

She was so upset that it took a while to get it out of her, but at last she blurted that he had started to take his clothes off.

I sat down again. "Well, what did you expect him to do?" I said tartly. "I don't know where you've worked before, Maureen, but the men here always take their clothes off." She stared at me in such utter bewilderment that I finally caught on. "Don't you know what kind of a place this is? Didn't Edgar L. tell you what business I'm in?"

"He—he just said," faltered Maureen, "that you were someone who helps girls."

I explained to her as gently as I could where she was, and said it had been an unfortunate misunderstanding and I was sorry she had been upset, but there was no harm done and she was free to go. She started toward the door, then hesitated, turned and came back. Opening her handbag, she took out the change purse and showed me its contents—three nickels and a dime. "I think I'd like to keep the date," she said.

Later in the evening she came again to my room and showed me the hundred-dollar tip she had received.

I said to her, "Well, was it so bad?"

"No," she said. "But then you see we didn't—we didn't do anything."

"*What?*" I said. "Maureen, what are you talking about?"

"We didn't sleep together." She smiled. "I talked him out of it."

I was flabbergasted. I have done some conning in my time, but never anything to equal that. It must be true that the Irish can blarney their way out of anything. Maureen never worked for me again, nor for any other madam. The proceeds of her "date" enabled her to keep going until she landed the radio job she'd come to New York to get. During the war she married and moved to Boston, which seems sort of a letdown. But even without a fairy-tale ending, the story of Maureen remains, so far as I know, unique in the history of prostitution.

II

The Second World War meant boom times again on Broadway and saw the appearance of a new crop of fat-cat spenders —the under-the-table traders known as black marketeers. It seems hardly necessary to say that my business was flourishing. The more desperate the times, the more men seek the great escape of sex. The streets swarmed with "V-Girls," but it was a question whether the V stood for victory or venereal.

They were, as one of my patrons ironically remarked, the kind of girls who give prostitution a bad name.

As a result of the shortage of hotel accommodations, men who previously had engaged hotel suites in which to entertain now brought their parties to my house, and my bar did a thriving business. Also as a result of this shortage, I had some customers who were, I think, less interested in spending the night in amorous pursuits than they were in having a roof over their heads.

Like everyone else with relatives and friends serving in the armed forces, the war touched me very nearly. My four brothers were in uniform and so were many of my patrons, including a number whom I regarded as more than mere business acquaintances. And just as everyone else did, I wrote letters and sent cigarettes and socks and candy bars to my "boys." This in itself kept me busy, for by V-J Day there were several hundred of them to be remembered. To my favorites I sent gold Mazuzahs. (A Mazuzah is a little case, like a locket, containing a miniature scroll on which is written the Ten Commandments.) It did not matter that most of the chaps to whom I sent them were not of the Jewish faith. They understood, as I meant them to, that the Mazuzahs were the symbol of my hope that all was well with them and of my wish for their safe return.

A boy named Arthur told me he was sure the Mazuzah had saved his life. One day when he was home on leave, he saw me on Fifth Avenue and came rushing up and gave me a big hug, calling me "Mom," as did many of the young kids who came to my house. And he went on to tell me how, at Bougainville, eleven enemy fighter planes circled over his ship and they brought down every one. "After it was all over," he said, "I felt something sharp biting into my palm. I had to pry my fingers back—that's how stiff I'd been scared—and then I saw that I'd been clutching your good-luck token. I'd held it so hard the flesh of my palm was grooved." He showed his hand as if he expected the mark still to be there. "I kept it with me always from then on, and it became the good-luck charm of the whole crew. When I was relieved by Captain Kiley, I passed it on to him."

I could hardly speak, I was so grateful that this big handsome boy had come safely home.

During the first year of the war, the cops did not favor me with their attentions. In fact, my only contact with the law had been a warning not to receive enlisted men in my house. (I have often wondered about this. Is a soldier's sex life supposed to be determined by his rank? If so, then presumably a general is entitled to a whole harem, while a second lieutenant would probably rate only a wink.) In any case, I resented the police warning and ignored it. How could I shut my door on a regular customer just because he wasn't brass? My younger patrons always called on me when they were on furloughs or before they left for overseas duty, and in my house they got as warm a reception as if they'd been wearing a shoulder full of stars or a four-striped sleeve.

However, the cops had not forgotten my existence. They were just waiting till I was down to kick me. In January of 1943 I had been ill with pleurisy for several weeks, so ill that I had closed the house and had not been in business for more than a month. Since nurses were difficult to find, I was being looked after by my old friend, Dora Maugham, a well-known night club entertainer and sketch writer. On the night of January thirteenth three of my girls—Joan, Eleanor and Shirley—had stopped in to inquire how I was, but Dora had left strict instructions that I was not to have visitors, so I didn't even know the girls were there. The medication I was taking kept me in such a fog that it was hard to know what was real and what was a dream, and certainly I hoped it was a dream when I opened my eyes and saw a policeman standing at the foot of my bed.

It *must* be a dream, I told myself. It can't be a raid. I'm not in business. I shut my eyes hoping the vision would go away, but when I looked again, there were *two* policemen. *What's in these pills?* I thought woozily. *That doctor is giving me goofballs.* . . . But finally I recognized one of the policemen as Bill Lenahan, whom I knew to be that rarity, an honest cop.

"It's all set, Bill," the other cop was saying. "The brunette's confessed."

"Polly, it's not true!" cried Joan, pushing past him into the room. "We only stopped to inquire about you, but this cop keeps saying I'm here to keep a date."

"Bill Lenahan, are you framing me?" I said, hardly able to get the words out I was so blurred with sedation. "I give you my word I had no idea Joan was here."

Bill sighed. "If it were up to me, Polly, I'd walk right out of here. But the boss is with us."

I asked to speak to his boss, but after the sergeant came in he paid no heed to what I was saying. He was interested only in the medicine bottles on the night table. Seeing my doctor's name on a label, he at once telephoned him to ask about moving me to the prison hospital ward at the House of Detention. When the doctor said there was a good chance I'd cork off if I was moved, the sergeant sent for a policewoman to stand guard at my bedside, and the three girls were bundled off to the police station. They did not dare pinch Dora. She was too well-known and too well-respected, and if they had arrested her they would have faced a suit. However, they insisted that she leave the apartment.

The policewoman had requested that the cop on the beat stop in every hour, so all through the night I was kept awake by the ringing of the doorbell. (As I was easily capable of lifting my head a good two inches from the pillow, it is a wonder they didn't chain me to the bed.) At eight o'clock another policewoman, Mrs. O'Connor, came on duty. Apparently she did not feel she had to be "protected" from me. She changed my bed linen and nightgown and brought me a cup of tea. I was so overcome by her consideration that I fainted.

I came to just in time to hear Mrs. O'Connor saying, "Please don't move her in a patrol wagon. She may die. Can't you call a taxi? At least they have heaters." I tried to get to the telephone to call my lawyer, but collapsed before I could do so. The next thing I remember is looking up to see a city doctor and a nurse standing over me, and I heard the doctor tell the sergeant I was too ill to be moved. But this cut no ice with that sweetheart of a cop, and after endless palaver I was carried out on a stretcher and filed in an ambulance bound for Bellevue. There, it turned out that the only space available was in the psychopathic ward. At this point I didn't care. All I wanted was a place to lie down, but the matron in charge announced there was no bed empty. While minds were being made up what to do with me and endless red tape being unwound, I spotted a grimy-looking, sheetless, pillowless cot— an unoccupied one. I weaved over to it, crawled aboard and blacked out.

Later in the day I swam back to consciousness to find my attorney, Mrs. Gottlieb, looking sadly down at me. I was done up in a ragged hospital gown and covered with a tattered blanket. Mrs. Gottlieb questioned me on details of the arrest and I, in turn, asked how I had happened to land in the psychopathic ward. Was it just a hunch on the city's part or had I qualified for membership? Mrs. Gottlieb said she would see about arranging a transfer, but I told her not to bother. Here I had a bed. I might not be so lucky again.

During my sojourn in the "locked wing," I was pestered constantly by attendants who had not bothered to read my chart and so treated me as if I were minus a majority of my buttons. One matron insisted that I trim my fingernails. I might, she implied, run amok and carve up the ward. The doctor, a young woman who appeared to be operating on the premise that she was the only human being there and the patients were laboratory specimens, took one look at me and declared that I was obviously a drug addict. I replied with considerable heat that she should dust off her crystal ball and look again. So, ray of sunshine that she was, she obliged with the statement that if I wasn't a hophead, then I must have syphilis—the pupils of my eyes did not dilate. She forestalled any rejoinder on my part by ramming a thermometer under my tongue.

Annie, the patient in the next bed, had a healthy sense of humor, although as she remarked to me somewhat mournfully, a fat lot of good it did her. She had told the judge before whom she appeared on a streetwalking charge, "Go easy on me, Handsome, and I'll meet you on Fourteenth Street after the trial." But the judge, said Annie, had no sense of humor at all. . . . While I cannot say that I enjoyed my sojourn in the psychopathic ward, I did learn that there are no crazy people—only sick ones—and that, as usual, when society does not understand a problem, it conveniently forgets all that it preaches about the brotherhood of man.

When my health report came in, I was eligible for bail. I got in touch with Mrs. Gottlieb and asked her to have Dora post bond so that I might leave the next day. During these proceedings an attorney snidely insinuated that a professional connection must exist between Dora and me, otherwise why would "Miss Maugham give up her work and her canteen activities just to nurse Miss Adler in questionable surroundings?"

Dora asked the judge if she might address the court in her own way and received permission to do so. Then, as she afterwards laughingly related to me, "I drew myself up in the chair and asked the lawyer if what he was trying to say was that I had 'worked' for you. He got very flustered, and hemmed and hawed and spluttered, and finally assured me that such a thought never entered his head. He just couldn't see how I, so long a respected member of the theater world, could 'enjoy' a close and lasting friendship with a lady of ill repute! Well, at this crack I hit the ceiling. I told him that I had known you for many years, and in all these years you had never asked me to take part in your business operations—and I had never asked you to sing a song!"

That fixed the lawyer's wagon all right, and there were no more difficulties made. The papers carried the story next day, and the publicity quite melted the matrons. I was swamped with hot coffee and fresh pillow slips. As I was leaving, the doctor (who, I decided, probably owned a full set of lampshades made of human skin) came in to hurl one last bouquet.

"If I'd known who you were," she said, "I'd have known you couldn't be syphilitic. You get arrested too often." And then, frowning, "I still can't understand why your pupils don't dilate."

I explained that during my illness I had taken a lot of medication, including opiates.

"Of course!" she said. "Why didn't I think of that?"

"Perhaps," I said sweetly, "because you are only capable of thinking mean and ugly things."

On January twenty-seventh, my case came to trial. Officer Martin took the stand and testified that Joan had admitted that her presence at my apartment the night of her arrest was for the purpose of committing an immoral act. The judge gave him a doubtful look. What prostitute would make this damaging admission to a cop? Although the sergeant and Bill were present, they did not take the stand to corroborate Martin's testimony. Nor did my girls or I testify. Mrs. Gottlieb moved for a dismissal and the Judge pronounced my two favorite words: *Case dismissed.*

(Later on, Mayor LaGuardia asked to see the minutes of the case because the charge was so flimsy. And who knows? LaGuardia may have thought the cops were bribed to present a weak case against me. It probably never occurred to him that the vice cops were again practicing the same methods of trapping victims as were in vogue before the Seabury investigation.)

III

Your heart often knows things before your mind does, and I think from this time on, psychologically speaking, I was already retired from the business I had been in so long. Although I opened up the house again, the Bellevue experience on top of my long illness had left me so drained and depleted that I spent the next few months in Connecticut convalescing, and when I finally got back in harness, I felt like the Ghost in *Hamlet* "Cut off even in the blossoms of my sin . . . With all my imperfections on my head." Everything was an effort, the ringing of the business phone was like a dentist's drill on an exposed nerve, and though I would try to be gay and amusing, I usually ended the evening locked in my room crying into my pillow. How could I play Polly the clown, Polly the *joie-de-vivre* kid, when everything seemed "weary, stale, flat and unprofitable" ("Seems, madam! Nay, it is"), and the only future I could imagine for myself so utterly bleak and meaningless? Finally, I decided I would have to get clear away from the house and its problems or else crack up completely.

I called my attorney to tell her where I would be. I had first known Mrs. Gottlieb in the Twenties when I was playing the market. At one of the brokerage houses at which I traded she was a customers' woman, and even then, although I knew her only slightly, I was impressed by her brilliant mind and compelling personality. She told me that it was her ambition to practice law, but I lost track of her after I gave up trying to be another Hetty Green. I never knew that she had followed through and become a lawyer until, some months before, I had read a newspaper story about one of her cases. I had called her in regard to drawing my will, and since then she had handled all my affairs. I respected Mrs. Gottlieb as I have respected few people in life. She stood for all the things and had all the qualities I most admired. And while she had never in word or look expressed an opinion about my profession, I was in no doubt that she had one.

Now I told her I was going to Fire Island for an indefinite stay. "I'm going to sit in the sun," I told her, "and not think about anything."

"Good enough," said Mrs. Gottlieb. "But, Polly, when you're ready to do some thinking—some real thinking—come and see me, please."

"Some real thinking about what?" I asked suspiciously.

Mrs. Gottlieb laughed. "Why, about whatever it is that you're going to Fire Island not to think about," she said.

Fire Island, which is two hours from New York, is less an island than a beach surrounded by water. Since there were no rooms available in the only hotel, I decided to try my luck at one of the best-known of the boardinghouses on the dunes between the Atlantic and the Great South Bay. At the door I was met by an elderly woman whose shrewd blue eyes measured me from head to foot. "Yes, I've a room available," she decided at last. "Step in, Miss—what did you say your name was?"

"I didn't say. It's Miss Davis."

The room was reached via a balcony over the living room, and as I stood at the door peering in, my landlady, who had stayed below stairs, yelled up to ask how I liked it. "Can't tell yet," I yelled back. "I have to crawl into it first." But though in its size and furnishings it was a bit reminiscent of my digs at the Jefferson Market Jail, the view out the window was something no Ritz could supply.

For the first few days I did exactly as I had told Mrs. Gottlieb—lay in the sun, and, well, I guess "unwound" is the best word. And when I wasn't soaking up sunlight, I drifted passively along on the currents of summer-resort life, making no overtures but nonetheless gradually being drawn into things. From Monday to Friday, I found, the days slid by placidly; the scene was peopled mostly by women and children. But on weekends what a change of pace! On weekends Fire Island really blazed. Then Flynn's, the most popular eating place, became a sort of Stork Club with Greenwich Village overtones, for the island was popular with the long-haired boys and the short-haired girls, and they showed up in swarms. But you also saw a sprinkling of heterosexuals, even on weekends.

Before long I had geared my life to that of the little community and found peace and contentment in the quiet daily round—up early, walking, sunning, lunch on the beach, an afternoon of reading, another stroll before dinner, then early to bed. I spent quite a bit of time snubbing the advances of a stocky, pale man who always seemed to be tagging after me. There was a peculiar and (to me) nauseating odor about him, which provided a more-than-sufficient clue to his whereabouts. He seemed always to be right behind when I was waiting my turn to use the telephone (there were only three on the island), and usually dogged me to Flynn's, where he'd ask me to join him in a drink. "Thank you, I don't drink," I'd say. And then—by way of telling the pest to drop dead, get lost and leave me alone—would instantly ask the bartender to serve me a Scotch and water.

One Friday I had cocktails at Flynn's with two friends of mine from New York, Deborah and Marge, who had secretarial jobs with a picture company. There was a large party at an adjoining table, among whom was Wolcott Gibbs, the *New Yorker* dramatic critic. One of the members of the party invited us to join them, which invitation was duly snapped up. We had an amusing evening, but word got around who I was, and the aftermath was not so amusing—at least not to me. (However, as the old saying goes, it's an ill wind which doesn't blow some man good, and the reaction of the respectable Fire Islanders to the news that there was a madam in their midst provided Mr. Gibbs with considerable literary material. In fact, a madam called "Molly" is one of the chief characters in *Season in the Sun,* his hit comedy about life on Fire Island.)

Saturday at breakfast, Deborah, Marge and I were joined by Terry, a friend of theirs also out for the weekend. "I'm just sick I missed all the fun at Flynn's last night," she said. "I hear there was a terrific party—and but swarming with intelligentsia—and, of all people, Polly Adler!"

"Yes, yes, we know," said Deborah quickly. "We were there."

"Well, as you can imagine, everyone's absolutely up in arms and appalled and horrified that this Adler creature's roaming around loose on the island, and *they say* on a talent hunt."

Deborah eyed me apprehensively and Marge almost swallowed her spoon. I sat quietly waiting for more.

"It's perfectly disgraceful," said Terry, turning to me. "Don't you think so?"

"If the Adler woman is doing what she's accused of," I said, "I agree. She should be put off the island along with that other woman."

"What other woman?"

"Why, that woman everyone calls a tramp—the one who doesn't seem to know that the walls here are paper-thin, or no doubt she'd tell that big-mouthed cloak-and-suiter not to make so much noise when she entertains him in her bedroom." And, as she flushed scarlet, "Who are you to call me disgraceful? I'm Polly Adler."

"I don't believe you! You're not—you couldn't be Polly——"

Nobody said anything, and after a moment Terry jumped up and fled from the room. She left on the afternoon boat, and I wish I had too, for, as I was soon to discover, not just the weekend visitors but everyone on the island had learned my true identity, and already the line was forming at the rock pile.

Previously I had agreed to lunch on Monday with a Mrs. Atkins, a widow with two grown daughters, who seemed to have taken a great shine to me and was always harping on what a marvelous person I was. But now when I turned up at her cottage, she all but reached for the Winchester.

"How dare you come here?" she said. And, after I reminded her I'd been invited, "Well, but of course I didn't know *then* who you were."

"I haven't changed," I assured her. "I'm the same woman you asked to lunch."

"You've got a nerve, sneaking around pretending to be respectable, forcing yourself on——"

"Mrs. Atkins," I cut in, "be fair. I didn't force myself on you. When we met, I didn't ask you to like me. It was your idea that we be friends. And I wasn't pretending to be anything."

"Humph! I notice you didn't say what business you're in."

"Because it doesn't concern you."

"Doesn't concern me? *Doesn't concern me!*" she squeaked. "When I have two daughters? And to think I introduced them to you!"

Mrs. Atkins's attitude was typical. As Pearl Davis, I had been hailed as a lamb and a card and a perfect dear, but now that word had seeped around that Pearl Davis and Polly Adler were one and the same, there was a hasty furling of welcome mats, virgins of all ages were whisked off the beaches, and matrons, who the day before had been all over me like a shower, either looked pointedly the other way or eyed me as if, overnight, I had sprouted an extra head.

I made arrangements to leave the island the next day, and then went defiantly to Flynn's for dinner. But I chose a table in the small room, away from the main dining room facing the bay. I was afraid to look at anyone. I didn't think I could stand any more snubs. Just as I was finishing my coffee, I smelled a familiar odor and looked up to see the pale-faced man who was always dogging me. And suddenly I realized why he was so attentive. He was paid to be; he was a cop. My self-control snapped. I threw down some money for my check and ran out of the restaurant like a crazy woman, the tears streaming down my face.

The next morning when my landlady came to see why I hadn't come down for breakfast, I guess I must have looked as if I were competing for the title of Miss Sad Sack of All Time.

"I'm sorry you had to hear all that rotten gossip," she said. "That Atkins woman started it, accused you of picking up young girls on the beach. Made me so mad I told her no one would rent her a cottage here next year, not so long as we old settlers have the say."

I looked at her. "Then you knew all along who I was?"

"Sure did," said my landlady, patting my hand. "I've seen you before. Used to run a restaurant in the Village. Fannie Brice was one of my customers, Gene Fowler too. Yep, I recognized you right off when you came to the door that day. Knew you'd be an ideal boarder and that's what you've been. Call yourself any name you like, you'll always be welcome here."

Wasn't she shocked at my profession? I asked her. "Men are men, aren't they?" she said. "And women are women. And the twain got to meet someplace. People don't do anything at your house that don't happen every day in every hotel and boardinghouse and motel in the country. You just are kind of more organized for it. . . . No point in your setting up here brooding. I'll heat up the coffee, and you go out and get some sun."

As I took my last walk on the beach, the thoughts that, as Mrs. Gottlieb had said, I came to Fire Island not to think, finally caught up with me. When I saw an inward-bound convoy, I could not help remembering the ship *Naftar*, which had passed by here some thirty-odd years before carrying me and my potato sack to the Golden Land. Had I really traveled so far since then? I wondered. True, I had graduated from the potato-sack class. I had bags and trunks and things to put in them, and surely I could no longer be called a greenhorn. Though I was still shy an education, I was hep to a lot of things that aren't taught in school. I knew how to bribe a cop and fly a plane and eat an artichoke and cure a hangover. I knew that Sunday was the night gangsters went out with their wives and Monday the night that socialites went to the opera. I knew who to go to for what, and how the smart money was bet, and all the Broadway rumors about where the bodies were hidden. I knew the names that made news, and they knew mine.

A cynical person might say that my life had been a typical American success story. From the arrival at Ellis Island up the ladder rung by rung—five dollars a week, ten dollars a week, a hundred dollars a week, a mink coat, a better address —from neighborhood trade to an international clientele— from a nobody to a legend. And yet, like the little kid with a tag on her coat, wasn't I still an alien with a label? It might seem I had come a long way from Second Avenue, but wasn't I still living from day to day? Now, just as much as then, wasn't uncertainty the only "constant" factor in my life?

And suddenly it seemed to me there was no direction to my life at all. I had been tacking back and forth for years over the same waters, running before the storm in bad weather and hoving to when it was calm. Yes, and I had been wrecked and in drydock and refitted. I'd even learned the compass and a star or two, but I was just keeping afloat; I wasn't going anywhere.

I knew that so long as I stayed in my present profession, it would be the same portless voyaging. I knew that, even supposing I had the money to do so, if I retired and lived on my "ill-gotten gains," I'd still, in a sense, be a member of the profession. The only difference would be that instead of being an active madam, I'd be a madam emeritus. It wasn't enough merely to disassociate myself from the business, to get away from the whorehouse, I'd still be adrift unless I had a destination. Like a mariner taking his bearings, I had to get a fix on myself and the future. If I knew where I was and what port to make for, then I could line out my course and head for land—and not golden land, either, but land to grow things in and build on.

Chapter 11

Call Me

Miss

The most shocking fault of women is that they make the public the supreme judge of their lives.

Stendhal   FRAGMENTS

I

My attorney had asked me to call her when I was ready to do some "real thinking," and so on my return to New York I made an appointment to see her. After we had chatted in desultory fashion for a few moments, I saw she was looking at me with concern.

"How are you feeling, Polly? Did Fire Island do you some good?"

"Fire Island was fine," I said. And then, unable to restrain my bitterness, "Maybe I'd be doing people a favor if I went around like the madams in the movies—complete with dirty feather boa, hypodermic syringe and a pimp. I ran into some of my 'public' on the island, and they seemed to resent it that I was disguised as a human being."

Mrs. Gottlieb flicked up the key to her interoffice communicator and asked her secretary to see that she was not disturbed. Then she turned to me.

"Polly," she said, "all this last year I've watched you becoming more and more strained and nervous, physically sick, emotionally disturbed. I've seen your vitality ebbing away—your warmth and your buoyancy and your capacity for laughter—and it's been like watching a death. But do you know what seems to me the saddest thing of all? Here you are driving yourself and destroying yourself to achieve something from which you derive so little satisfaction."

I was deeply moved by her concern. She was talking from the heart. She really cared what became of me. "What should I do?" I asked despairingly. "I don't know which way to turn. Everywhere I look it's a dead end. I've been hoping you could tell me——"

Mrs. Gottlieb frowned and made an impatient gesture. "I can't say to you: *Polly, do this* or *Polly, do that*. A decision another makes for you means nothing. But I can say that I don't for a moment believe what you've told me so often—that society won't let you be anything but a madam. No, Polly! With your drive and determination and courage, the only person who can keep you from doing anything is yourself." I started to interrupt, but she checked me. "Yes, I know you've tried before to make the break. And don't think I'm underrating the hardships and handicaps of your position. I'm well aware that no matter what enterprise you might embark on, you'd start with strikes on you, and the going would be tough. But my God, Polly, has anything ever been handed to you on a silver platter? When hasn't the going been tough? Since you were a child you've fought tooth and toenail every step of the way. Don't you think now it's high time to stop and consider what it is you are fighting for? Isn't it time to ask what you want—not out of life, but out of yourself?"

Her words hit me hard, but it wasn't an easy question to

face. "How does anyone know what to think these days?" I hedged. "It's not only me. Everybody's values are all mixed up. I mean look at the people I see in my house—educated, successful people who run things and tell others what to think. Would they be there if they weren't mixed up too, if they knew what they wanted of themselves?"

But Mrs. Gottlieb refused to be sidetracked. "There's a line Henry James wrote that you should take to heart, Polly," she said and quoted, " 'Remember that every life is a special problem which is not yours but another's, and content yourself with the terrible algebra of your own.' "

"There are too many X's in my problem," I said. "I'm a Madam X who never studied algebra, so how could I ever figure myself out?"

She would not be put off by flippancy either. "Have you ever really tried? Have you really sat down and considered the case of Polly Adler, examined the record from beginning to end?"

"Of course I've thought about my life—often. But you know how it is when you remember. It's a jumble of bits and pieces like a scrambled-up jigsaw puzzle."

"Then why not collect the pieces and put them in order? Write them down."

"Write? Me?" The notion was ridiculous.

"Yes, why not?"

"But I don't know how to write."

"You know how to remember," said Mrs. Gottlieb blandly. "You have an astonishing memory."

"But—but I wouldn't know how to express myself. How could I? Me and my eight hundred words plus slang?"

"Don't worry," said Mrs. Gottlieb. "Just write down the truth. People who tell the truth don't need a dictionary to do it. It's those who evade it who need a large vocabulary. . . .

I'm serious about this, Polly," she went on. "In the end each person must be his own judge, and no judge can hand down a decision until he is thoroughly familiar with the evidence. Think through your life. Set it down in black and white where you can study it and evaluate it. You'll find that having to express things concretely helps you to focus on them. And sometimes what loomed so large will dwindle into insignificance, while feelings you never even knew you had turn out to be the dominant ones. If you'll put yourself down on paper, you'll learn a lot about yourself, I promise you."

I looked at her. "Including," I asked dubiously, "what occupation I'm best suited for?"

"Including that," said Mrs. Gottlieb with a smile.

After leaving Mrs. Gottlieb, I walked for blocks mulling over what she had said. Was she warning me that I was a candidate for a snakepit? I realized that in proposing I write down my life story she was in fact prescribing a form of psychotherapy—a voyage of self-exploration in the hope that it would help to resolve the doubts and conflicts that were stymying me. I knew that to salvage my peace of mind more was required than simply running away. And perhaps perspective would point the way; perhaps if I saw myself in relation to the past, I would be able to get that badly needed fix on the future.

I stopped off at a stationery store and bought a thick pad of paper and an extra bottle of ink, but for the time being that ended my literary activity. Whenever my eyes fell on the pad gathering dust on my desk, I thought, "Supposing when those pages are filled, I read them over and find I've been twenty-five years in the wrong business? Maybe I'd better let well enough alone."

However, the seed had been sown and finally on June 17,

1945, "Operation: Autobiography" got officially under way at a milk farm in New Jersey. In two days I managed to write about fifteen hundred words, at which point pride of authorship reared its head, and I showed the fruit of my labors to the owner of the farm. "You should explain more about Yanow and yourself," she said, and this remark, although I didn't suspect it then, was the opening shot in a bombardment of literary advice and criticism which was to continue intermittently for the next seven years.

This comment had a somewhat dampening effect on the newly kindled creative fires, but I continued to work weekends and by the end of July had written more than a hundred pages. It was both fascinating and painful, this reliving of my life, and there were many times when the past became more real to me than the present. Yet reading the pages over, I would see so many places where I had failed to make the words say what I wanted them to say, where I knew what I meant but my lack of know-how had prevented me from communicating it to paper.

The remedy, when finally it dawned on me, was breathtakingly simple. I'd go to school and learn how to express myself! All my life I'd been yearning for an education—well, what was stopping me from getting one? No one was holding a gun on me, forcing me to stay ignorant!

I was full of plans and blazing on all burners when, one August night, I paid a backstage call on Charlie Barnett, who was appearing at the Strand Theater. I told Charlie of my decision to go to school, adding that now it was just a question of where I'd settle down.

"Poll, I've just the place for you," he said. "I'm going on the road for four months and you can use my house in Los Angeles. It has a swimming pool, and I'll throw in the use of my Cadillac."

"Sounds good! What will you charge per month—an arm or leg?"

"No charge at all. Is it a deal?"

"You just sold me, Charlie," I said. "Next week I'll be leaning out your bedroom window, plucking the makings of my breakfast orange juice."

A few days later I was standing alone in my bare apartment, waiting for the expressman to pick up my trunks. One of them, tagged "Memory Trunk," held the souvenirs and mementos of my thirty-two years in "Goldine Madina." There was a pile of old address books, a card file of girls who had worked for me, ledgers marked "Profits and Payoffs," and enough "stiffs" (bad checks) to paper the mansions of some of the men who had issued them. There were newspaper clippings and a stack of magazines containing articles about me, letters from friends, theater programs, banquet menus, Christmas and birthday cards. And at the very bottom of the trunk, almost buried under layers of mothballs, were the bird of paradise Joan had given me, a pair of green sequin dancing shoes with high heels (the first I ever owned), my grade-school diploma, and a torn shawl and a little girl's undershirt—all that remained of the "traveling outfit" in which I had set out, so eager for adventure, from Yanow.

I gazed at the trunk with stinging tears—and then I had to laugh. Although the little girl had headed west to America instead of east to Pinsk, she was still on her way to Gymnazia. . . . Wrong-Way Corrigan had nothing on me!

II

The road to a higher education was a long uphill one still. I had two years of high school to make up before I could enter college, and at the same time I was learning how to cook, keep house and garden, and also was active in several charity organizations. So I was, to say the least, a busy kid. Yet sometimes—especially at night—time hung heavy. I lived alone, and I was living with a stranger—a woman whose sudden crying spells bewildered me, whose bitterness unnerved me. I tried unburdening myself on paper, but now that the first impetus was spent, I found it harder than ever to write and wondered that I'd ever had the nerve to attempt such a thing.

I saw many old friends from my New York days, but I was timid and self-conscious about meeting new people. All too often I would shrink within myself, wondering whether they were secretly laughing at me, pretending to be friendly while regarding me with a cold, clinical eye, studying me like a specimen on a slide. Sometimes I would cut loose and kid about my former profession, make jokes about myself, get in the cracks before anybody else could. But more often I would sit self-conscious and tongue-tied, afraid that if I joined in the conversation I would make some grammatical blunder or reveal my ignorance of the topic under discussion. When I was a madam, it wouldn't have mattered, but now it was different. I was in the process of evolving from a "character" into a person. As the doctor in T. S. Eliot's play, *The Cocktail Party,* said, I had "lost touch with the person I thought I was" and not yet having found my new self, I felt all the insecurity of a d.p.

As was perhaps to be expected, most of my New York friends were astonished when I matriculated at a West Coast college, but once they were over the initial shock they applauded my determination, and I was constantly being urged to report on my career as a coed. (If incongruity is the root of humor, no doubt my audiences were softened up before I even started to give. Just the idea of the "most notorious woman in the history of New York vice" being a college freshman seemed to them irresistibly comic.)

However, none of my teachers or fellow-students had any idea I was the erstwhile proprietor of the nation's number one bordello, and, as a result, I found myself constantly involved in situations whose irony only I could appreciate. For example, in speech class I was chairman of a discussion group among whose members was a police lieutenant. I shall never forget what a kick it gave me when I called on him for a few comments on *Kon-Tiki*. What a twist for Polly Adler to be telling a copper to talk!

Then, in composition class, my teacher innocently proposed that I write a theme based on my past life and experiences. "If you keep a scrapbook," she said, "perhaps something in that might suggest something." For obvious reasons I didn't adopt her proposal, but she was a good joe and the joke was too good to keep. At the end of the semester she drove over to my house to drop off my grades (mostly B's— how'm I doing?), and on an impulse I trotted out one of my scrapbooks.

"What would you have said," I asked her, "if I'd written you a theme based on this part of my past life?" and I began to flip over the pages, pausing for her to take in such headlines as VICE QUEEN SOUGHT IN INQUIRY. . . . POLLY ADLER'S POLITICAL PULL CITED BY D.A. . . . MIDTOWN MADAM OF MANY MAGDALENS MISSING. . . . DEATH THREAT DELIVERED TO RED-LIGHT CZARINA. After a truly colossal double-take (and after comparing my features with a newsphoto), my teacher hauled the scrapbook over onto her lap and perused its pages in silence for several minutes. Then she looked up, a wicked glint in her eye.

"Miss Adler," she said solemnly, "if you had written a

composition based on this material and read it in class"—she paused—"well, all I can say is the expression 'a liberal education' would have taken on a new meaning. In fact," she added, "a new dimension."

Since a major incentive in going to college was to learn how to express myself, I followed the suggestion of the school counselor that I enroll for English 85, a course in etymology. (Walter Winchell announced in his column that I was studying Greek and Latin, and in a sense this was true because etymology was certainly Greek to me.) I found myself gleaning such tidbits as that the word "tram" was derived from Benjamin L. Outram, who invented the flanged wheel (I am still waiting for the conversation to turn to flanged wheels, so I can spring this one), and "extravagant" from the Latin words for *outside* and *to wander*. To wander outside was what I often wanted to do during this class. How could I hope to master correct English usage when the Greeks and Romans and Anglo-Saxons and Teutons had been bollixing up the language for so many centuries? But the instructor urged me to stay in there and pitch, and by dint of beating out my brains I managed to keep up with the others.

More important, I learned how to use a dictionary and how to consult reference works. Ever since I had begun my autobiography, my bookshelves had been sagging with dictionaries—the Oxford, the American Collegiate, Webster's Unabridged (a heavy rascal), Webster's Biographical, a Roget and Fowler's *English Usage*. Hitherto, they had just been dust-catchers—in fact, it used to make me mad to look at them and think of all the knowledge locked up in them and inaccessible to me—but now that I had found the key I became a dictionary buff, and often rocked my friends by nonchalantly coming out with a sixteen-dollar word.

Meanwhile, various columnists had reported that I was at work on my memoirs. People kept asking me when the book would be finished, and, realizing I had put myself on the spot, I steeled myself to get on with my *magnum opus*. Every night I would vow that first thing in the morning I'd get to the desk, and every morning I'd trump up excuses to keep away from it. I would clean closets, wax floors, polish silver, weed flower beds, paint lawn furniture—anything to avoid taking pen in hand.

"How can a person make herself write?" I finally asked a writer friend, Eileen Shannon. "By writing," she replied, and I shuddered and changed the subject. But next morning she telephoned and, dispensing with the usual good morning, asked, "How many pages will you do today?" "Three," I said, caught unawares. "Fine," said Eileen. "I'll ring up this afternoon, and you can read them to me." For more than a month, she called every morning to get me started and every afternoon to check up, hoping in this way to get me in the habit of regular work.

But I was still looking for an easy way out. I rented a dictaphone and had it installed next to my bed. Then, when genius burned as it often did (or seemed to) in the small hours, I would gab away like mad until, convinced I'd spouted at least a chapter, I'd sink back on the pillows and drift off to dreamland, much pleased with myself. The only drawback was that more often than not I'd forget to hold down the recording button, and when I turned on the playback next morning would find my golden words had gone with the wind.

In the end, I got wise and set up a schedule which I followed faithfully (except such times as I kicked over the traces and played truant at Palm Springs or Las Vegas). I would be up at eight and have coffee and orange juice at the kitchen table, getting to the desk at eight thirty. At eleven thirty I would knock off for lunch, then another three hours' work, after which I took a breather until six when, on four nights a week, it was time to go to school. Classes were over at nine, and from nine thirty to eleven I prepared the next day's lessons, then read until one. Nor did I skim through the pages as I formerly had. Now that I had some inkling of the agony of literary creation, I felt I owed the author my most respectful attention.

For, believe me, agony is a mild word for it. Often, as I sat there at my desk, I'd find myself thinking nostalgically of the good old days when I was wrestling with cops and drunks instead of nouns and verbs. Compared to writing a book, running a house had been a breeze! Certainly if I'd had any idea of the skull-popping headaches in store for me, wild horses hitched to lawyers could never have induced me to set pen to paper. But when first I embarked on the enterprise I had the courage of ignorance, and when I finally began to realize all that I was up against, pride and stubbornness kept me from quitting. Since it was known I was working on a book, I'd have to finish it or it would be a slow boat to China for "Author" Adler!

III

While I was plugging away eight and ten hours a day, the weeks slipped by, spring turned into summer (I was working outdoors now, under a huge Chinese elm), and my younger pup celebrated the equivalent of a poodle's bar mitzvah. But though my script had grown a little too, I began to have the feeling that I'd be longer writing the story of my life than I had been living it.

However, thanks to Dora Maugham, one bothersome problem had been settled—my book now had a title. Previously, an appeal to my friends for suggestions had elicited a flattering number of responses, but they were all either too facetious or, as the saying goes, not for the family trade. (Martha Raye, I remember, came up with *Forever Adler* and Swifty Morgan contributed *10,000 Nights in a Sing-Song House: or Brother, Can You Spare a Yen?* . . . When I remarked that this title would be more appropriate for an Oriental madam, Swifty replied, "What the hell, Polly! You operated on the East Side, didn't you?") But though dreaming up titles developed into quite a popular parlor pastime, it wasn't until Dora came to visit that we contacted the jackpot.

Then one day I happened to be spraying a rosebush in my back yard, and Dora, who was taking a sunbath, was profoundly impressed by this spectacle of suburban domesticity.

"I wonder what the cops would say," she mused, "if they could see you now."

"Oh," I said, "probably they'd be disappointed that my home is not a house."

Dora's reaction to this remark was so unusual that she frightened me into dropping the spray can. "Eeyow!" she squealed. "Hold everything!" And, as I stared at her wondering if maybe she'd been out in the sun too long, "Turn that around and you've got it!"

"What on earth are you talking about?"

"The perfect title for your book—*A House Is Not a Home!*"

I rushed over to Dora and gave her a hug that nearly knocked her down. So far as I was concerned, I told her, it was the most inspired piece of thinking anyone had done in a garden since the day Isaac Newton got conked by an apple.

To which Dora replied drily that I should watch it, my college education was showing.

Perhaps having a title acted as a spur. At any rate, I really got cracking and by the middle of September, three years and three months after going to the post, I came breezing (or maybe I mean wheezing) across the finish line. However, my first feelings of elation were rapidly followed by a terrible attack of cold feet. Would I be making a fool of myself if I submitted the script to a publisher? Rejection I could take, but not ridicule. It seemed to me my story was interesting, but as for the way it was written—well, what was the use of kidding myself?—Shakespeare could relax. I decided the thing to do was to ask a few friends of mine, writers and newspapermen, to read the script, get their reactions, and ask their advice about ways of improving it.

Then came the deluge! I had meant to show my script to only three or four people at most. But word gets around, and after I'd shown it to one, it was hard to refuse it to others. Anyway, it wasn't long before I found myself ringed three-deep in literary advisers, each one of whom had a different idea how the story should be written and whose suggestions pulled me in all directions at once. I was told that the book would be meaningless without a detailed account of my family background and childhood—and that nobody would be interested in my pre-madam years; that I should include a "good big picture" of the Twenties—and that the Twenties had been done *ad nauseam*; that the gangster material was old hat—and the Dutch Schultz chapter the best in the book; that I should avoid anything smacking of *True Confessions*—and that the confessional slant was sure fire; that the treatment should be semi-fictional and the tone light and frothy—and that my approach should be clinical, stressing the sociological implication of my story, and annotated by a psychiatrist, social worker or legal eagle.

Well—I had asked for it. And if, as a result, I lost months of time and (very nearly) my mind, I have no one to blame but myself. I was, and am, deeply grateful for my friends' interest and their desire to help. The trouble was that I crossed them up no less than myself by following suggestions blindly and indiscriminately.

Dazed and confused by the avalanche of advice thundering around me, much of which, moreover, was couched in a foreign language (What did I know of *continuity* and *reader-identification* and *transitional paragraphs* and *telegraphing?*), when changes were recommended, I didn't put up any arguments. And being convinced that everybody knew more about writing a book than I did, I played no favorites. Meekly at the behest of whichever in the procession of Svengalis happened to be sitting in, I revised and excised, interpolated and transposed, played up and toned down. With nary a murmur of protest, I abandoned my plan of beginning the book with my birth and narrating my story in chronological sequence (a scheme so obvious that it instantly branded me as a literary "square"), and instead, volubly coached from the side lines, made free use of such flossy devices as flashbacks and stream-of-consciousness passages. I added a foreword and footnotes, an appendix and a glossary of underworld slang, and if I hadn't been so anxious to get the book done by Christmas, there would have been statistical tables and a psychograph of the composite prostitute as well. (A request to America's foremost authority on sex that he write an introduction had laid an egg.) In short, by the time the overhauling had ended it seemed to me the only thing unchanged was the title. Don't think it hadn't been suggested, but on this one point I was a rock.

The day the book came back from the typist's, five pristine copies of it, as I gazed at the massive pile of typescript I experienced something approximating the thrill of the moment I had tried on my first mink coat. (Thousands and thousands of words, all mine!) The only difference was that I felt no desire to "try on" the book—to see how it read now that every infinitive had been welded together, every comma was in place. Somehow just the thought of ploughing through the four-hundred-plus pages induced a sensation of dizziness and an overwhelming compulsion to go quietly off and lie down. I contented myself with gloating over the beautiful title page and table of contents, and trying to picture how the magic words "By Polly Adler" would look in print.

That afternoon an old friend of mine, a man well-known in the publishing world, came to pay a pre-Christmas call. He had known about my autobiographical project almost from its inception. In fact, he was one of the very few who had seen that first battered and blotted manuscript I had brought with me from New York, and had promised to advise me on placing the book when the time came. Now, in response to his inquiry on "work in progress," I informed him the last coat of paint had just been applied to my *House,* and proudly showed him the script. How soon would he be able to read it?

He was going away over the holidays, my friend said, but he knew how anxious I was to get the script on its way, and as he had a couple of hours to spare, would I have any objections to his giving it a quick once-over now? To the contrary, I said, nothing would suit me better, and after seeing him settled with the top copy, I went off to get him some tea and a glass of sherry.

When I came tiptoeing back and put down the tray, he looked up at me with a puzzled expression. "This is nothing like that first draft you showed me, Polly," he said. "It doesn't read as if the same person had written it."

"Thank you for the compliment," I said. "Maybe I'm learning something, after all." And I explained about seeking advice from my friends and about all the revising I had done. "When I remember how crude and badly written that first draft was, it makes me blush for shame to think that anyone ever saw it. This is a big improvement, don't you agree?"

"Well, I can see you've done a lot of work," my friend said. He resumed reading, and I took up another copy of the script and pretended to read too, but I was far too much on edge to concentrate. I watched covertly as he skimmed through a few pages, then skipped over to the next chapter and sampled several parts of that, occasionally turning back to re-read a passage. He went through the entire script in this fashion, and then, stacking it in a neat pile, he sat for what seemed an interminable time, his elbows planted on the desk, his head in his hands.

Finally, I could stand it no longer. "Doctor, please tell me, what's the verdict? This suspense is killing me."

"There are a lot of good things I could tell you, Poll," he said slowly, "but not, I'm afraid, what you want most to hear. Because, frankly, I'm disappointed. This is nowhere near the book that your first draft had led me to expect." And, as I let out a bleat of mingled anguish and indignation, "I don't say you couldn't find a publisher for it. It's slick, it's professionally put together, and quite possibly if I'd never met you, if I were acquainted with you only through what's written here, my opinion of the book would be altogether different. I'd think this was all there was to the Adler story, and

I'd be satisfied. But because I do know you, I can't help knowing that you've left out the most important part."

I looked at him in utter bewilderment. "I don't understand what you mean. There's nothing left out. I've put in all the facts."

"Oh, you put the facts in," he said, "but you failed to put in Polly Adler. What I miss here, Polly, is you, yourself." He pushed his chair back from the desk and stood up. "Gosh darn it, my dear, you mustn't be afraid to write your own book! Don't listen to what people say to you. Forget the rules. It's *your* story. Tell it your own way. . . . Now in that first version you showed me, the one you're so ashamed of, maybe it wasn't the most polished performance in the world, maybe the syntax was a little weird, but it was the Book of Polly— it was alive; it had salt and spontaneity; it rang true, and, above all, the person that is you materialized. While in this" —he tapped the beautiful new script and shrugged—"Well, it's an empty *House*. Adler doesn't live here any more."

I sat in stricken silence, and presently my friend came over and placed a sympathetic hand on my shoulder. "I know what you're thinking," he said, "and I don't blame you. Go ahead and say it. I'm a pusillanimous, picayunish, wrong-headed, hair-splitting, sour-spoken, misbegotten son of a——"

"Don't go putting thoughts in my head," I said. "Actually, I was just recalling the pet saying of an old madam named Vicki Shaw."

"Oh? And what was that?"

"Too many cooks," I said glumly, "spoil the brothel."

When he had gone, I walked over to the desk and stared down at the thick white slab of typescript which now seemed to resemble nothing so much as a tombstone. I had begun that book with the object of getting a line on myself, of collecting the evidence so I could hand down a decision in the case of Polly Adler. But if, as my friend said, I had failed to put Polly Adler in the story, then what I had here was of no value to anyone, and least of all to me.

Just tell the truth. Tell the story in your own way. It sounded so simple, I thought bitterly, but what *is* my own way? And suddenly there flashed in my mind the memory of a long-ago conversation with Robert Benchley. During the years of our friendship I had told him much of my life story, and one evening when I had been reminiscing he had urged me to write my memoirs. Thinking he was joking, and, as always, self-conscious about my lack of education, I had reminded him that I was no Vassar girl—the only degree I held was from Jail University.

"It's not a college degree that makes a writer," said Bench. "The great thing is to have a story to tell. And, Polly, you certainly have a story."

"Fine," I said. "Now all I need is to know how to write it."

"Write it the way you've lived it," said Bench. "Write it with your heart."

I shoved the beautiful typescript to one side and hauled a tablet out of the drawer. "Hang on to your hats, kids," I muttered to myself. "Here we go again." Then I picked up my pen. *I was born in Yanow,* I wrote, *a White Russian village near the Polish border, on the second Sunday before Passover. . . .*